MATTY MATHESON
HOME STYLE COOKERY

Matty Matheson

PHOTOGRAPHY BY
QUENTIN BACON

Abrams, New York

To Rizzo Louise Matheson

Contents

Seekers of the Truth

I NEVER THOUGHT I'D HAVE THE OPPORTUNITY TO WRITE A COOKBOOK IN MY LIFE, LET ALONE TWO. More than a decade ago, my sous chef at Parts & Labour and I used to talk for hours and hours about food, chefs, and everything else in our industry, but one of the things I remember the most was seeing Canadian chefs with huge food icons on social media. It would completely freak us out every time we saw any big-name chef come to Canada. How the fuck could that ever even happen? Daniel Boulud hanging out in the woods with the guys from Joe Beef or Anthony Bourdain eating at Martin Picard's Au Pied de Cochon. The fact that Americans were eating in Canada and people were posting about it was insane. Then, the tables started turning. Through the restaurants of Montreal, the world started recognizing the bountiful food of Canada and giving opportunities for younger chefs to shine.

Still, it was unfathomable for a normal Canadian chef to have a cookbook. I only knew of three chefs from here that ever had one. Fellow Canadian chefs and I used to talk about what we would do if we ever had the chance to write one of our own: what would be in it, what the pictures would look like, what stories we would tell, who we'd include—our farmers, our staff, our food. I thought that there would only be opportunities for chefs to write restaurant cookbooks. I never thought anyone would be interested in a home cookbook from anyone in my country.

In the days before social media and Amazon, we would search actual cookbook stores for copies of books by these titans of food to read. It was a lot like searching for new punk music. Finding a bookstore with a good cookbook section was hard, but when we did find them, it was like discovering Valhalla. When I discovered *The Nouvelle Cuisine of Jean & Pierre Troisgros*, it was like the first time I listened to *Victim in Pain* by Agnostic Front. Finding and reading *Letters to a Young Chef* by the master Daniel Boulud in a bookstore was like the first time I listened to a tape of *The California Takeover . . . Live* with Strife, Snapcase, and Earth

Crisis. And I stole *The Complete Nose to Tail* cookbook by Fergus Henderson of St. John restaurant from an Indigo store in Ottawa (I'm sorry Indigo!) because I was on tour with my friend's band and had no money. Reading the first lines of that book was like creepy crawling to the Cro-Mags' "Seekers of the Truth," the nastiest riff of all time. All those experiences with food and music were life-changing and made me the chef that I am today.

Honestly, I never thought that I would be a chef. I never had that moment of falling in love with the craft before I went into my career. I only wanted to cook to make money because I genuinely loved being a cook. It never really clicked that it would be my path or that I would become a Canadian legend.

Now, when I started thinking about writing my first cookbook, it took me a long while to figure out what it would be like. Would it contain all my drug stories? My fucked-up cooking stories? I didn't know if it should reveal the twisted mental stories of kitchens that I lived through and am very happy I made it out of alive or stories about farmers and fisherfolk. In the end, I decided to put myself out there because your story is the easiest one to tell, since no one else has that story. It is yours and yours alone.

I wanted to tell that story of my life through a culinary lens, and I think I did a pretty bang-up job. It's so fucking scary to write and put something out there, like I did in that book. I made a book proposal, and when I started having meetings with publishers, they all told me that I needed a cowriter to tell my story. I asked several writers to work with me, and every one couldn't do it for legitimate reasons. Regardless, I found impostor syndrome kicking in. *Why doesn't anyone like me? Why don't publishers and cowriters believe in my book? Why won't anyone help me? Am I not far along enough in my career to write a cookbook?* I'm lucky that I found Garrett McGrath and Abrams. They were happy to take a chance because they saw potential in me and my story that no other publisher did. I'm lucky they believed in me to write my own story. They helped me and pushed me to write honestly and be true to myself. That helped the book flow like my favorite beverage of all time, cold water from a hose on a hot day.

And now my first book has become a *New York Times* bestseller because you—my fans—believe in me! My fans are the greatest fans in the world. You guys made a college dropout a bestselling author. It's true that I still don't know what a semicolon is or where a period should really go. I also think that every sentence should be a paragraph long, an exclamation point should end every sentence I write, and WRITING IN ALL CAPS IS OKAY! But you all have embraced me, who I am, and the way I write. It's beautiful and pure. Thank you for your understanding.

Okay, okay, okay, I'm getting a little crazy here, but I'm fucking proud of myself and proud of where I am and where I'm going! Right now I'm flying to Australia. I'm writing my second book on my phone like I wrote my first book because I don't know how to use a laptop or a keyboard, and I can type faster on my phone, so fuck it all! My editor and publisher are equally excited about that as well.

I'll admit that maybe my first book was selfish because I didn't worry about people cooking from it. My goal was to tell the story of my culinary lineage and the restaurants that made me the chef that I am today. It's fucked up, but I didn't think enough about whether people would make recipes that will take four days. Cooking is difficult and some dishes are hard to make, but a lot of those recipes are brutal, and I'm sorry. I always laugh to myself when people tell me that my recipes don't work, or it doesn't look like the photo in the book. That's right, I've made most of these dishes a bunch of times. Who in their right mind thinks that if they are a novice cook but follow a recipe they will end up with a perfect dish? If I read a recipe word for word, step by step, I know I wouldn't be able to make it perfectly the first time. If you were to give me the blueprints for carpentering a scooch box, I'm sure it would take me ten or fifteen tries to put together so that my scooch box is scooch-able. I just couldn't do it on the first try. My brain is fragile that way. It takes time, and it takes fucking it up a few times to find your

groove and that space where time stands still and you cook effortlessly and tastefully. Please be patient with cooking. Like most good things, it takes time.

Now what the fuck is this cookbook going to be? Why am I making this? Simply: I want to share home cookery with you so you can cook for the people you love. That's it. I always cooked for my friends throughout the years, but now that I have a home and a growing family, I cook for them more than anyone else because of the joy that it brings them and it brings me. They love eating Daddy's food. But let's be real: It's also because I don't have any restaurants open right now. But I want to make a home cookbook that builds your self-confidence through sharing food with one another.

I think the biggest problem people have with cooking is the main idea. Like, I bought a chicken, now what the fuck do I do with it? Coq au vin, grill it, stuff it, fry it, make a stew, make a soup, make a pasta? It's daunting, so I want this book to help just a little and give some ideas and some easy techniques for all you lovely freaks out there. This book starts with recipes for basics like breads, stocks, vegetables, and dips. Next, we move on to dumplings and pastas, curries, soups, and a stew, and the underappreciated sandwiches. And we close the book with the bangers: fried foods, roasts, smoked meats, and grilled dishes. I haven't forgotten desserts. I hate making them, but I love eating them. I know in my first cookbook there are only three desserts. Don't worry, we got Matty's top ten big boys holding down the last section. They will break your pantry and your brain. Baking is science, and I am not a scientist

I wanted a book for real building blocks and stepping stones, and by the end of reading through it and hopefully cooking one or forty-seven or however many you have the willingness to commit to, I hope that you find that one dish that you cook for your girlfriend, boyfriend, friends, family, grandmother, anyone. I truly hope that you cook for someone you love, which will begin to make you love yourself more. Let's build up that self-love, baby! Dance hard or die.

CHAPTER 1

Bread

Bread Is Life, Flour Is Not the Enemy, Grind Your Grains

GROWING UP WITH MY MOM'S GRAIN GRINDER IS SUCH A BEAUTIFUL MEMORY FOR ME NOW, BUT WHEN I WAS A KID I WAS EMBARRASSED TO HAVE WHOLE-WHEAT BREADS OR LARGE PULLMAN LOAVES IN MY SANDWICHES AT LUNCH. All the other kids had Wonder Bread. How lucky they were in my misconstrued mind. Now I wish I had the time to make bread at home or grind wheat to flour. My family was so lucky; we were so well fed, but I'm sad that I mostly resented it. It's funny how hindsight is 20/20, ya know. It's so fucking badass that my mom made fresh bread weekly and that we had that in our young lives.

Every family has traditions. Every part of the world has their breads, that mixture of flour, water, and yeast that gives so much back to your home. As I've traveled the world I have found that people are so proud of the breads that they make and serve with their meals. I've broken bread on almost every continent.

The reason why I'm starting this book with breads is because of this pride. These are my favorite kinds. They are blocks of the world. With them you can go in hundreds if not thousands of directions. The only thing holding you back is your imagination. These are the most basic and most loved breads that will help you on your culinary journey.

Bread can take time and can fuck up real bad, real fast, and I want you to know that I understand that. I fuck up all the time, in a lot more than just bread-baking. Not letting up is the key, though—to keep going is the gift that keeps giving, to get it right is the miracle.

There are some things you will have to understand before baking. If you have dusty-ass packets of active dry yeast, buy new ones because the old ones will not work. It does matter if you overwork or underwork your dough. It definitely takes making breads a couple times to even begin to understand what this all is. Was your water too warm? Maybe! Was the dough too cold because your kitchen is drafty? Unfortunately, it all matters so much. I always say I'm not a scientist 'cause bread and baking are 100 percent science and 100 percent love, so that's fucking 200 percent! Fuck! Hahaha. I have the love, though, and I hope you will, too. We all gotta keep going. Please keep trying and please don't get discouraged.

These breads will give you so much to look forward to. Dipping homemade Roti (page 29) into the Lamb Neck Dizi Sangi (page 186) or Yellow Curry Clams (page 185) will feel way better than buying some roti from down the street. Don't feel bad if your hands are full with making the curry. Maybe buy the roti the first time, then buy some curry next time and make the roti, ya know. Don't take on the world. Crawl, walk, run is always best with life and cooking.

In this chapter are eight of my favorite breads. Make them and love them. Trust the process. Understand that the process doesn't stop the first time you make one. That's just the beginning. Remember one thing: Always save your apple juice cans 'cause you never know when and where you'll need to pump out some molasses bread! Hopefully, there's snow on the ground, a fire roaring in the fireplace, and rabbit stew on the stove. Godspeed, my little boulangers.

Sesame Seed Rolls

MAKES:
6 (6-INCH/
15 CM) ROLLS

PREP TIME:
1 HOUR 15 MINUTES, PLUS
1½ HOURS INACTIVE TIME

This is the best bread for cheesy garlic bread, a submarine sandwich filled with the finest and thinnest cold cuts, or crisp French toast. Your friends or children will love you forever when you hit the sesame seed French toast with hot maple syrup and fresh whipped cream.

1	cup (240 ml) warm water (115 to 127°F/46 to 53°C)
2	teaspoons active dry yeast
1	tablespoon granulated sugar
1	tablespoon kosher salt
¼	cup (60 ml) plus 1 teaspoon olive oil
3	cups (450 g) all-purpose flour, plus more for kneading
	Canola oil, for the bowl and plastic wrap
½	cup (75 g) toasted sesame seeds

In the bowl of a stand mixer, combine the warm water, yeast, sugar, salt, and olive oil. Let the mixture sit for 8 to 10 minutes, until the mixture becomes foamy and fragrant; this indicates the yeast is active and alive.

Add 1⅓ cups (200 g) of the flour and mix with the dough hook on low speed for 2 minutes. Add an additional 1⅓ cups (200 g) of flour until well incorporated. Continue adding the remaining ⅓ cup (50 g) flour one-third at a time until a soft dough forms. The dough should still be sticky. Pull the dough off the sides of mixing bowl and continue kneading for 2 to 3 minutes, or until the dough has come together but is still a little sticky at the bottom. Unload the dough onto a lightly floured work surface and continue kneading until smooth and soft to the touch. Place the dough into a lightly oiled large bowl. Cover the dough with a damp kitchen towel and let proof for 45 minutes.

After the dough has risen (it may not double in size, but it should be noticeably puffy), turn it out onto a clean work surface and divide it into six. Roll each piece of dough into a long, skinny loaf shape about 6 inches (15 cm) long and 1½ inches (4 cm) wide. Once shaped, roll each piece in the sesame seeds, making sure the rolls are completely covered in seeds. Place onto a baking sheet lined with parchment paper, allowing least 1½ inches (4 cm) of space between the loaves. Cover with greased plastic wrap and allow the rolls to rise until they double in size, about 45 minutes.

While the rolls are rising, preheat the oven to 350°F (175°C).

Remove the plastic wrap and bake the rolls for 25 minutes. When the seeds are toasted and the bread is golden brown and feels light, place on wire racks and let cool for 20 minutes. Serve warm.

Seeded Rye Bread

MAKES:
1 LOAF

PREP TIME:
1½ HOURS, PLUS 6 HOURS AND
20 MINUTES INACTIVE TIME

This bread was designed for eating with smoked fish, salty things, and acidic things. Fry it in butter. Slice it thin then top with cultured butter and beef tartare and you'll love me forever. The first time I had rye bread was in Copenhagen. It was just a slice served with butter, a nice ham, and a boiled egg. A perfect breakfast in a perfect city.

3	cups (700 ml) plus 2 tablespoons warm water (115 to 127°F/46 to 53°C)
1	tablespoon active dry yeast
1	tablespoon granulated sugar
⅓	cup (32 g) sunflower seeds
⅓	cup (32 g) pumpkin seeds
⅓	cup (32 g) sesame seeds
6	cups (900 g) rye flour
2	cups plus 3 tablespoons (327 g) bread flour, plus more for kneading
½	cup (120 ml) molasses
⅓	cup (32 g) cracked rye
½	teaspoon salt
	Canola oil, for the bowl
½	cup (120 ml) ice

In a small bowl, combine ⅓ cup plus 4 teaspoons (100 ml) warm water, the active dry yeast, and the sugar. Mix well and let sit for 8 to 10 minutes, until the mixture becomes foamy and fragrant. This indicates the yeast is active and alive.

In another small bowl, combine the sunflower, pumpkin, and sesame seeds.

In a stand mixer, combine the rye flour, bread flour, yeast mixture, molasses, half of the seed mixture, the cracked rye, salt, and the remaining water. Mix with the dough hook on medium speed until a dough has formed, about 2½ minutes. Let the dough sit, covered with a towel, for 20 minutes.

Transfer the dough to a lightly floured work surface and knead until it is smooth and has a nice elastic bounce, about 5 minutes. Move the dough to a lightly oiled mixing bowl. Cover with a damp kitchen towel and place in a cold oven to slightly inflate, about 1 hour. Transfer back to your workspace, flatten the dough, then fold the top and bottom edges toward the middle. Return the dough to the bowl, then back to the cold oven. Let sit until doubled in size, about 3 hours.

Transfer the dough back to your work surface. Positioning your hands on the outside of the dough, rotate the dough over the surface to form a taut dome, pinching the edges underneath. Transfer, seam side up, to a large oiled colander and loosely cover with plastic wrap. Let the dough double in size again, about 3 hours.

One hour before baking, place a large cast-iron skillet on the bottom rack of the oven. Position another rack above the skillet and place a pizza stone on top of it. Preheat the oven to 400°F (204°C).

Invert the dough onto a rimless baking sheet lined with parchment paper. Spray the dough with water and roll in the remaining seed mixture. Using the paper, slide the loaf onto the stone. Place the ice in the skillet—the ice will melt and add steam in the oven, which will help the loaf not to burn and helps the loaf to rise. Bake until dark brown, about 1 hour. Let the bread cool on a wire rack to room temperature before serving.

Molasses Bread in an Apple Juice Can

SERVES:
8

PREP TIME:
1 HOUR, PLUS 1 HOUR
INACTIVE TIME

Apple juice in cans is gonna fly off the shelves from this day on, I swear. Every family in the Maritimes has made a version of this recipe. Making cylinder-shape bread using a large apple juice can is scrappy and great for recycling. You get to drink shitty apple juice, which is great as well. Please make the effort to find these cans; it'll make this process way funnier and an instant family tradition that your kids will love forever.

1	cup (240 ml) warm water (115 to 127°F/46 to 53°C)
1	teaspoon granulated sugar
1	tablespoon active dry yeast
⅔	cup (160 ml) molasses, such as Crosby's Fancy, plus more for serving
1	cup (90 g) old-fashioned rolled oats
1	cup (240 ml) hot water
2	cups (300 g) whole-wheat flour
4½	cups (660 g) all-purpose flour
2	teaspoons kosher salt
2	(1.05 L) cans Allen's Apple Juice, or other similar-size cans
	Unsalted butter
	Sea salt (optional)

In a medium bowl, combine the warm water and sugar, then sprinkle the yeast over the top. Let sit for 8 to 10 minutes, or until the mixture becomes foamy and fragrant; this indicates the yeast is active and alive.

In another medium bowl, combine ⅔ cup (160 ml) of molasses and the oats; stir to incorporate. Pour the hot water into the molasses and oat mixture, stir with a whisk, then add the yeast mixture; whisk to fully incorporate. Transfer to the bowl of a stand mixer fitted with the dough hook attachment. With the mixer running, add the whole-wheat flour slowly (so you don't get flour all over yourself). Then add the all-purpose flour and kosher salt and let it come together. Raise the speed to medium and knead the dough for 2 minutes, or until the dough just comes together. Turn the dough out onto a clean work surface and cut in half.

Grease the inside of the cans with butter. Transfer the dough halves into the cans. Drape a kitchen towel over them and place in a warm area for 1 hour, or until the dough is double in size.

While the dough is rising, preheat the oven to 350°F (175°C).

Place the cans on a baking sheet and bake for 45 minutes, or until the bread has a crispy shell and you can puncture the center with a wooden skewer and it comes out clean.

Set the cans on a wire rack and let the bread cool for 30 minutes. Remove the bread from the cans and let cool further. Once you're ready to dig in, slice a thumb-wide piece and smother with cold butter, molasses, and a pinch of sea salt, if you like, for a real treat. Wrap leftovers in plastic wrap and store in the fridge for up to a week. After a week, the bread can be turned into bread pudding (see my first cookbook for the recipe).

Bannock "Ghost Bread"

SERVES:
6

PREP TIME:
1 HOUR, PLUS 1 HOUR
INACTIVE TIME

My love for bannock started in sixth grade after me and this kid Danny got into a fight because he fouled my best friend at the time, Nick, on the basketball courts at Garrison Road Public School. Go Greyhounds! We both got sent to the principal's office, and we both cried 'cause we both had bloody noses. Then we learned we lived down the street from each other, and I went over to his house after school, and his mom made Indian tacos with this fresh fried donut, and I was like, What is this Mrs. General? and she was like, Call me Cathy, and this is called bannock, but we call it ghost bread. We are Mohawk and our family is Turtle Clan, and this bread has been made by our people for more than 14,000 years. And then I became obsessed with Indian tacos, and every time Cathy made them I was there at the Generals' dinner table. Danny is still my best friend, and Cathy still makes the best bannock I've ever had. She wouldn't share her recipe because she told me to just figure it out, so here's my version.

2	cups (480 ml) whole milk
3	tablespoons instant dry yeast
1	tablespoon granulated sugar
4	eggs
2	tablespoons sour cream
1	cup (240 ml) canola oil, plus more for the bowl and frying
2	teaspoons kosher salt
8½	cups (1 kg) all-purpose flour, plus more as needed

Combine the milk and 1 cup (240 ml) water in a medium pot and heat over medium-low heat until a thermometer reaches just above body temperature, 99.5°F (37.5°C). Add the yeast and sugar and let sit in a warm place until foamy and fragrant, 8 to 10 minutes.

In the bowl of a stand mixer fitted with the whisk attachment, mix the eggs and sour cream at medium speed until incorporated. Reduce the speed to medium-low and slowly pour in the oil until thoroughly combined. Slowly add the yeast mixture.

Turn off the mixer and replace the whisk attachment with the dough hook. Turn on mixer and set to medium-low speed. Slowly add the salt and flour at a medium pace until the dough is completely combined and slightly tacky.

Place the dough in a lightly oiled bowl and allow to proof in a warm area for 1 hour. The dough should double in size.

Fill a large Dutch oven halfway with oil and heat over medium heat until reaches 325°F (165°C).

Place the dough on a lightly floured surface, punch it down, and roll it 1¼ inches (3 cm) thick. Using a cookie cutter, punch out 4 (6-inch/15 cm) circles. Re-roll the remaining dough to the same thickness and punch out 2 more rounds. Place the rounds on a floured tray.

Fry the dough until golden brown, about 3 minutes per side, flipping it back and forth with a spider. It will puff up like a pita. Transfer to a wire rack to drain and cool, then serve warm.

Roti

Making roti at home is kinda like making cinnamon rolls or croissants: Lots of work, but the end result is worth the time and consideration. Giving the paratha that scrunch up after it's perfectly cooked is one of the best feelings ever. You can do it with two spatulas, like chopping it up with both hands gently and slightly turning it, or you can just grab it with your big old greasy hands and give it a nice scrunch, which will flake and bust this perfect roti into a brand-new creature that has more creases and cracks for sauces and dip. It's the Voltron of roti.

1½	cups (192 g) durum flour, plus more for dusting
¼	teaspoon kosher salt
2	tablespoons canola oil, plus more for the bowl
¾	cup (180 ml) hot water
1	tablespoon unsalted butter, melted

Place 1¼ cups (160 g) of the flour into a medium bowl. Add the salt, oil, and hot water and mix with a fork. Lightly dust your work counter with the remaining flour; remove the dough from the bowl and place it onto the counter. Adjust the dough with more flour or water if it is too sticky or dry.

Knead the dough until it is soft and pliable, about 5 minutes. The kneading is super important to work the gluten. Once the dough is the right consistency, place it in a large oiled bowl and cover with a kitchen towel. Rest the dough for 10 minutes.

Cut the dough into 4 portions. Working one piece at a time, roll out the dough to roughly 10 inches (25 cm). Spread with butter, then fold upward, back and forth like an accordion, 1 inch (2.5 cm) at a time; curl it up like a pinwheel. Repeat for all 4 pieces, then chill, about 30 minutes. Once completely chilled, roll each piece into 10-inch (25 cm) circles.

Preheat a large cast-iron skillet on medium-high. Throw a roti into the dry pan and cook for 1 minute. Flip and press down the roti to ensure even cooking on the other side. When the roti rises and forms brown, even bubbles, it's ready to come out. Repeat with the remaining roti. Serve hot.

Grilled Naan

I love naan so much. There's nothing like grilling a bread and lathering it with a room-temperature garlicky butter that melts and pools when brushed on. OMFG, this is everything already, but then top it with freshly chopped and tossed za'atar and sumac. This bread by itself is a champ, but use it to wrap a grilled chicken shawarma or stuff it with sabbich or tear and dip it. The whole block will light up with love.

2	cups (480 ml) whole milk
2	tablespoons instant dry yeast
2	tablespoons granulated sugar
4	eggs
2	tablespoons sour cream
1	cup (240 ml) canola oil, plus more for bowl and brushing
2	teaspoons sea salt, plus more for finishing
8½	cups (1 kg) all-purpose flour, plus more as needed
2	tablespoons za'atar
2	tablespoons dried sumac

Combine the milk and 1 cup (240 ml) water in a medium pot and heat over medium-low heat until a thermometer reaches just above body temperature, 99.5°F (37.5°C). Add the yeast and sugar and let sit in a warm place until foamy and fragrant, 8 to 10 minutes. This indicates the yeast is active and alive.

In the bowl of a stand mixer fitted with the whisk attachment, mix the eggs and sour cream until incorporated. Reduce the speed to low and slowly pour in the oil until thoroughly combined. Slowly add the yeast mixture and the salt.

Turn off the mixer and replace the whisk attachment with the dough hook. Slowly add the flour at a medium pace on medium speed until the dough is completely combined and slightly tacky.

Place the dough in a lightly oiled bowl, cover with plastic wrap, and allow to proof in a warm area for 1 hour. The dough should double in size.

While the dough is rising, preheat your grill. You can use a gas grill or charcoal grill.

Place the dough on a lightly floured surface, punch it down, and roll it 1¼ inches (3 cm) thick. Using a floured bench scraper, cut the dough into whatever shape you want. They are not supposed to be perfect. Place the dough on a floured tray.

Grill the naan on your super-hot grill: Let the naan puff and get a nice char on the bottom side, about 1 minute. Flip and repeat. Make sure to keep your eyes on each side—don't burn it, you fucking kooks. Put on a wire rack, lightly brush with oil, and season with a generous amount of za'atar, sumac, and sea salt. Repeat with the remaining naan.

Cornbread

MAKES:
8 WEDGES

PREP TIME:
1 HOUR

Cornbread is maybe the most iconic bread in North America. Like barbecue, it's a basis of American cuisine. Everyone should have a cast-iron pan and everyone should know how to season it, and everyone should know how to make a cornbread. Some add flour, some don't; some use bacon grease, some use butter. I like to use whatever's in the fridge: If I have bacon fat, then hell yes, I'm gonna use that to crisp up my cornbread. Once again, you can take your cornbread in so many directions. Add cheese, pickles, ham, sausage, bacon—you could literally throw anything in there. Just make sure it's cooked in a cast-iron pan that was handed down to you. If you don't have that, then buy one and start the tradition, and hand it down to your children or friends from your deathbed.

	Unsalted butter, at room temperature
4	eggs
2	teaspoons kosher salt
⅓	cup plus 2 tablespoons (100 g) granulated sugar
1¼	cups (300 ml) buttermilk
3	tablespoons sour cream
¼	teaspoon baking powder
¼	teaspoon baking soda
2	cups (300 g) all-purpose flour
1	cup (228 g) instant cornmeal
¼	cup (30 g) diced jalapeño chile
¼	cup (30 g) diced pickled jalapeño chile
½	cup (50 g) grated smoked Gouda cheese
½	cup (50 g) grated Monterey Jack cheese
⅓	cup plus 1 tablespoon (100 g) unsalted butter, frozen then grated on the large holes of a cheese grater

Preheat the oven to 375°F (190°C). Grease a large cast-iron skillet with the room-temperature butter.

In a large bowl, whisk the eggs, salt, and sugar until combined. Add the buttermilk, sour cream, baking powder, and baking soda and whisk to combine. Add the flour, cornmeal, both jalapeños, both cheeses, and the frozen grated butter. Do not overmix.

Pour the batter into the prepared cast-iron skillet and bake for 40 minutes, or until nice and golden brown on top and a cake tester comes out clean. Let that cornbread rest for 15 minutes on a wire rack, then pop the cornbread out of the skillet onto a cutting board and slice into 8 wedges.

Focaccia

SERVES:
8 TO 10

PREP TIME:
1 HOUR, PLUS 2 HOURS
INACTIVE TIME

This bread, with its pockets of bubbling olive oil and crunchy summer savory; crispy, airy top; and roasted bottom, is perfect for holding thinly sliced mortadella or some fresh picked arugula. Smother it with fresh pepper, sea salt, and more good olive oil. This bread is perfect for any time of the year, whenever you need a pick-me-up or some divine moments in your mouth.

1⅓ cups (315 ml) warm water

2 teaspoons active dry yeast

1 tablespoon granulated sugar

5 cups (750 g) all-purpose flour, plus more as needed

2 teaspoons kosher salt

1 cup (240 ml) extra virgin olive oil, plus more for drizzling

½ cup (100 g) chopped summer savory
    Sea salt (preferably Newfoundland sea salt)

In a small bowl, combine the warm water, yeast, and sugar. Mix well and let sit for 8 to 10 minutes, until the mixture becomes foamy and fragrant; this indicates the yeast is active and alive.

In the bowl of a stand mixer fitted with the dough hook, combine the flour, kosher salt, ½ cup (120 ml) of the olive oil, and the yeast mixture and mix on low speed. Once the dough has come together, continue to knead for 2 to 3 minutes on medium speed, until the dough becomes smooth and soft. Add a little more flour if the dough is still tacky.

Transfer the dough to a clean, lightly floured work surface and knead two or three times more, again adding a touch more flour if needed. Coat the inside of a large bowl with oil. Put the dough in the bowl and cover with a kitchen towel. In a warm spot in your kitchen, let the dough double in size, at least 1 hour.

Coat the inside of an 18 by 13-inch (46 by 33 cm) half sheet pan with the remaining ½ cup (120 ml) olive oil—this oil creates the crunchy crust of the focaccia. Put the dough onto the sheet and press the dough out to all edges of the baking sheet. As you are doing this, spread your fingers out to make little finger holes in the dough—this gives the focaccia its bubbly look. If you don't do this step, your focaccia will be flat and smooth.

Now rest your dough. You want your dough to grow double in size again; leave it for another hour.

While the dough is rising, preheat the oven 450°F (220°C).

Sprinkle the top of the focaccia with chopped summer savory and sea salt and drizzle a little more olive oil on top. Bake until golden brown, 25 to 30 minutes. Remove from the oven and let cool to room temperature before slicing.

CHAPTER 2

Stocks

Stocks Are Broths?
Broths Are Stocks?
Fortify Your Life.

BROTHS ARE IMPORTANT BUILDING BLOCKS IN THE CULINARY CASTLE OF THE WORLD.
Or maybe they're the moat that protects the castle. Yeah that's it. Broth and stocks protect us from what we don't know. For sure the bread is the drawbridge. I recently watched *Braveheart*, which is my favorite movie. Maybe that's why I'm talking about castles and drawbridges. It's going to stop here, because I don't want this book to turn into a medieval cookbook. This is just how my mind works.

Broths and stocks have magic in them. Beef and bone marrow broth can cure you. A court bouillon can make sure your mussels are poached perfectly and full of flavor. With great stocks you can make great soups. With shitty stocks you can make shitty soups. In some restaurant kitchens, stocks are garbage cans. I fucking hate when I see cooks just throwing food scraps into stocks. If they are really dumb fucking cowboys they don't even take off the elastic. Like who the fuck would do that? A fucking animal would make something that poorly and with that kind of disrespect.

The stocks in this chapter are simple and timeless. I am just giving you the paintbrushes and the canvas. You can start painting in your style shortly, but let's make just a nice simple painting of a tree-filled hill before we go deep on some far-out Impressionist shit, ya know? We need to master the basics, Bob Ross–style, before we can get to the big show. Simplicity is so key, and restraint is vital when making stocks. All it takes is bones, onion, and water. If simmered properly, in twenty-four hours you should have a broth that is so filled with body and love that when you strain and finally add salt and awaken its true beauty, your head will explode—so be careful. Once again, restraint is key: Please don't start off by adding all these herbs and spices; just make the stocks, then fortify with a secondary flavor. By making these simple stocks you will be left with such power, such grace.

I love broth so much, and I know you will fall in love with it forever. Spread that love as well—if a friend is suffering from a flu or a hangover, bring over a pot of chicken stock to their house. Nothing feels better than bringing food to someone in need. Stock is love and life!

Celeriac Stock

MAKES:
4 QUARTS (4 L)

PREP TIME:
7 HOURS AND
15 MINUTES

We used to make this at Parts & Labour, to go in our cauliflower dish. The deep flavor these roots develop after roasting whole creates a beautiful stock. With the protection of the outer skin, the celeriac root caramelizes through in the hours of the bake. The water steeping method extracts the pure essence of this phenomenal vegetable. This can be easily reduced to a celeriac demi or added to and fortified like any other stock.

4	large unpeeled celeriac (celery root)
2	unpeeled yellow onions, cut in half
6	sprigs thyme
4	bay leaves
5	quarts (5 L) cold water
½	cup (170 g) kosher salt

Preheat the oven to 325°F (165°C).

Rinse the celeriac under water to wash away dirt or sand. Place the celeriac on a wire rack set into a baking sheet. Bake for 4 hours or until the celeriac gets a deep caramelization all over. With an hour remaining, throw your halved onions in with the celeriac to roast. Remove from the oven.

Place the roasted celeriac, onions, thyme, and bay leaves into a large stockpot and cover with the cold water. Bring to a gentle boil over high heat, then turn down heat to medium-low and simmer uncovered for 2 hours. Turn off heat and let the celeriac steep in its tea for 45 minutes, then add the salt.

Ladle out the celeriac, onions, thyme, and bay leaves and discard them. Note: There may still be sand coming off the celeriac, so let the tea settle for 30 minutes before you strain. Strain the tea through a fine chinois or strainer, discarding the last little bit (about a centimeter) so you don't get any leftover sand. Strain the tea again through a coffee filter that you set into the fine chinois or strainer. You can reduce the tea by half again to intensify the flavor if you like.

The tea will last up to 1 week in the fridge. Or you can put it into 1-quart (1 L) ziplock bags and freeze it. Quick tip: Use a small pot to hold the ziplock bag in place as you ladle the tea in. Take out excess air, seal, and freeze.

Rutabaga Nage

MAKES:
2 QUARTS (2 L)

PREP TIME:
3 HOURS

Root vegetables make beautiful stocks. I love making separate stocks of rutabaga, turnip, celery root, or celery instead of combining them into a vegetable stock. This makes sense to me. I think of it like a tea, and everyone loves tea, especially vegetable tea. Bone broth is definitely having its time in the sun, but vegetable tea should be on the rise. I'm loving it.

4¼	pounds (2 kg) rutabaga, peeled and chopped
2	large yellow onions, cut in half
2	tablespoons kosher salt
3	quarts (3 L) cold water

Combine the rutabaga, onions, and salt in a large stockpot. Add the water, place over medium heat, and bring to just under a boil. Turn down heat to low and lightly simmer for 2 to 2½ hours, never letting the stock boil. It's important that you don't let the rutabaga break down and cloud your stock. Turn off heat and let the stock steep for 30 minutes.

Strain your stock through a fine chinois or strainer, then strain again through a coffee filter that you set into the fine chinois or strainer. After straining, you could also reduce the stock again by half to intensify the flavor.

If not using the stock immediately, let it cool to room temperature and refrigerate for up to 1 week. Or you can put it into 1-quart (1 L) ziplock bags and freeze it for up to 2 months. Quick tip: Use a small pot to hold the ziplock bag in place as you ladle the stock in. Take out excess air, seal, and freeze. Bring to a boil before using.

Mushroom Stock

MAKES:
3 QUARTS (3 L)

PREP TIME:
1 HOUR AND
20 MINUTES

Mushrooms are the "beefiest" of all the vegetables, which gets me excited. This stock can be made like any other stock and can be poured and strained into many directions of flavor-building. Mac loves it when we make a mushroom stock at home 'cause he can play Whack-a-Mole with the floating, bobbing mushrooms. I love watching my kids play with food; I think everyone should play with food. It creates a unifying emotion of joy that can develop into a lifelong love affair. More kids should play with their food.

6	pounds (3 kg) cremini mushrooms, washed and cleaned
1	bouquet garni (2 sprigs thyme, 3 sprigs parsley, and 1 bay leaf tied together with butcher's twine)
1	(6-inch/15 cm) piece dried kombu
2	onions, cut in half and roasted for 1 hour at 325°F (165°C)
½	cup (65 g) black peppercorns, toasted

Place all mushrooms into your pot and cover with 5 quarts (5 L) water. Add the bouquet garni, kombu, roasted onions, and peppercorns.

Bring the stock up to a boil over medium-high heat, then reduce heat to low, cover, and simmer for 30 to 45 minutes. Remove from heat and strain the solids through a fine chinois or strainer. Strain the stock a second time through a coffee filter that you set into the fine chinois or strainer. You can reduce the stock by half again to intensify the flavor if you like.

The stock will last up to 1 week in the fridge. Or you can put it into 1-quart (1 L) ziplock bags and freeze it. Quick tip: Use a small pot to hold the ziplock bag in place as you ladle the stock in. Take out excess air, seal, and freeze.

Court Bouillon

MAKES:
5 QUARTS (5 L)

PREP TIME:
1½ HOURS

This stock is a special one for me. You can poach vegetables, shellfish, fish, or even poultry in this recipe. Court bouillon is a fundamental stock in most French kitchens and allows you to add that gentle magic touch to many dishes. Why would you poach mussels just in salted water? I'm not saying court bouillon should be made with scraps, but those kinda dried-out vegetables and herbs would be great in building a broth full of flavor. If you're lucky enough to be able to buy or grow fresh tarragon or lemon thyme, then holy cow, you're one lucky household.

2	white onions, quartered
1	leek, sliced
3	carrots, peeled and sliced
1	whole head garlic, cut in half crosswise
6	ribs celery, sliced
3	tomatoes (5 ounces/150 g total), quartered and seeded
1	quart (1 L) white wine
6½	quarts (6 L) cold water
1	tablespoon black peppercorns
1	tablespoon white peppercorns
1	tablespoon pink peppercorns
2	tablespoons coriander seeds
2	tablespoons cardamom pods
2	bay leaves
7	sprigs parsley
4	sprigs tarragon

Place the onions, leek, carrots, garlic, celery, and tomatoes in a large stockpot and cover with the wine and cold water. Bring the stock to a hard boil over high heat.

In a small skillet over medium heat, toast the peppercorns, coriander seeds, cardamom, and bay leaves until fragrant. Add to the stock along with the parsley and tarragon and boil for 30 minutes. Turn off heat and let steep for 30 minutes, then strain through a fine chinois or strainer, discarding the solids. Strain a second time through a coffee filter that you set into the fine chinois or strainer.

Let the stock cool to room temperature and refrigerate for up to 3 days. Or you can put it into 1-quart (1 L) ziplock bags and freeze it for up to 2 months. Quick tip: Use a small pot to hold the ziplock bag in place as you ladle the stock in. Take out excess air, seal, and freeze. Bring to a boil before using.

Fish Fumet

MAKES:
3 QUARTS (3 L)

PREP TIME:
1 HOUR

Please never boil this stock, ever. All you need to do is just slightly raise to a gentle simmer, then turn way down low and allow it to come together. You do not want cloudy fish stock. That shit is so gross. And please, please, please use a fresh fish head. Once again, you don't have to use the most perfect vegetables, but it helps to do so. You must not cook this stock for longer than one hour. Allowing it to steep is important, and letting it settle before ladling from the top and working your way down is important to make sure you have nice, clear fish stock. Once you have this fish fumet, you could reuse and fortify it with shrimp shells, which make for an even more amazing stock that can be reduced and used for soups, cooking vegetables, and sauces. I love just using this stock with some fresh sliced white fish, store-bought udon, and napa cabbage with chili oil, cilantro, lime juice, and maybe a little white pepper.

1	large grouper head (5 pounds/2.2 kg), split and rinsed
5	quarts (5 L) cold water
1¼	cups (300 ml) white wine
½	cup (50 g) peeled and diced ginger
1	stalk lemongrass, tenderized with the side of your knife
3	shallots, cut in half
4	scallions, cut into 2-inch (5 cm) pieces
⅓	cup (30 g) coriander seeds, toasted
½	cup (50 g) cilantro sprigs
½	cup (50 g) tarragon sprigs
2	tablespoons kosher salt

Place the fish head in a large stockpot and cover with the cold water and white wine. Bring to a soft boil over medium heat. Skim off the scum (impurities) that floats to the top of the stock and wipe off with a paper towel any scum that is stuck to the sides of the pot. Once the stock is beautiful and clear, about 20 minutes, add the remaining ingredients except the salt.

Simmer your fumet super lightly over low heat for 45 minutes; don't overcook, or it will become milky and cloudy. Strain through a fine chinois or strainer, then strain again through a coffee filter that you set into the fine chinois or strainer. Season with salt.

Let the stock cool to room temperature and refrigerate for up to 3 days. Or you can put it into 1-quart (1 L) ziplock bags and freeze it for up to 2 months. Quick tip: Use a small pot to hold the ziplock bag in place as you ladle the stock in. Take out excess air, seal, and freeze. Bring to a boil before using.

Chicken Stock

MAKES:
4 QUARTS (4 L)

PREP TIME:
3 HOURS AND
15 MINUTES

Chicken stock is "the" stock, right? It's the most-used one in my house, for sure. I love chicken stock—blond, dark, smoked, boxed. Yes, that's right, I love using boxed stock. Is there anything better than reducing dark chicken stock into a jus and drowning warm buttery mashed potatoes in it, then plopping a crisp fried chicken thigh on top? I love chicken so much, and bad chicken, for all you water-bleached economy-chicken eaters, is not chicken. Find a butcher and ask for a heritage chicken or even a Chantecler chicken and eat that and tell me it ain't the best chicken you've ever had. If you make stock with a good chicken, guess what, your stock, filled with free-range love, will be an even better stock.

1	(3-pound/2.3 kg) whole fresh chicken, rinsed
5	quarts (5 L) cold water
1	onion, sliced in half
1	stalk lemongrass, tenderized with the back spine of your knife
2	scallions, white and green parts, chopped
1	bird's eye chile
½	cup (50 g) cilantro sprigs
1	whole head garlic
1	thumb-size piece ginger
1	tablespoon each black and white peppercorns, toasted

Place the chicken in a large stockpot, cover with the cold water, and bring to a soft boil over medium heat. Skim off the scum (impurities) that float up to the top of the stock and wipe off with a paper towel any scum that is stuck to the sides of the pot. Once the stock is beautiful and clear, about 20 minutes, add the remaining ingredients.

Turn down heat to low and gently, gently, gently simmer for 2 hours, skimming any scum or fat that rises to the top. Turn off heat and steep the stock for 1 hour, then strain through a fine chinois or strainer. Reserve the chicken meat for a million different things, discarding all the other solids. Strain a second time through a coffee filter that you set into the fine chinois or strainer.

If not using immediately, let the stock cool to room temperature and refrigerate for up to 3 days. Or you can put it into 1-quart (1 L) ziplock bags and freeze it for up to 2 months. Quick tip: Use a small pot to hold the ziplock bag in place as you ladle the stock in. Take out excess air, seal, and freeze. Bring to a boil before using.

Pork Stock

MAKES:
6½ QUARTS (6 L)

PREP TIME:
13 HOURS AND
35 MINUTES

A pork bone stock is the other white meat stock. It could be used perfectly with a bean soup, as a chili base, or even for braising more pork. Almost ten years ago, I had a beautiful pork broth and frozen Concord grapes in a great French restaurant, Le Chateaubriand, and it was the first bite of one of the best meals of my life. Pork stock is also perfect for ramen or kimchi stew. It's a little more intense than chicken stock, and I do love making it because I love pork so much.

5	pounds (2.5 kg) skinless pork neck bones, rinsed
5	pounds (2.5 kg) pork rib bones
10½	quarts (10.5 L) cold water
2	white onions, quartered
2	ribs celery, each cut into 5 chunks
2	tomatoes, quartered and seeded
1	head garlic, cut in half crosswise
6	sprigs parsley
4	bay leaves
2	tablespoons black peppercorns, toasted

Place the pork neck and rib bones in a large stockpot, cover with the cold water, and bring to a soft boil over medium heat. Skim off the scum (impurities) that floats up to the top of the stock and wipe off with a paper towel any scum that is stuck to the sides of the pot. Once the stock is beautiful and clear, about 20 minutes, add the remaining ingredients.

Turn down heat to low and gently, gently, gently simmer for 12 hours, skimming any scum or fat that rises to the top. Turn off heat and steep the stock for 1 hour, then strain through a fine chinois or strainer, discarding the solids. Strain a second time through a coffee filter that you set into the fine chinois or strainer.

If not using immediately, let the stock cool to room temperature and refrigerate for up to 3 days or freeze for up to 2 months. Bring to a boil before using.

Beef and Bone Marrow Stock

MAKES:
6 QUARTS (6 L)

PREP TIME:
13½ HOURS

Marrow is maybe the most important part of this stock. The way the marrow renders, the tendon softens—I love it so much. Whenever I make beef stock I always throw in some marrow bones, and at the end, for a special few bites, I make some toast that I scrape the marrow and tendon onto, with some sea salt and fresh cracked pepper, and wash it down with a cup of beef stock. The stocks in this chapter are all so simple and leave you with a blissful liquid that freezes and serves up some sips and soups and bases for great meals year-round. I love these building blocks. Build yourself a soup castle and enjoy your day.

1	pound (450 g) chuck roll
6	(2-inch/5 cm) pieces beef bone marrow
10½	quarts (10 L) cold water
1	onion, halved
2	bay leaves
2	tablespoons black peppercorns, toasted

Place the chuck roll and bone marrow in a large stockpot, cover with the cold water, and bring to a soft boil over medium heat. Skim off the scum (impurities) that float up to the top of the stock and wipe off with a paper towel any scum that is stuck to the sides of the pot. Once the stock is beautiful and clear, about 20 minutes, add the remaining ingredients.

Reduce heat to low and gently, gently, gently simmer for 12 hours, skimming any scum or fat that rises to the top. Turn off heat and steep the stock for 1 hour, then strain through a fine chinois or strainer, discarding the solids. Strain a second time through a coffee filter that you set into the fine chinois or strainer.

If not using immediately, let the stock cool to room temperature and refrigerate for up to 3 days. Or you can put it into 1-quart (1 L) ziplock bags and freeze it for up to 2 months. Quick tip: Use a small pot to hold the ziplock bag in place as you ladle the stock in. Take out excess air, seal, and freeze. Bring to a boil before using.

Lamb Stock

Lamb stock is another stock that maybe you don't need, but let me tell you, it's so worth it and has such distinct taste. Fortify it with a chicken stock or reduce it to a jus for roasting lamb or making a lamb curry. A lot of people say lamb is too gamey, and I think those people are just buying from bad butcher shops, or overboiling or underseasoning it and really bringing out the worst in lamb. When people think of animals like lamb, goat, or rabbit, they think of them in a bad way. I love lamb so much, and I love all stocks. They are vehicles of flavor. I hope you all make some at least once and see how many ways you can take these stocks and build your little flavor worlds.

6	lamb shanks
10½	quarts (10.5 L) cold water
2	white onions, quartered
4	carrots, peeled and sliced
4	ribs celery, sliced
3	tomatoes, quartered and seeded
1	head garlic, cut in half crosswise
7	sprigs parsley
7	sprigs thyme
2	bay leaves
2	tablespoons black peppercorns, toasted

Preheat the oven to 400°F (200°C).

Place the lamb shanks on a wire rack set in a baking sheet and roast until golden brown, about 40 minutes.

Place the roasted lamb shanks in a large stockpot, reserving the fat from underneath the rack. Cover the shanks with the cold water and bring to a soft boil over medium heat. Skim off the scum (impurities) that floats up to the top of the stock and wipe off with a paper towel any scum that is stuck to the sides of the pot.

Braise the lamb shanks for 3 hours, skimming any scum or fat that rises to the top. Add the remaining ingredients and the collected fat drippings to the stock and cook for 1 hour. Remove from heat and steep the stock for 1 hour, then strain through a fine chinois or strainer, discarding the solids. Strain a second time through a coffee filter that you set into the fine chinois or strainer.

If not using immediately, let the stock cool to room temperature and refrigerate for up to 3 days. Or you can put it into 1-quart (1 L) ziplock bags and freeze it for up to 2 months. Quick tip: Use a small pot to hold the ziplock bag in place as you ladle the stock in. Take out excess air, seal, and freeze. Bring to a boil before using.

CHAPTER 3

Vegetables

I Love Cooking Vegetables and You Should Too

WELCOME TO THE LONGEST CHAPTER IN THIS BOOK. GUESS WHAT, IT'S THE VEGETABLE SECTION! Guess what again, there's some meat and some fish in some of these vegetable dishes! If you don't want there to be meat or fish, then don't use any, and add mock meat or soy cheese or whatever you want. I just love cooking vegetables as much as cooking meat. This chapter is to show you guys that that's kinda true, I guess; or maybe I do love cooking meat and seafood a little more, but I'm trying harder to love vegetables.

In this chapter there are pickles, salads, soups, composed dishes, and family-style dishes. I hope they spark excitement and creativity in your kitchen. I think less is more, even with vegetables. That's why I love pickles and preserves so much, same as curing meats or smoking fishes or charcuterie. It's the ability to preserve the product, to hold it in time, and make it nonperishable. It's a way of honoring your ingredients.

Let's make the most of vegetables and treat them with the respect they deserve. If there are eyes on your potatoes you can just cut them off and still cook them perfectly for a vichyssoise or my favorite, Aligot Potatoes, or Cheesy Stringy Potatoes (page 108). All it takes is a little time and care. It's important to make time for vegetables. Let's line the halls of your cold, dark spaces with pickles, preserves, and krauts. Making preserves is a labor of love. Don't DM me if you don't clean out your jars properly and someone gets a little frothy from some sketchy carrot sauerkraut you made a year ago. That's not my problem. Good rotation is very important. Labeling is massive when pickling, so you know when you made it.

Even though some of these dishes have meat or seafood, I want to show you that the vegetables are still the stars. I want to show you that sometimes a small amount of meat can make a vegetable shine brighter. I want to show the unity in food. I want to break down the walls. I don't want everything to be so cut and dry.

I hear you, my vegetarian fans. I'm trying to give you dishes to get something out of this chapter. The vegetables don't stop here. Instead of making a soy tofu turkey roll or whatever you call it, check out my beautiful Thanksgiving Stuffing Butternut Squash (page 110). When it comes to vegetables and food overall, your imagination is the only thing to blame.

Pickled Radish (page 69)

Carrot Kraut (page 69)

Hot Pepper Agrodolce (page 68)

Nannie's Blood-Red Beets (page 68)

Dilled Pickles (page 70)

Pickled Hot Peppers (page 67)

Bread and Butter Pickles (page 71)

Yuzu Cucumbers (page 65)

Black Radish Kraut (page 65)

Fish Sauce Green Tomatoes (page 66)

Yuzu Cucumbers

SERVES: 6 TO 8

PREP TIME: 20 MINUTES, PLUS 12 TO 24 HOURS INACTIVE TIME

Quick and easy with high impact for a joyous crunchy time. I love making these often in the summer. They're great with literally anything—grilled pork, steamed fish, or just a snack 'cause you're a snack, so enjoy this snack, snack.

⅓	cup (75 ml) yuzu juice
⅓	cup (75 ml) lime juice
2	tablespoons malt vinegar
1	tablespoon toasted sesame oil
2	tablespoons sambal oelek
3½	tablespoons olive oil
1	cup (35 g) cilantro stems, minced
2	tablespoons grated garlic
2	tablespoons grated ginger
2	tablespoons granulated sugar
6	mini cucumbers, cut into straight 1-inch (2.5 cm) coins

Whisk together the yuzu and lime juices, malt vinegar, sesame oil, sambal oelek, olive oil, cilantro stems, garlic, ginger, and sugar in a large bowl.

Add the cucumbers to the marinade and toss to coat. Cover and refrigerate for 12 to 24 hours. Take out of the marinade and serve immediately, with grilled fish, Korean BBQ ribs, or curries.

Black Radish Kraut

MAKES: 2 QUARTS (2 L)

PREP TIME: 15 MINUTES, PLUS 6 WEEKS INACTIVE TIME

This was my favorite pickle ever from the amazing Allison Roberts, who was our first pastry chef and who pickled and preserved at Parts & Labour. The cumin and the black radish that turns pretty much into sauerkraut is the greatest gift. This punchy radish ferment is perfection on a snappy pork hot dog, in a wild boar terrine, or on a borscht with some sour cream!

4¼	pounds (2 kg) black radish, cleaned and grated on the large holes of a box grater
⅓	cup (40 g) toasted cumin seeds
3	tablespoons kosher salt (or 2 percent of the weight of the radish)
1½	tablespoons granulated sugar (or 1 percent of the weight of the radish)

Preheat the oven to 350°F (175°C). Wash 2 (1-quart/1 L) mason jars and lids and pop the jars in the oven for 15 minutes to sterilize.

In a sterilized bowl, mix the grated black radish, toasted cumin seeds, salt, and sugar until the radish is well coated. Pack into your jars up to the rim. Place a piece of folded plastic wrap at the top and seal the jars tight.

Leave the jars to ferment at room temperature, 69°F (18°C), in a dark place, for 3 weeks. Open the jars, check for any unhealthy black mold, wipe the sides of the jars, add a new piece of plastic wrap, and continue fermenting for 3 more weeks. Discard the jar if you see any mold on the kraut. Open the jars and taste for desired acidity and funkiness. Store in the fridge for up to 1 year.

Fish Sauce Green Tomatoes

MAKES:
2 QUARTS
(2 L)

PREP TIME:
1 HOUR, PLUS
12 HOURS
INACTIVE TIME

Who doesn't love a funky, deep-flavored, fish-sauced pickled tomato? The best thing about these sliced pickled tomatoes is that you could chop them up for a relish, or add them to a mignonette for oysters, or add some of their liquid to a Bloody Mary punch bowl. The world is yours, and it's raining green tomatoes and fish sauce.

3	cups (680 ml) white vinegar (preferably Allen's 5% acidity)
1½	cups (360 ml) fish sauce
¾	cup (170 g) granulated sugar
⅓	cup (60 g) halved and seeded jalapeño chiles
2	tablespoons kosher salt
4	pounds (1.8 kg) large green tomatoes, cut in half

Preheat the oven to 350°F (175°C). Wash 2 (1-quart/1 L) mason jars and lids and pop the jars in the oven for 15 minutes to sterilize.

Put the vinegar, fish sauce, 1½ cups (360 ml) water, and sugar in a large nonreactive pot and bring to a soft boil; boil until the sugar is completely dissolved. Add the jalapeños and salt.

Pack the tomatoes into your jars; you want to pack one tomato at a time, cut side down, followed by the next tomato cut side down. Fit as many as you can without squishing them. Aim to fill the jars to just below the rim.

Carefully pour the hot brine over the tomatoes, making sure the tomatoes are completely submerged. You may need to shuffle some of the tomatoes and add more brine, but make sure there is around ½ inch (1 cm) space between the brine and the lid.

Use a chopstick to stir around the jar and remove any air bubbles in the brine. Seal the jar with a lid.

To heat-process, place the jars in a large stockpot with a kitchen towel underneath the jars to protect them from breaking. Cover with warm water, bring to a boil over medium-high heat, and boil for 20 minutes to seal the tops. Using canning tongs, carefully remove from the hot water and place upside down on a dry kitchen towel.

Once pickled, store unprocessed in the fridge for up to 6 weeks. The longer you allow the tomatoes to age, the better. If you are happy with your seals, store processed jars in a cool dark place for 6 weeks or more.

Pickled Hot Peppers

MAKES:
4 QUARTS
(4 L)

PREP TIME:
1 HOUR, PLUS
24 HOURS
INACTIVE TIME

I truly think the reason for making these is to blend them up and make an agrodolce to cover any kind of grilled meat. I used to confit and deep-fry half a pig's head, then cover it in a pickled pepper agrodolce, and now you can, too. This is the beginning of opening your spicy mind's eye.

1½	quarts (1.5 L) white vinegar (such as Allen's 5% acidity)
3	cups (750 g) granulated sugar
2	tablespoons canning salt
1	pound (450 g) jalapeño chiles, seeded and chopped
1	pound (450 g) Anaheim chiles, seeded and chopped
1	pound (450 g) serrano chiles, seeded and chopped
1	pound (450 g) poblano chiles, seeded and chopped
1	pound (450 g) pimento chiles, seeded and chopped
1	pound (450 g) red bell peppers, seeded and chopped
8	garlic cloves, peeled
8	bay leaves

Note: Use gloves when handling chiles, and do not touch your eyes after handling them!

Preheat the oven to 350°F (175°C). Wash 4 (1-quart/1 L) mason jars and lids and pop the jars in the oven for 15 minutes to sterilize.

In a nonreactive pot, combine the vinegar, 1½ quarts (1.5 L) water, sugar, and salt. Bring to a boil over medium-high heat and boil for 10 minutes. Combine the hot and sweet peppers. Wearing gloves, pack the mixed hot and sweet peppers into your jars up to ½ inch (1 cm) from the mouth of the jars. Add 2 garlic cloves and 2 bay leaves to each jar.

Carefully ladle the hot pickling liquid into the jars, leaving ½ inch (1 cm) at the top. Remove air bubbles with a quick stir and adjust the headspace, if necessary, by adding more hot pickling liquid. Wipe the rims and screw the tops on until fingertip tight.

Heat-process the jars, following the instructions on page 66. The hot peppers are ready to eat within 24 hours, or store up to 6 months in a cool, dark area.

Nannie's Blood-Red Beets

MAKES: 4 QUARTS (4 L)	PREP TIME: 1 HOUR, PLUS 24 HOURS INACTIVE TIME

Nannie's blood-red beets are a valuable asset to any table, and I still have no idea why at literally every meal there was a jar on the table. I'm starting to think it was the only thing Nannie could pickle, haha. Jokes aside, I love you and miss you, Nannie, and I know you could make other pickles. I'm literally chirping my deceased grandmother.

¼	cup (50 g) whole cloves, toasted
¼	cup (50 g) whole allspice, toasted
2½	cups (600 ml) red wine vinegar (preferably Allen's 5% acidity)
1¼	cups (300 g) granulated sugar
1	tablespoon canning salt
4	pounds (1.8 kg) medium red beets, boiled, peeled, and quartered
4	bay leaves
8	garlic cloves, peeled
2	cinnamon sticks, broken in half

Preheat the oven to 350°F (175°C). Wash 4 (1-quart/1 L) widemouthed mason jars and lids and pop the jars in the oven for 15 minutes to sterilize.

Wrap the cloves and allspice in a double layer of cheesecloth and tie with kitchen twine to make a sachet.

In a nonreactive pot, combine 2½ cups (600 ml) water, the vinegar, sugar, spice sachet, and salt and bring to a boil over medium-high heat; boil for 10 minutes. Remove from heat and remove the sachet.

Pack the beets into your jars up to ½ inch (1 cm) of the mouth of the jars. Place 1 bay leaf, 2 garlic cloves, and ½ cinnamon stick in each jar.

Heat-process the jars, following the instructions on page 66. The beets are ready to eat within 24 hours, or store up to 6 months in a cool, dark area.

Hot Pepper Agrodolce

MAKES: 1 QUART (1 L)	PREP TIME: 20 MINUTES

This is the best: Use it to cover a crispy pig's head, fried fish, a buttery terrine, or a beautiful air-dried, perfectly grilled squab.

1	quart (1 L) Pickled Hot Peppers (page 67), with liquid
2	cups (250 g) granulated sugar
⅓	cup (50 g) chopped shallots
2	tablespoons grated garlic
2	tablespoons grated ginger

Strain the liquid from the jar of hot peppers into a medium saucepan and reserve the peppers. Add the sugar, shallots, garlic, and ginger to the liquid. Cook over medium heat until reduced and the liquid starts to caramelize.

Run your knife through the pickled peppers until chopped. Add the chopped peppers to the saucepan and stir until the peppers are nicely coated in the sweet and sour reduction.

Carrot Kraut

MAKES: 2 QUARTS (2 L)

PREP TIME: 25 MINUTES, PLUS 24 HOURS INACTIVE TIME

This is another Allison Roberts preserve that was served on the terrine board at Parts & Labour and that I truly love. It's almost a kraut, and if you were to add a ton of sugar and cook it down you could transform it into a marmalade. I love this 'cause you can use carrots all year round, and if you're so lucky to have great carrots from a farmers' market then they will be even better. There's nothing cooler than seeing people leave a farmers' market with a tote stacked with vegetables, those carrot tops waving to the farmers like an Olympic athlete who just broke a world record.

2	cups (500 g) granulated sugar
2	cups (480 ml) white vinegar (Allen's 5% acidity)
1	cup (240 ml) apple cider vinegar
2	tablespoons mustard seeds
1	tablespoon celery seeds
3	pounds (1.3 kg) carrots, grated on the large holes of a box grater
4	bird's eye chiles, cut lengthwise and seeded
4	bay leaves

Preheat the oven to 350°F (175°C). Wash 2 (1-quart/1 L) widemouthed mason jars and lids and pop the jars in the oven for 15 minutes to sterilize.

In a nonreactive pot, combine the sugar and 2 cups (480 ml) water and bring to a boil over medium-high heat, stirring to dissolve all the sugar. Once the simple syrup is ready, add the vinegars, mustard seeds, and celery seeds to build your sweet pickling liquid.

Pack the carrots between the 2 jars. Add the chiles and bay leaves and really pack the carrots in tightly.

Heat-process the jars, following the instructions on page 66. The kraut is ready to eat within 24 hours, or store up to 6 months in a cool, dark area.

Pickled Radish

MAKES: 1 QUART (1 L)

PREP TIME: 10 MINUTES, PLUS 24 HOURS INACTIVE TIME

Little sour orbs of crunch: I love pickled whole radishes. Pickling whole is a great way to keep the integrity of a small radish or other smaller vegetable, even if you want to quarter or slice it after. The fact is, it will be a pleasant experience for all. Radishes grow like weeds in gardens—so fast and so fresh. Pickling a couple bunches will end in happiness.

1	cup (240 ml) white vinegar (preferably Allen's 5% acidity)
½	cup (120 g) granulated sugar
1	teaspoon kosher salt (or 1 percent of weight of all liquid)
1	pound (450 g) round red radishes, sliced in half if large
1	tablespoon crushed garlic

Preheat the oven to 350°F (175°C). Wash a (1-quart/1 L) widemouthed mason jar and lid and pop the jar in the oven for 15 minutes to sterilize.

In a small nonreactive saucepan, combine the vinegar, 1 cup (240 ml) water, the sugar, and the salt and bring to a boil over medium-high heat. Remove from heat.

Pack the radishes in your jar and pour the hot pickling liquid over them. Add the garlic to the jar and let cool to room temperature without the lid, then tighten the lid on and refrigerate. Allow the pickles to sit for 24 hours before eating. They can be kept in the fridge for up to 1 month.

Dilled Pickles

MAKES:
4 QUARTS
(4 L)

PREP TIME:
50 MINUTES,
PLUS 36 HOURS
INACTIVE TIME

Who doesn't love a dill pickle? C'mon, guys! It's the original pickle. I've even said, if a sandwich doesn't come with a pickle, throw that sandwich on the floor. (I'm only half-joking 'cause throwing food on the floor is for babies, and if you do it as an adult you have a lot to learn about being a real-life human being and not some idiot.) Pickles rule, so make these!

¾	cup (165 g) canning salt
2	quarts (2 L) cold water
6	pounds (2.75 kg) pickling cucumbers, quartered lengthwise
2½	cups (600 ml) white vinegar (preferably Allen's 5% acidity)
1⅓	cups (300 g) granulated sugar
4	sprigs dill
8	garlic cloves, peeled
8	dried hot chiles

Preheat the oven to 350°F (175°C). Wash 4 (1-quart/1 L) mason jars and lids and pop the jars in the oven for 15 minutes to sterilize.

In a large food-safe container, dissolve ½ cup (110 g, or 10 percent) of the salt into the cold water and add the cucumbers for soaking. Saltwater soaking removes excess water from the cucumbers and adds flavor back into them. Cover and soak the cucumbers overnight in the fridge. Strain the cucumbers from the liquid before pickling.

In a stockpot, combine 5 cups (1.2 L) water with the vinegar, sugar, and the remaining ¼ cup (55 g) salt and bring to a boil over medium-high heat; boil for 10 minutes.

Pack the cucumbers into your jars up to ½ inch (1 cm) of the mouth of the jars and place in each jar 1 dill sprig, 2 garlic cloves, and 2 chiles.

Heat-process the jars, following the instructions on page 66. The pickles are ready to eat within 24 hours, or store up to 6 months in a cool, dark area.

Bread and Butter Pickles

MAKES:
4 QUARTS
(4 L)

PREP TIME:
50 MINUTES,
PLUS 36 HOURS
INACTIVE TIME

I don't know a pickle person that doesn't love a bread and butter. These can be made crinkle-cut, sliced, diced, or left whole and eaten with joy and fulfillment. I love these so much diced, as a relish on a lobster roll or tossed in a leafy green salad. These scream summer in the height of cucumber season, when they grow faster than grass and can be pickled just as fast. Unfussy and easy to make, these are a perfect condiment or side for any occasion.

¾   cup (165 g) canning salt

1   quart (1 L) cold water for brine

3   pounds (1.3 kg) pickling cucumbers, crinkle cut ½ inch (1 cm) wide

2½   cups (600 ml) white vinegar (preferably Allen's 5% acidity)

3   pounds (1.3 kg) white onions, cut in half and sliced

2½   cups (600 g) granulated sugar

2   tablespoons toasted cumin seeds

¼   cup (30 g) ground turmeric

2   tablespoons mustard powder

¼   cup (50 g) celery seeds

8   garlic cloves, peeled

8   sprigs tarragon

Preheat the oven to 350°F (175°C). Wash 4 (1-quart/1 L) mason jars and lids and pop the jars in the oven for 15 minutes to sterilize.

In a large food-safe container, dissolve ½ cup (110 g) of the salt into the cold water. Place the cucumbers in the brine for soaking. Saltwater soaking removes excess water from the cucumbers and adds flavor back into them. Cover and soak the cucumbers overnight in the fridge. Strain the cucumbers from the liquid before pickling.

In a stockpot, combine 5 cups (1.2 L) water with the vinegar, onions, sugar, cumin, turmeric, mustard powder, celery seeds, and the remaining ¼ cup (55 g) salt. Bring to a boil over medium-high heat; boil for 10 minutes.

Pack the cucumbers into your jars up to ½ inch (1 cm) of the mouth of the jars. Add 2 garlic cloves and 2 sprigs tarragon to each jar.

Heat-process the jars, following the instructions on page 66. The pickles are ready to eat within 24 hours, or store up to 6 months in a cool, dark area.

Favorite Salad of All Time

SERVES:
4 TO 6

PREP TIME:
20 MINUTES

What can I say? Is there anything better than a perfectly dressed lettuce leaf salad? No! The answer is no! With a bit of tuna and chopped vegetables, this is not just a side, it can be the main attraction.

½	cup (100 ml) white vinegar
1	cup (40 g) chopped flat-leaf parsley
3½	tablespoons canola oil
3½	tablespoons extra virgin olive oil, plus more for finishing
1	teaspoon sea salt
¼	cup (40 g) green olives, pitted and chopped
⅓	cup (30 g) diced celery
¼	cup (30 g) finely chopped shallot
½	cup (55 g) sliced cooked green beans
½	cup (30 g) diced cucumber
1	(5-ounce/142 g) can albacore tuna, drained and flaked
2	heads (200 g) green leaf lettuce
	Freshly ground black pepper

In a small bowl, combine the vinegar, parsley, canola oil, and olive oil and blast it with an immersion blender until incorporated. Season with salt.

In a medium bowl, combine the green olives, celery, shallot, green beans, cucumber, and tuna and dress with half the dressing.

In a separate medium bowl, toss the lettuce with the remaining dressing and season with salt and pepper.

Start by layering 3 leaves of lettuce in a tight pile and spoon over the tuna mixture to cover the lettuce. Repeat 3 times, until you have a mountain of salad; finish the top layer with the tuna mixture and splash the top with olive oil and salt.

Kitchen Sink Salad

SERVES:
6 TO 8

PREP TIME:
30 MINUTES

OMG guys! This salad is so perfect. It's like a submarine sandwich in a salad. If you hate bread or are "allergic" to bread but love subs, then this is the salad for you. Salami, hot peppers, cheese, olives, celery—so many crunchy, salty, minerally yummy bites in the greatest lettuce of all time: the iceberg lettuce. I love this salad, I love subs, I love you!

½	cup (120 ml) white vinegar
1	tablespoon dried basil
1	tablespoon dried oregano
½	tablespoon garlic powder
¼	cup (50 ml) vegetable oil
¼	cup (50 ml) olive oil
	Salt and freshly ground black pepper
1	head (450 g) iceberg lettuce, cut into quarters
½	pound (240 g) Italian salami, diced
½	pound (240 g) nice Cheddar cheese, torn into pieces
1½	cups (300 g) sliced pepperoncini
2	cups (350 g) corn (steamed, cut into niblets)
½	head (150 g) cooked broccoli, florets only
1	pint (250 g) cherry tomatoes, cut in half
6	to 8 hard-boiled eggs, cut in half
1	red onion, thinly sliced

In a medium bowl, blend together the vinegar, basil, oregano, and garlic powder with an immersion blender. Slowly blend in the vegetable oil until incorporated, then do the same with the olive oil. Season the vinaigrette with salt and pepper.

Make sure you do all your knife work and vegetable prep before you start building your salad. Once you have everything cut and organized in separate containers, in a large bowl, gently toss together the lettuce and dressing. Taste for seasoning. Add the salami, cheese, pepperoncini, corn, broccoli, tomatoes, and eggs on top of your dressed salad. Finish with paper-thin onion rings.

Zucchini Greek Salad

SERVES:
2

PREP TIME:
35 MINUTES

What's better than a diner Greek salad that's always mostly just onions and oregano with little to no good olive oil—maybe some canola oil, if you're lucky? Grilling and slicing zucchini and serving them in the style of a Greek salad. You can make this for packed lunches 'cause there's no lettuce to fade away into oblivion from the acid. Zucchini, instead, will just marinate and get better. I'm a new lover of feta, and I don't know why it took me so long, or why I considered it to be more of a diner condiment than a cheese. But hey, I'm always learning and loving new ingredients, and so are you.

1	pound (450 g) zucchini, half sliced ¾ inch (2 cm) thick, half thinly sliced into ribbons on a mandoline
3	tablespoons extra virgin olive oil, plus more for drizzling
½	teaspoon sea salt, plus more for sprinkling
1	(8-ounce/225 g) brick feta cheese (highest quality you can find)
⅔	cup (100 g) pepperoncini
⅓	cup (50 g) Kalamata olives
1	cup (150 g) unpeeled, roughly chopped cucumber
3	cherry tomatoes
¼	cup (5 g) arugula
¼	red onion, thinly sliced into rings
2	teaspoons drained (and rinsed, if salty) capers
2	teaspoons champagne vinegar
2	tablespoons dried oregano

Grill the zucchini ribbons on both sides, over medium heat, until charred and fork-tender. Cool.

Put the zucchini ribbons and slices in a medium bowl and toss with the olive oil and salt.

Place the feta in the center of the plate; arrange both types of zucchini around the feta. Place the pepperoncini, olives, cucumber, tomatoes, arugula, red onion, and capers around the zucchini. Drizzle vinegar and olive oil onto the cheese and vegetables. Sprinkle with sea salt and the oregano.

Burn Your Tongue Caesar Salad

SERVES:
2 TO 4

PREP TIME:
25 MINUTES

If your Caesar salad dressing doesn't burn your tongue, it's not good, and that's a fact. There needs to be enough garlic to burn your tongue, so if my recipe doesn't do it or you have a higher garlic burn–tongue ratio, then add more and add just enough anchovy. That's the key: burn-your-tongue garlic and just enough anchovy. I guess I'm trying to mess up your first dates or your kids' breath. Now mixing lettuce with this kind of dressing is no joke—you need to add it little by little to make sure you're not overdressing because with a burn-your-tongue dressing, going over the line can destroy this whole process. It's not about really fucking up your shit, it's just supposed to hit and punch up a mundane Caesar salad.

6	anchovy fillets packed in oil, drained
2	garlic cloves, grated on a Microplane
	Kosher salt
2	egg yolks
1	tablespoon Dijon mustard
4	teaspoons red wine vinegar
1	tablespoon freshly ground black pepper, plus more as needed
2	tablespoons olive oil
⅓	cup (75 ml) vegetable oil
3	tablespoons finely grated Parmesan cheese, plus more for topping
2	tablespoons lemon juice
6	slices (100 g) of your favorite bread
¼	cup (60 ml) melted butter
1	pound (450 g) romaine hearts, cut in half

Preheat the oven to 350°F (175°C).

On a cutting board, chop together the anchovy fillets, garlic, and a dash of salt. Use the side of your knife to mash the mixture into a paste. Scrape the paste into a medium bowl. Add the egg yolks, mustard, vinegar, and pepper and whisk until emulsified. Slowly add the olive oil, drip by drip, until fully incorporated, then do the same with the vegetable oil. Whisk until the dressing is thick and glossy. Whisk in the cheese, adjusting the consistency with water, and season with salt and more pepper if needed. Add the lemon juice.

For the croutons, tear the bread slices into medium pieces, toss them in melted butter, then toast in the oven until golden, 10 to 15 minutes.

In a medium bowl, gently toss the lettuce using your hands, adding the dressing a couple spoonfuls at a time until you reach your desired amount. Give the lettuce a taste to check for seasoning. Start building your salad on a large flat plate, putting the halved romaine hearts down. Then, throw some croutons on there. Keep going until you have a mountain of salad. Top with more cheese until fully covered.

Bulgur Tabbouleh Salad

SERVES:
6

PREP TIME:
30 MINUTES

Loose grain salads are great for you. As a "doctor," I prescribe you to eat bulgur wheat tabbouleh every other day for one month, and you will receive great health. The fresh herbs and the perfectly diced vegetables will give you the strength and hope to carry on your day. Serve it with Grilled Naan (page 30) and Chopped Baba Ghanoush (page 119) for a Middle Eastern–inspired meal.

¾	cup (120 g) medium-grind bulgur wheat
1½	teaspoons sea salt, plus more to taste
⅓	cup (80 ml) olive oil
4	hothouse tomatoes, skinned, quartered, seeded, and cut into small dice
2	heirloom carrots, peeled, cut in half, and sliced into half-moons
2	cups (50 g) finely chopped flat-leaf parsley
½	cup (13 g) mint leaves
1½	cups (75 g) thinly sliced scallions
	Zest from 1 lemon
¼	cup (60 ml) lemon juice
1	teaspoon freshly ground black pepper

Combine the bulgur, ¾ cup (180 ml) water, salt, and 2 teaspoons of the olive oil in a medium saucepan. Bring to a simmer over medium heat, then cover, reduce heat to low, and cook until tender, about 12 minutes. Remove from heat and let stand, covered, for 10 minutes. Fluff with a fork and spread on a baking sheet to cool.

In a medium bowl, mix together the cooked bulgur, the remaining olive oil, the tomatoes, carrots, parsley, mint, scallions, lemon zest and juice, salt, and pepper. Mix well. The tabbouleh should taste fresh, light, and acidic.

"Good" Canned Tuna Chickpea Salad

SERVES:
4 TO 6

PREP TIME:
25 MINUTES

Finding good canned tuna isn't hard—you just have to buy the cans that aren't ninety-nine cents (though I do love those as well). This salad is so perfect, and the way I present it here is GENIUS! A can of tuna in good olive oil surrounded by chopped mirepoix salad with lots of parsley tossed in lemon juice and more olive oil is literally my dream salad. Fiber and tuna are a match made in my mind, and probably as old as time, but it's beautiful and new to me.

½	cup (120 ml) white vinegar
2	cups (45 g) parsley leaves
¼	cup (60 ml) canola oil
¼	cup (60 ml) extra virgin olive oil
1	teaspoon kosher salt
2	(15-ounce/425 g) cans chickpeas, drained
½	red onion, diced
1	carrot, peeled and diced
4	ribs celery, thinly sliced on a bias
1	(4-ounce/100 g) can tuna in olive oil
½	teaspoon sea salt
	Freshly ground black pepper
4	white anchovy fillets, chopped
1	cup (45 g) chervil leaves
4	pieces (300 g) grilled bread, such as Grilled Naan (page 30)

In a small bowl, combine the vinegar, parsley, canola oil, and the olive oil and blast it with an immersion blender until incorporated. Season with ½ teaspoon of the kosher salt.

In a medium bowl, combine the chickpeas, red onion, carrot, and celery. Toss with the vinaigrette and season with the remaining ½ teaspoo`n kosher salt.

Keep the tuna in its can and center it on a plate. Build the chopped white anchovy fillets in a circle around the tuna can. Next add the chickpea salad over the anchovy fillets. Cover with chervil and serve with grilled bread.

Waldorf Sweet Potato Salad

SERVES:
2 TO 4

PREP TIME:
1 HOUR AND
10 MINUTES

This dish came to me in a whirlwind storm of classics and smashing waves of sweet potato dreams. Of course, the texture of the baked and caramelized sweet potato pairs perfectly with the blue cheese and bread crumbs. The tarragon rounds out all the flavors. Then you have to go over the top with the warm maple vinaigrette. This dish is a must in the winter season for dinner parties that will bring your mouth and soul back to the 1920s, where the Waldorf belongs.

1	pound (450 g) sweet potatoes or yams
1	tablespoon vegetable oil
½	cup (30 g) coarse bread crumbs
¼	cup (60 g) butter
2	tablespoons maple syrup
2	tablespoons lemon juice
½	teaspoon sea salt, plus more for finishing
⅔	cup (150 g) crumbled blue cheese (Roquefort)
⅔	cup (100 g) white grapes, sliced
¼	cup (25 g) tarragon leaves
1	teaspoon cracked black pepper

Preheat the oven to 375°F (190°C).

Scrub the sweet potatoes well and pat them dry with a dish towel. Place each sweet potato in a foil square and drizzle with vegetable oil. Using your hands, rub the oil into a thin, even layer all over the sweet potatoes. Wrap the sweet potatoes up tight in the foil and place in the oven.

Depending on the size of your sweet potatoes, it will take between 45 minutes and 1 hour for them to be done. Check at 45 minutes by inserting a sharp knife or fork into the center. It should feel quite soft and the knife should easily glide all the way through. If not, return to the oven and check again in 10 minutes. Once cooked through, pull out of the oven and unwrap.

Meanwhile, spread the bread crumbs in a baking pan, place in the oven, and bake until toasted, 8 to 10 minutes.

Melt the butter in a small saucepan at medium-high heat; allow to bubble for about 3 minutes. Cook enough to let the fat solids caramelize and create brown butter. Add the maple syrup, lemon juice, and salt to finish your vinaigrette. Set aside and keep warm.

Once the sweet potatoes are cool enough to handle, peel and forchette (fork) the flesh into large hunks and place in a bowl with the toasted bread crumbs. Sprinkle the blue cheese all over the sweet potatoes. Place the grapes randomly on top, spoon the brown butter vinaigrette all over, sprinkle with tarragon leaves, and finish with some salt and pepper.

All the Tomatoes Tomato Salad

SERVES:
4 TO 6

PREP TIME:
35 MINUTES, PLUS
45 MINUTES INACTIVE TIME

Tomatoes rule and should be eaten at room temperature, and they should never be kept in the fridge. Tomatoes are the greatest fruit in the world. This tomato salad with lots of cornbread crumbs is one for the books. If you don't have cornbread, just fry lots of torn day-old bread in olive oil until golden and crunchy, then throw in garlic and some herbs and place it all on a paper towel; let the oil drip and then pulse in a food processor. Or really, you should just be eating these tomatoes with some good olive oil and sea salt. But that wouldn't be a cookbook recipe. Imagine if we just actually left everything alone and ate things at the highs of seasons with no fuckery and enjoyed the real sensations of the purest of pure.

1	pound (450 g) heirloom tomatoes (different varieties)
1	pound (450 g) cherry tomatoes (different varieties)
4	tablespoons plus 1 teaspoon (65 ml) olive oil
2	tablespoons lime juice
	Zest of 1 lime
2	teaspoons sea salt
1	teaspoon freshly cracked black pepper
1	cup (200 g) crumbled Cornbread (see page 33)
1	garlic clove, peeled
½	cup (140 g) crumbled feta cheese
1	cup (30 g) chopped basil leaves

Slice all the tomatoes in different shapes and sizes; arrange them randomly on a serving plate. Brush the tomatoes with 3 tablespoons (45 ml) of the olive oil, then drizzle with the lime juice and sprinkle with the zest, salt, and pepper. Allow the tomatoes to marinate for 45 minutes.

Meanwhile, preheat the oven to 300°F (90°C). Line a baking sheet with parchment paper.

Put the cornbread into a medium bowl. Grate the garlic into the cornbread and splash in the remaining 1 tablespoon plus 1 teaspoon (20 ml) olive oil. Spread the crumble mixture evenly onto the prepared baking sheet and bake for 15 minutes, until the cornbread is dry and crunchy. Take the cornbread out of the oven and let cool.

Lightly sprinkle a thin layer of the cornbread crumble over the tomatoes, then crumble the feta all over the salad and finish with a handful of the basil on top.

Escarole Bean Brodo

SERVES:
6 TO 8

PREP TIME:
1 HOUR, PLUS
12 HOURS
INACTIVE
TIME IF USING
DRIED BEANS

I have such equal love for all three parts of this simple dish: the brodo, the beans, the escarole. Make this dish on a cold day and let the beans cook all morning, and by lunch you'll have a perfect bean texture. The broth will be just right, with the earthiness of beans, and then at the perfect moment add the cleaned escarole—make sure you really wash it 'cause it can be chock-full of sand. You could also add smoked white fish, or some chicken, or even some salt pork, but I think, once again, restraint is so important. This dish can stand on its own bean toes high and mighty and proud.

2	tablespoons unsalted butter
½	yellow onion, diced
1	leek, white and light green parts only, diced
3	ribs celery, sliced
¾	cup (200 ml) dry white wine
1	(15-ounce/425 g) can cannellini beans, drained
1	(15-ounce/425 g) can navy beans, drained
1	(15-ounce/425 g) can butter beans, drained
2	quarts (2 L) Chicken Stock (page 51), or store-bought
1	pound (450 g) escarole, cut into 2-inch (5 cm) wedges
2	teaspoons kosher salt
	Freshly ground black pepper
	Splash of white wine vinegar
½	cup (100 g) grated Parmesan cheese

In a medium Dutch oven, melt the butter over medium heat. Once the butter is bubbly and frothy, add the onion, leek, and celery and cook until the onions are translucent but with a little color and caramelization, about 10 minutes. Deglaze with the wine, scraping the browned bits from the bottom of the pot with a wooden spoon, and reduce by two-thirds. Add the beans and cook for 2 minutes. Add the chicken stock, bring to a boil, then reduce heat to medium-low and simmer for 30 minutes, adding the escarole during the last 5 minutes of cooking. Add the salt, pepper to taste, and vinegar.

Ladle the bean and escarole mixture into serving bowls with an equal amount of broth. Sprinkle with the cheese to finish.

If you're using dried beans: Soak beans, any type of bean, overnight in ratio of 25 percent beans to 75 percent water. The next day, strain the beans, place in a medium-size Dutch oven, and cover with cold water 3 inches (7.5 cm) from the top of the beans. Bring to a simmer; avoid boiling beans because that will break them apart. Add aromatics like onion, garlic, chiles, and herbs (rosemary, thyme, sage, bay leaves) if you want. An hour into cooking, the beans should be tender; turn off heat and season the water with salt. Let the beans rest in the cooking liquid for 30 minutes before using in the recipe or serving, or cool completely to room temperature before refrigerating.

Kombu-Steamed Fingerling Potatoes

SERVES:
6

PREP TIME:
45 MINUTES

I love the mineral flavor of fingerling potatoes. Kombu adds just enough sea tones that you'll think you've picked these potatoes right off the shores of Prince Edward Island. And there's nothing better than potatoes and warm butter and lots of green onions and sea salt.

2¼	pounds (1 kg) fingerling potatoes
7	ounces (200 g) dried kelp (kombu)
1¼	cups (300 g) cultured butter, cubed
	Zest of 1 lemon
2	tablespoons lemon juice
2	teaspoons sea salt (preferably Newfoundland)
2	cups (220 g) thinly sliced scallions

Rinse the fingerling potatoes. Fill a large saucepan with 2 inches (5 cm) water and add the kelp. Set the potatoes in the steamer basket and place over the water (it's easier to start over no steam so you don't burn yourself). Make sure the lid is tight. Turn on heat to high, and once you see steam escaping, turn down heat to low, just enough to keep the water simmering, and cook until the potatoes are fork-tender, 20 to 25 minutes.

Turn off the heat under the steamer, pour out the remaining water, and let the potatoes hang out. Place a large skillet over medium heat, melt the butter in the skillet, then let the butter get all golden frothy and bubbly. Now the butter is ready (be careful—don't let the butter burn at this stage).

Add the potatoes to the skillet, shaking it back and forth to evenly coat all the potatoes in the nice frothy butter. Add the lemon zest and juice and salt. Transfer the potatoes to a serving bowl and pour any remaining butter from the skillet onto the potatoes. Cover with a TON of scallions. DONE!

Broccoli and Mussel Escabeche

SERVES:
2 TO 4

PREP TIME:
1 HOUR, PLUS
OVERNIGHT
MARINATING

I love this salad during late summer to early fall. That sentence alone is the most cookbook thing I've written so far. I hope you guys make mussels escabeche, and I hope you make squid ink aioli, and I really hope you serve them with marinated broccoli. This is seafood-vegetable crudités with style and grace and just enough spice and acid that you'll remember this dish for weeks if not months and hopefully years.

FOR THE ESCABECHE:

4½	pounds (2 kg) mussels
1¼	cups (300 ml) dry white wine
4	bay leaves
⅓	cup (80 ml) extra virgin olive oil
1	yellow onion, thinly sliced
2	tablespoons thinly sliced garlic
	Kosher salt
⅔	cup (160 ml) chardonnay vinegar
1	tablespoon sweet smoked paprika
1	teaspoon black peppercorns

FOR THE MARINATED BROCCOLI:

⅓	cup (70 ml) fish sauce
⅓	cup (70 ml) malt vinegar
⅓	cup (70 ml) soy sauce
⅓	cup (70 ml) sambal oelek
1	teaspoon toasted sesame oil
4	teaspoons grapeseed oil
½	cup (50 g) thinly sliced whole scallions
6	sprigs cilantro, leaves and stems, minced
3	tablespoons grated ginger
1	head (1 pound/450 g) broccoli, stem and florets sliced ½ inch (12 mm) thick
½	teaspoon kosher salt

FOR THE SQUID INK AIOLI:

3	egg yolks
⅓	cup (50 g) black garlic cloves
1½	tablespoons lemon juice
1	teaspoon squid ink
1	teaspoon kosher salt
¾	cup (200 ml) grapeseed oil

FOR SERVING:

1	teaspoon Korean chili powder
	Olive oil
½	lime
	Sea salt

recipe continues

Make the escabeche: Scrub the mussels and pull out any hairy beards. Rinse well and drain. Place the mussels in a wide, heavy-bottomed saucepan and add 1 cup (240 ml) of the wine and the bay leaves. Cover and cook over medium heat, shaking the pan occasionally, for 5 minutes, or just until the mussels begin to open. As soon as they open, remove from the pan and place in a colander set over a bowl. Allow to cool, removing the mussels from their shells. Discard any mussels that have not opened.

Heat the olive oil in a 10-inch (25 cm) heavy-bottomed saucepan over medium heat. Add the onion, garlic, and a pinch of salt and cook for 5 minutes, or until the onion is lightly colored. Add the vinegar, paprika, peppercorns, and remaining ¼ cup (60 ml) wine, then bring to a boil over high heat. Reduce the heat and simmer for 8 minutes, then remove from heat and leave to cool for 10 minutes.

Stir the mussels into the escabeche and pour into a shallow dish. Leave to cool, then cover and refrigerate overnight.

Make the marinated broccoli: Combine the fish sauce, vinegar, soy sauce, sambal oelek, toasted sesame oil, grapeseed oil, scallions, cilantro, and ginger in a medium bowl and whisk until incorporated. Toss in the broccoli, season with the salt, and let marinate at room temperature for 30 minutes.

While the broccoli is marinating, make the aioli: In the bowl of a food processor (or you can whisk by hand), combine the egg yolks, black garlic, lemon juice, squid ink, and salt. With the machine running, pour in a steady stream of oil through the hole in the lid until the mixture starts to thicken; keep adding the oil until the aioli holds a soft peak. Check for seasoning.

To serve: Lay down the broccoli stems and florets randomly all over the bottom of your serving bowl. Strain out the mussels and fill all the holes in the bowl with mussels, resting them on the broccoli for added height and texture. Spoon in the mussel escabeche liquid to cover the bottom of the bowl as the sauce. Next, dollop 1 tablespoon of the aioli with a sprinkle of Korean chili powder on top, randomly in the center of the bowl. Finish the dish with a drizzle of olive oil, a squeeze of the lime, and a sprinkle of sea salt.

Leek and Mackerel Terrine

MAKES:
1 (4 BY 12-INCH/10 BY 30.5 CM) TERRINE

PREP TIME:
1 HOUR, PLUS 36 HOURS INACTIVE TIME

Now, here we go. This is another it's-totally-worth-it dish. Making food at home should always be a beautiful night. This is great for summer, when the leeks are coming out of the gardens and you're picking them up at a local farmers' market, and the mackerel is swimming off the coasts.

I love the idea of you guys making this and slicing it and unveiling it to yourself first, enjoying it 'cause you earned it, then showing it off to your family and friends. Eat this on an old wood table under a tree with some shade and drink lots of ice-cold unsweetened tea, and trust me, you'll feel very good about yourself.

FOR THE FIRST CURE:

2	large mackerel (as fresh as possible)
⅓	cup (75 g) kosher salt
2	tablespoons granulated sugar

FOR THE BRINE AND SECOND CURE:

⅓	cup (80 ml) rice wine vinegar
2	tablespoons granulated sugar
¼	cup (60 ml) water
2	tablespoons kosher salt

FOR POACHING THE LEEKS:

1	quart (1 L) Fish Fumet (page 48)
3	large (300 g) leeks, mostly whites, 10 inches (25 cm) long, cut in half and washed out
5	gelatin sheets
1	tablespoon mirin
½	teaspoon kosher salt

FOR FINISHING:

2	tablespoons olive oil
1	teaspoon sea salt
1	teaspoon lemon zest
½	cup (15 g) parsley leaves, chopped
½	cup (15 g) chervil leaves, chopped
½	cup (15 g) tarragon leaves, chopped
¼	cup (30 g) finely chopped shallot
2	tablespoons capers, diced
1	teaspoon lemon juice
	Freshly ground black pepper

recipe continues

Cure the mackerel: Set yourself up with a secure cutting board and a kitchen towel folded lengthwise across it. Lay the mackerel on its side with the belly facing away from you. Fillet the top side of the mackerel first along the spine, then flip the fish and fillet the second fillet (if you don't feel comfortable doing this, ask your fishmonger to fillet and pin bone for you). Mix the salt and sugar together to make the cure. Place the mackerel fillets on a rimmed baking sheet and pack the cure around both sides of the fillets. Place another baking sheet on top to weight down the fillets and wrap plastic wrap fully around both sheets to create pressure. Cure overnight (12 hours) in the fridge.

Brine the mackerel: In a medium saucepan, combine the vinegar, sugar, water, and salt and bring to a light simmer. Remove from heat and let cool to room temperature. Take the mackerel fillets out of the cure, using a damp paper towel to clean off any remaining cure. Now you want to pin bone the fillets and peel off the outer skin of the mackerel: Start at the tail end and slowly remove the clear outer skin, leaving the shiny silver/blue skin attached. Once the brining liquid is cooled, drop the fillets back on the baking sheet, skin side up, and pour brining liquid up to the bottom of the skin. Place the second baking sheet on top, wrap plastic wrap fully around both sheets again, and refrigerate overnight (12 hours) again.

Poach the leeks: In a medium saucepan, bring the fish fumet to a light simmer over medium heat. Poach the leeks until tender, 5 minutes; test with a cake tester to the core layers. Remove the leeks from the fumet and cool them on paper towels, separating the layers and keeping them in their rectangular shape. Reserve 4 cups (1 L) of the poaching liquid and strain through a fine chinois or strainer.

Bloom the gelatin in a small bowl of ice water for 5 minutes. Remove the bloomed gelatin and whisk it into the still-warm fumet. Add the mirin and salt. Keep in a warm place; do not let gelatin fully set yet.

Build the terrine: Remove the mackerel from the brining liquid, place on paper towels, and pat dry. Line a terrine pan or loaf pan with plastic wrap, leaving excess over each edge to be able to fully wrap the terrine once it's built. Place the first mackerel fillet at the bottom of the terrine pan, cover the whole fillet with 3 or 4 layers of leeks, and spoon the seasoned fumet on top just to cover and fill any gaps. Repeat this process 3 more times, until the terrine is full and all the mackerel is in the terrine. Wrap excess plastic wrap hanging over the sides to seal in the terrine. Cut a piece of cardboard to fit perfectly into the top of the terrine, place it on top, and lay a brick of butter (or something else on hand that's similar in size and weight) on top to press the terrine into place. Set in the fridge for minimum 6 hours, or overnight.

To plate: Slice the terrine ¾ inch (2 cm) thick with a super-sharp knife. Place on a flat white plate. Brush the terrine with some of the olive oil and season with some of the sea salt and the lemon zest. Combine the parsley, chervil, tarragon, shallot, and capers in a small bowl and season with the remaining olive oil and sea salt, the lemon juice, and black pepper. Place the herb relish in a tight little pile on each slice of terrine.

Roasted Cauliflower and Hazelnuts

SERVES: 4

PREP TIME: 45 MINUTES

This salad, warm or cold, is great for any season, and shaved hazelnuts just look beautiful. I kinda hate nuts because they get stuck in my teeth, but shaving them with a Microplane allows for the light, fluffy hazelnut to spread its tasty wings and create a perfect partner with the sweet cauliflower puree and the toasted cauliflower florets.

FOR THE CAULIFLOWER PUREE:

1	head (1 pound/450 g) cauliflower
⅓	cup (100 ml) water
⅓	cup (85 g) unsalted butter
1	tablespoon maple syrup
½	teaspoon kosher salt
1	tablespoon lemon juice

FOR THE BROWN BUTTER VINAIGRETTE:

⅔	cup (150 ml) brown butter (see page 100)
2	tablespoons maple syrup
2	tablespoons apple cider vinegar
1½	tablespoons Dijon mustard
1	teaspoon kosher salt
½	teaspoon freshly ground black pepper

FOR THE MILLE-FEUILLE:

1	head (1 pound/450 g) cauliflower, leaves trimmed, cut into quarters lengthwise with stem attached
1½	tablespoons olive oil
	Sea salt

FOR SERVING:

⅓	cup (50 g) toasted hazelnuts
	Sea salt

Make the cauliflower puree: Roughly cut the cauliflower into ⅓-inch (1 cm) thick slices. Place the cauliflower, water, and butter in a medium saucepan and cover with the lid. Heat over high heat to start steaming quickly, then reduce heat to medium and continue cooking until tender and there is just a little liquid left. Strain the cauliflower, reserving the liquid. Place the cauliflower in a blender and puree, adding the reserved cooking liquid through the hole in the lid. To ensure the consistency you are looking for, add a little liquid at a time and taste until it is smooth and silky. Pass the puree through a fine chinois or strainer and stir in the maple syrup, salt, and lemon juice.

Make the vinaigrette: Combine all the ingredients in a blender and blend until smooth. (You could also use a food processor or immersion blender.)

Make the mille-feuille: Preheat the oven to 365°F (165°C). Slice the cauliflower into ½-inch (12 mm) pieces and season with oil and salt. Place on a baking tray in the oven and roast for 20 minutes, until golden brown.

To serve: On a large flat plate, dollop 5 spoonfuls of cauliflower puree. Place the roasted cauliflower to cover all dollops of puree. Spoon the vinaigrette over and use a Microplane to grate the toasted hazelnuts, thinly covering the cauliflower. Season with sea salt.

Butter-Basted Cabbage with Sunflower Seed Sabayon

SERVES:
4

PREP TIME:
1 HOUR

If anyone makes this at home, I hope we meet and you can hug me, and I'll hug you back. This dish is def a restaurant-style dish that you could make at home. Making a sabayon and slow-roasting and basting a cabbage might seem like a lot, but let's push ourselves and make more interesting food at home. Okay? Okay!

FOR THE CABBAGE:

2   tablespoons grapeseed oil

1   small (675 g) green cabbage, outer leaves removed, cut in half

¼   cup (60 g) unsalted butter, or more if needed

2   teaspoons apple cider vinegar

FOR THE BROWN BUTTER AND SABAYON:

½   cup (120 ml) butter, diced

3   egg yolks

3   tablespoons white wine vinegar

2   tablespoons white miso

1   tablespoon warm water (optional)

FOR SERVING:

2   to 4 tablespoons sunflower seeds, toasted and chopped

½   teaspoon sea salt

2   tablespoons thyme leaves

Make the cabbage: Heat the grapeseed oil in a large cast-iron skillet over medium-high heat. Add the cabbage; brown undisturbed until the underside is almost blackened (the edge of the sides will start to brown as well), 10 to 15 minutes.

Reduce heat to medium-low and let the pan cool, 1 to 2 minutes. Add the butter to the skillet; shake the pan to get butter in, around, and under the cabbage. When the butter is melted and foaming, tilt the skillet toward you and spoon the browning butter over the cabbage, making sure to bathe the area around the core (thick and dense, this part will take the longest to cook), about 30 seconds. Stop basting and cook the cabbage undisturbed for 3 minutes, then baste again for 30 seconds. Repeat the cooking and basting process twice (the butter will continue to get darker as it cooks; add a knob or two more to bring it back from the brink). At this point, the cabbage should be tender (a cake tester inserted into the core should meet with no resistance) and the outer leaves will have pulled away from one another. If the cabbage is not done, repeat the cooking and basting process once more, for 2 minutes. Add the vinegar and quickly baste.

Make the brown butter and sabayon: Place the butter in a medium saucepan; bring to a boil over medium-high heat and allow milk solids to caramelize and brown. Once the butter has obtained a beautiful golden hue, strain it through a coffee filter and discard the brown milk fats. You should be left with clear brown butter.

In a medium metal bowl, whisk together the egg yolks, vinegar, and miso. Set the bowl over a medium saucepan with a little simmering water (make sure the bottom of the bowl doesn't touch the water) and whisk constantly until the eggs are nice and fluffy, then remove from heat. Slowly drizzle in the brown butter; continue to whisk until the sabayon thickens, 6 to 8 minutes. Add the warm water to loosen, if needed. Once consistency is reached, set aside and wrap with plastic; store in a warm place.

To plate: Arrange the cabbage on a plate or in a bowl. Add a huge spoonful of the sabayon on top and cover with the sunflower seeds, sea salt, and thyme.

Root Vegetable Bouillon Soup

SERVES:
4

PREP TIME:
30 MINUTES

This may be my favorite dish in this chapter. It's beautiful, and it's a perfect dish. The power of the root vegetables coming together in the stock: There isn't anything better—this should bring people to bliss and joy and all things surrounding happiness. This is the soup of soups. The mother of dragons soup. The *Bad Boys II* of soup. It's the welcome-to-Earth-punch-in-the-face-from-*Independence-Day* soup. That's two-Will-Smiths-in-one-soup-description soup, soup. Soup.

2	quarts (2 L) Court Bouillon (page 47)
1	(6-inch/15 cm) piece dried kelp
3	medium turnips, peeled and cubed
1	large daikon, peeled and cubed
1	large rutabaga, peeled and cubed
1	small butternut squash, peeled and cubed
2	celeriac (celery root), peeled and cubed
1	tablespoon lime zest
2	teaspoons sea salt
2	tablespoons toasted sesame seeds
½	cup (100 ml) olive oil (the nicest oil you have)

In a medium stockpot, combine the bouillon and kelp and heat over medium heat until you see steam. Never boil your dashi, because you want to just accentuate the savory flavor of umami in your broth. Turn off heat and steep the kelp in the broth for 10 minutes, then discard the kelp. Add the turnips, daikon, rutabaga, squash, and celeriac and return to medium-low heat to lightly poach in the dashi until fork-tender, about 15 minutes.

Scoop out the vegetables with a slotted spoon and place them in a large shallow bowl.

Add the lime zest, salt, toasted sesame seeds, and olive oil to the hot broth, whisking gently to break up the olive oil into little dot shapes throughout the broth. Pour the broth over the root vegetables and dig in.

Fingerling Potato Supreme

SERVES: 4 TO 6

PREP TIME: 35 MINUTES

This is an ode to you-know-what, and I'm okay with that. Everyone loves nachos, and everyone loves a fries supreme. Making fries at home is pretty annoying, but making this at home is, guess what, super easy, and smashed fingerlings are an incredible food, so this whole dish is just a giant you're-welcome to your family, friends, children, loved ones, dogs, cats, fish, or iguanas, if you're into that kinda thing. All are welcome!

FOR THE QUESO:

1	teaspoon neutral oil, such as vegetable or canola oil
1	white onion, chopped
⅔	cup (150 ml) milk, plus more as needed
1	pound (450 g) American cheese
⅓	cup (50 g) pickled jalapeño chiles, chopped
3	tablespoons yellow mustard (preferably Heinz)
½	teaspoon kosher salt

FOR THE POTATOES:

2¼	pounds (1 kg) fingerling potatoes
	Kosher salt
2	teaspoons neutral oil, such as vegetable or canola oil
½	white onion, cut into small dice
½	cup (60 g) pickled jalapeño chiles, sliced into rings
1½	cups (50 g) chopped cilantro stems and leaves
1	cup (55 g) chopped scallions

Make the queso: Heat the oil in a medium saucepan over medium-high heat. Add the onion and cook until translucent, 8 minutes. Pour in the milk, reduce heat to medium-low, and when the milk is warm, slowly add the cheese, stirring constantly and adding more cheese as it melts and combines into the sauce. Add more milk to achieve your desired consistency; I like mine nice and thick. Add the pickled jalapeños, mustard, and salt; keep warm while you make the potatoes.

Make the potatoes: Boil the potatoes in a large pot of heavily salted water until par-cooked (just before fork-tender), 15 to 20 minutes. Strain the potatoes; let cool and dry on a baking sheet lined with paper towels.

Crush the potatoes in between your hands to form little potato patties. Don't break apart the potatoes too much, but allow the skins to come off a little so they can become all crispy as they fry.

Heat a large cast-iron skillet over medium-high heat. Add the oil, then the potatoes, and pan-fry until crispy and golden brown, 6 minutes, turning halfway. Place onto paper towels and season with salt.

To plate: Place the crispy potatoes on a serving plate and cover with the warm queso so the potatoes become ooey-gooey. Then cover with the onion, pickled jalapeños, cilantro, and scallions. Eat immediately with all your friends.

Butter "Chicken" Rutabaga

SERVES:
6 TO 8

PREP TIME:
2 HOURS AND
15 MINUTES

Who doesn't love butter chicken? It's a perfect meal. Now get rid of the chicken and just use rutabaga 'cause it's the greatest of all root vegetables, and with the paneer you have a match made in heaven. The earthiness of the rutabaga adds more to this curry than chicken. Vegetarians can literally swap out the chicken in most chicken dishes for a root vegetable. Making chicken and dumplings? Use rutabaga instead. A big pot of chili? Use beans and diced beets, parsnips, and turnips. Root vegetables rule, and so does this dish. You're welcome.

⅓	cup (80 ml) olive oil
6	garlic cloves, peeled
2	bird's eye chiles, stemmed, plus more chiles, sliced, for garnish
2	long red chiles, stemmed
2	yellow onions, roughly chopped
¼	cup (40 g) peeled ginger, minced
½	cup (120 ml) ghee
3	tablespoons tomato paste
1	tablespoon ground turmeric
2	tablespoons chili powder
2	tablespoons garam masala
2	tablespoons ground coriander
2	tablespoons ground cumin
2	quarts (2 L) Court Bouillon (page 47)
3½	cups (785 g) tomato puree
1	tablespoon dried fenugreek leaves
2	rutabagas (1⅓ pounds/600 g), peeled and chopped
½	cup (60 g) paneer, cut into ½-inch (12 mm) wedges
2	cups (480 ml) heavy cream
1	teaspoon kosher salt, plus more for serving
4	cups (630 g) cooked jasmine rice
½	cup (30 g) cilantro, leaves picked, stems chopped
½	cup (113 g) unsalted butter
1	cup (100 g) green peas, fresh or frozen

Combine the olive oil, garlic, both chiles, the onions, and ginger in a blender and blend until smooth.

Heat the ghee in a large Dutch oven over medium-high heat. Add the onion puree and cook until the mixture darkens slightly and softens, about 15 minutes.

Add the tomato paste, turmeric, chili powder, garam masala, coriander, and cumin and cook for 5 minutes, or until dark and sticky. Add the court bouillon. Using a wooden spoon, scrape up any browned bits at the bottom of the pot.

Stir in the tomato puree and fenugreek leaves and increase heat to high. Add the rutabagas and bring to a boil, then reduce heat to maintain a simmer. Cover and cook, stirring occasionally, until thick, about 1 hour. Add the paneer and cook until the paneer is cooked through, about 15 minutes more. Add the cream and stir to combine. Season with the salt and serve over the rice. Garnish with the cilantro and sliced bird's eye chiles.

Melt the butter on medium-high heat. Add the frozen peas and warm through. Season with kosher salt. Serve on the side.

Aligot Potatoes, or Cheesy Stringy Potatoes

SERVES:
4

PREP TIME:
1 HOUR

Potatoes can be used in so many ways: gnocchi, French fries, smashed potatoes, mashed potatoes, potato dauphinois, pomme puree, and, what I feel is the highest form of potatory, the aligot. When made well, it should be very smooth. I hate mealy aligot potatoes that happen when the potatoes aren't hot enough and are overworked at low temperature. I think making aligot potatoes and making the Infamous Cheesy Citrus Refried Beans (page 123) are very similar. You have to get the texture of your base just right before adding the cheese. Too much butter or fat or milk or juice and the whole operation could go sideways. Please follow the instructions and you will have perfect ribbons of cheesy potatoes, and maybe the key really is using the cheapest pre-shredded mozzarella, because I truly think that's the best kind.

4	Yukon Gold potatoes, peeled and quartered
	Kosher salt
1	cup (240 ml) heavy cream, warmed
½	cup (1 stick/115 g) unsalted butter
1	pound (450 g) fresh cheese curds
½	pound (225 g) fresh mozzarella cheese
1	teaspoon freshly ground white pepper

Place the potatoes in a medium pot and add water to cover by 2 inches (5 cm). Add salt so the water is nice and salty; bring to a boil over high heat, then turn down to maintain a light simmer. Cook until the potatoes are fork-tender, 15 to 20 minutes. Drain the potatoes through a colander.

Immediately pass the potatoes through a food mill and back into the pot. Set the pot over super low heat and stir in the warm cream and butter. Add half of each cheese, melt, then stir in the remaining cheeses. Continue stirring until the potatoes can be stretched with a spoon like melted mozzarella. Season with salt and the white pepper. Serve warm.

Thanksgiving Stuffing Butternut Squash

I think I'm a genius for this one. No longer will vegetarians have to submit to Tofurky or mock meats. Just stuff a squash with amazing buttery bread and herbs and roast and serve with thick vegetable-based gravy, and you'll be the hottest vegetarian dinner host ever in the whole universe. I'm sure some veggie people have done this. If not, here ya go, you absolute freaks.

FOR THE "POULTRY" SEASONING:

¼	cup (32 g) ground sage
2	tablespoons dried thyme
2	tablespoons dried marjoram
2	tablespoons dried rosemary
1	tablespoon ground nutmeg
1	tablespoon freshly cracked black pepper

FOR THE SQUASH AND STUFFING:

2	pounds (900 g) plus ⅓ cup (40 g) unsalted butter
2	white onions, diced
6	ribs celery, sliced
1	cup (150 g) coarsely grated butternut squash
1	cup (100 g) ready-cooked chestnuts, roughly chopped and soaked in hot water for 20 minutes
6½	cups (1.5 L) Court Bouillon (page 47)
1	large sourdough loaf, crust removed, sliced, lightly toasted, and torn into 1½-inch (3.75 cm) pieces
1	cup (50 g) chopped flat-leaf parsley
2	teaspoons kosher salt
1	large butternut squash, cut in half lengthwise, seeded, and hollowed out

FOR THE VEGETABLE GRAVY:

½	cup (100 g) unsalted butter
⅔	cup (100 g) all-purpose flour
1	quart (1 L) Celeriac Stock (page 41), reduced by half, infused with ½ cup (15 g) ground sage
⅓	cup (48 g) "poultry" seasoning
1	teaspoon kosher salt

Make the "poultry" seasoning: Combine all the ingredients in a small bowl.

Preheat the oven to 375°F (190°C).

Make the stuffed squash: In a large saucepan, melt 2 pounds (900 g) of the butter over medium-high heat. Add the onions and celery, reduce heat to medium-low, and gently sweat for 20 minutes, or until the vegetables are translucent. Add ⅓ cup (50 g) of the "poultry" seasoning and toast until fragrant, about 4 minutes. Add the grated squash and chestnuts and stir until completely coated; cook for 10 minutes. Add 4 cups (900 ml) of the court bouillon, bring to a simmer, and mix in the sourdough pieces. The mixture should be slightly wet. Add the parsley and salt and remove from heat.

With one squash half, cut off about 2 inches (5 cm) from the bulbous end to create a vent. Stuff the other hollowed-out squash half with the stuffing; pack it in with the stuffing crowning out of the squash by about ¾ inch (2 cm). Place the piece with the end cut off on top of the stuffed bottom and tie with butcher's twine. (If you have no idea what I'm saying, flip to the next page for a picture of how the vent should look.) Once securely tied, make sure that the stuffing is packed evenly into the squash.

Now melt the remaining ⅓ cup (40 g) butter into the remaining 2½ cups (600 ml) court bouillon for basting.

Place the whole squash onto a rack set in a baking sheet. Bake for about 1 hour, basting the squash with the court bouillon and butter mixture every 15 minutes, until the stuffing is golden brown and the whole squash is fork-tender.

Make the vegetable gravy: As the squash is cooking, melt the butter in a medium saucepan over medium heat. Add the flour, stir until the flour is fully incorporated into the butter, and cook until it starts to bubble and turn golden in color, about 2 minutes. Slowly pour in half the celeriac stock and blend with an immersion blender until thick. Add the rest of the celeriac stock, the "poultry" seasoning, and salt and cook for 10 minutes over medium-low heat. Blend again and check for seasoning. Keep warm until plating.

Slice the whole squash into 1-inch (2.5 cm) rounds and place on a serving platter; cover with vegetable gravy or serve gravy on the side.

CHAPTER 4

Dips, Purees, and Spreads

"Bring them dips." —Drake

YOU MIGHT BE ASKING YOURSELF: WHY THE FUCK AM I MAKING A CHAPTER ABOUT DIPS AND PUREES OR WHATEVER THESE THINGS ARE? It's because everyone loves chips and dips. Even Drake wanted his chips with a dip when the Raptors won the big basketball game. But, for real, this whole thing started with my citrus beans. I would always make them for my crew—especially Alex Snelgrove, who always asked me for them all the time when we used to party at her house with Marika. I pretty much lived on their couch from 2003 until 2005. Even now I sleep on the couch at Marika's house in Parkdale when I'm in Toronto 'cause I'm still punk. Dips are punk for sure!

Dip is great for parties. They are also great to crush on your own or for when you and your friend are going to binge-watch *Veep*. Like two days ago, Trish got mad 'cause I bought a shitty seven-layer dip. She wouldn't eat it, but then the next day she made the sickest seven-layer dip I'd ever seen. She did not fuck around, and we smashed the dip while watching *You* on Netflix! We got sucked into that weird, creepy show real fast and finished the whole dip as fast as that creepy dude from *Gossip Girl* could steal your girl, her phone, and another dude's personality, and kill someone and never get caught while being very obvious. What the fuck is that? Anyway, dips are crucial to the self-care lifestyle. As you will see on page 129, I learned and don't fuck around anymore with seven-layer dips. It is purely theatrical and in no way on earth is it functional. It is purely aesthetic and beautiful.

Chopping grilled eggplant for a bowl of baba ganoush, spreading a tapenade on some grilled bread, and whipping cream for smoked fish mousse will give you that pure cooking at home feeling. No one can take away the feeling you will get while making queso for a football-filled Sunday, your brother-in-law yelling at you about how great the Buffalo Bills are but you knowing that they are the greatest losers in American history.

Chopped Baba Ghanoush

SERVES: 4 TO 6

PREP TIME: 45 MINUTES, PLUS TIME TO FIRE UP THE GRILL

Grilling eggplants can be peaceful. I love the smell of the blistering skins. I don't love a pureed baba ghanoush, and I think eggplants hate it, too. I love hand-chopping and folding in the oils, minced garlic, fresh-cut herbs, and all that lovely smoky eggplant liquor that comes from the trapped steam of wrapped charred aubergines. Serve your smoky baba ghanoush alongside other dips with Grilled Naan (page 30), raw veggies, and grilled meats. Also, I always make my baba ghanoush in the middle of a grove, okay?!!!

3	medium eggplants
1	tablespoon canola oil
2	garlic cloves, grated on a Microplane
1	tablespoon olive oil
1	cup (25 g) chopped parsley
1	teaspoon kosher salt
1	teaspoon freshly cracked black pepper
	Zest of 1 lemon
2	tablespoons lemon juice

Start the charcoal 1 hour before cooking to make sure the coals are hot enough to give the eggplants a nice clean char. Group the coals into a pyramid shape at the bottom of a Konro grill (a regular charcoal grill works similarly). Ignite the coals using a butane torch (or with lighter fluid). Fan the coals with a foldable hand fan (or any extra cardboard hanging around), and keep fanning the embers until 50 percent of the charcoal is ignited.

Once the charcoal is raring to go, use a paper towel to rub a thin layer of the canola oil all over the eggplants to prevent flareups, which would leave the eggplants with a carbon flavor. NOT COOL!

Grill the eggplants for 5 to 8 minutes, until all the skin on that side turns nice and black. Rotate the eggplants 90 degrees and repeat on that side. Repeat 2 more times, until the eggplants are completely black and tender. To be sure they're cooked, insert a wooden skewer into the center of the thickest part of an eggplant and keep it there for 5 seconds. Pull the skewer out; touch the skewer to the bottom of your lip and hold it there. If it's warm, the eggplant is ready to come off the grill.

Put the eggplants in a medium bowl, cover with a kitchen towel, and let them come to room temperature. Peel off the charred skin. Strain the cooking juices released from the eggplants and reserve ¼ cup (60 ml) of the liquid.

Gently cut the eggplants into small chunks; don't overwork it. Place the eggplants back in the bowl and add the garlic, olive oil, eggplant cooking juices, parsley, salt, pepper, lemon zest, and lemon juice.

"Good" Canned Tuna Tonnato Sauce

MAKES:
1 QUART (1 L)

PREP TIME:
45 MINUTES, PLUS
25 HOURS INACTIVE TIME

Tuna mayonnaise is the best, period. When I was writing the outline of this book, I didn't realize how much I love preserved tuna, and I guess I really, really love canned tuna, or confit tuna, if you wanna get fancy. Tonnato sauce is a classic, with shaved veal, some Pecorino, and maybe a few choice leaves of arugula. The mayo can be used with veal carpaccio or as a dipping sauce for crudités—perfect for broccoli. Eat with toast, olives, or anything you want, really. Like with most things, I'm not really a traditionalist, so please, if you love mayo and tuna, start brushing your teeth with tuna mayonnaise. I think kids would love that.

½	cup (110 g) kosher salt, plus more as needed
⅓	cup (70 g) granulated sugar
1	pound (450 g) mackerel fillet, skin and pin bones removed
1	quart (1 L) grapeseed oil
⅓	cup (50 g) lemon peel
¼	cup (60 ml) lemon juice, plus more as needed
2	tablespoons Anaheim chile powder
1	cup (25 g) tarragon sprigs
2	egg yolks
1½	tablespoons Dijon mustard
4	teaspoons white wine vinegar
1	(5-ounce/142 g) can tuna
	Olive oil, for drizzling

Note: If you don't have a smoker, create your own fish mixture with really good canned tuna and dried bonito flakes (which can be found in Asian grocery stores).

In a medium bowl, mix together ½ cup (110 g) of the salt and the sugar. Place the fish in a baking pan. Evenly sprinkle the cure mixture over the fish and pack it all around the fillets, top and bottom. Cover and set the pan in the fridge to cure for at least 1 hour and up to 3 hours. Once cured, wipe off the cure using a damp paper towel (do not run under running water). Pat dry with paper towels.

While the fish is curing, turn the smoker to 300°F (150°C). Follow the instructions for your smoker. If you do not have a smoker, you can use a grill. Soak woodchips for 30 minutes, then drain and sprinkle them over the coals. You want to use woodchips made from fruit trees, like applewood or cherrywood, so the smoke flavor isn't as overpowering as it would be with mesquite or hickory.

Place the cured fish on a wire rack; place in the smoker and smoke for 30 minutes, or until it's a beautiful golden hue. Take care not to overcook it. Take the fish out and cool to room temperature.

In a medium saucepan, combine the grapeseed oil, lemon peel, lemon juice, chile powder, and tarragon and heat over medium-high. Once the oil is hot, take the pan off the heat and cool to room temperature. Strain the oil through a fine chinois or strainer into a container.

Pack the mackerel fillets in the oil, cover, and let sit in the fridge for 24 hours. Pull the fish from the fridge, remove the fillets, and pat dry. Let the oil come to room temperature again so it is de-solidified.

In a food processor, combine the mackerel, egg yolks, mustard, and vinegar. Through the hole at the top, in a slow and steady stream, add the oil that was used to store the fillets in until the mayonnaise holds at a hard peak and is nice and glossy; you won't use all of the oil. Check for seasoning; add lemon juice to thin out to desired mayo consistency.

Serve right away, topped with your favorite canned tuna and a drizzle of olive oil, or store in the fridge in an airtight container for up to 6 days.

The Infamous Cheesy Citrus Refried Beans

This one is for my family-not-family, the BSOD-Macdonell crew. I've told this story before: All my friends were vegetarian or vegan. I always had to cook for them when we hung out at their houses. Tacos were always a winner and easy to make: a bunch of salsa, tortilla chips, some guacamole, some refried beans, and these cheesy citrus beans, which are my go-to. I say citrus 'cause sometimes I'd use fresh grapefruit, other times orange juice, or whatever was at the house. I'd cook onions and garlic, add spices, deglaze with the citrus juice, add the refried beans and the canned beans, then finally add all the cheese and BABBABOOOOOOM! You got spicy, citrus cheesy beans that you can dip into, put in a burrito, or just eat with a spoon.

2	tablespoons vegetable oil
⅓	cup (60 g) finely chopped white onion
2	tablespoons finely chopped garlic
⅓	cup (50 g) chopped jalapeño chiles
2	teaspoons ground cumin
2	teaspoons ground coriander
2	tablespoons Mexican seasoning mix
1½	cups (360 ml) grapefruit juice
1	(15-ounce/450 g) can refried pinto beans
1	(15-ounce/450 g) can pinto beans, drained
1	teaspoon kosher salt
1	pound (450 g) mozzarella cheese, shredded

In a large skillet, heat the oil over medium-high heat. Add the onion, garlic, and jalapeños and cook for 12 minutes, or until the onions are translucent. Add all the spices and toast for 3 minutes. Deglaze with the grapefruit juice and bring to a simmer. Add the refried pinto beans, whole pinto beans, salt, and cheese, turn down heat to low, and stir to warm it all up gently so it's cheesy, beany, citrusy, and yummy—yum!

Smoked Whitefish Mousse Sundae

SERVES:
6 TO 8

PREP TIME:
45 MINUTES, PLUS
1 HOUR INACTIVE TIME

My first job at Le Select was making whitefish mousse—well, maybe not making the mousse, but picking the fish meat from the bones and making sure all the finger bones and rib bones and any smoke skin were taken out. They also never wanted the fatty bellies of the white fish in the mousse, so I would snack on those. You may be thinking, Ew, smoked fish and whipped cream, but let me tell you, this is one of the greatest dishes ever. Folding in the sour cream with your smoked fish, then pumping up the flavors with whipped cream, is something that will be such a winner at any party or snack tray. I just love Triscuits so much—the salt and the crunch make for the perfect vessel to pile this whipped smoked fish mousse onto. It looks like a sundae, and it tastes like marshmallow heaven.

½	cup (110 g) kosher salt
⅓	cup (70 g) granulated sugar
1	pound (450 g) pickerel fillets, or any whitefish, skin and pin bones removed
1¼	cups (300 ml) sour cream
½	cup (120 ml) heavy cream
	Sea salt
	Lemon juice
	Olive oil
	Pickled peppers
	Triscuits, or other crackers, or potato chips, for serving

Note: If you don't have a smoker, find a fish market and buy hot-smoked fish.

In a medium bowl, mix together the kosher salt and sugar. Place the fish in a baking pan. Evenly sprinkle the cure mixture over the fish, packing the cure all around the fillets, top and bottom. Cover and set the pan in the fridge to cure for at least 1 hour and up to 3 hours. Once cured, wipe off the cure using a damp paper towel (do not run under running water). Pat dry with paper towels.

While the fish is curing, turn the smoker to 300°F (150°C). Follow the instructions for your smoker. If you do not have a smoker, you can use a grill. Soak woodchips for 30 minutes, then drain and sprinkle them over the coals. You want to use woodchips made from fruit trees, like applewood or cherrywood, so the smoke flavor isn't as overpowering as it would be with mesquite or hickory.

Place the cured fish on a wire rack; place in the smoker and smoke for 30 minutes, or until it's a beautiful golden hue. Take care not to overcook it. Take the fish out and cool to room temperature.

Flake the fish into a medium bowl and mix in the sour cream. Work the fish and sour cream together, but don't overwork it—leave it a little chunky.

In a separate medium bowl, whisk the heavy cream to soft peaks. Using a spatula, fold the whipped cream into the fish mixture 1 tablespoon at a time. Keep adding dollops of whipped cream and fold, fold, fold until the mixture is nice and fluffy. Season with sea salt and lemon juice, then gently scoop the mousse into a serving vessel. Drizzle the top of the mousse with olive oil and finish with a sprinkle of sea salt and pickled peppers. Serve with Triscuits, other crackers, or potato chips.

Pickled Hot Pepper Queso and Braised Beef Ribs

SERVES:
6 TO 10

PREP TIME:
3 HOURS AND
35 MINUTES

This is 100 percent ripped off the barbecue beef and queso from Valentina's Tex Mex BBQ in Austin, Texas. I was blown away the first time I had this, and I loved it so much I couldn't stop dipping my breakfast taco into the beef and salsa-drenched cup of cheese. Thank you, Miguel and family, for making some of the best barbecue in the world and making me crave your food so much. We don't have real Tex-Mex in Canada, and certainly not good barbecue, so even writing this is making me miss Texas and your food.

FOR THE BRAISED SHORT RIBS:

4½	pounds (2 kg) beef short ribs, cut crosswise into 2-inch (5 cm) pieces (ask your butcher)
2	teaspoons kosher salt
1	teaspoon freshly cracked black pepper
2	tablespoons vegetable oil
1	yellow onion, diced
⅓	cup (50 g) diced celery
⅔	cup (100 g) diced green bell peppers
1	tablespoon tomato paste
1½	cups (360 ml) Mexican lager
5	sprigs thyme
½	cup (100 g) jalapeño chiles, charred, peeled, and chopped
4	cups (880 ml) Beef and Bone Marrow Stock (page 55), or store-bought
1	teaspoon Tabasco sauce

FOR THE QUESO:

1	pound (450 g) American cheese
½	cup (120 ml) milk
½	cup (50 g) grated sharp Cheddar cheese
½	cup (50 g) grated Monterey Jack cheese
½	cup (50 g) grated Oaxaca cheese
¼	cup (60 ml) yellow mustard
¼	cup (40 g) Pickled Hot Peppers (page 67), plus 3 tablespoons Pickled Hot Pepper liquid
	Kosher salt

FOR GARNISH:

⅔	cup (100 g) finely chopped white onion
2	scallions, thinly sliced
1	cup (55 g) chopped cilantro stems and leaves
⅓	cup (60 g) Pickled Hot Peppers (page 67)
1	bag (250 g) tortilla chips, preferably freshly fried

recipe continues

Make the braised short ribs: Preheat the oven to 350°F (175°C).

Season the short ribs with 1 teaspoon of the salt and the pepper. Heat the vegetable oil in a wide-bottom Dutch oven over medium-high heat. Working in 2 batches, brown the short ribs on all sides, about 8 minutes per batch; transfer to a plate. After the last batch, pour out about 70 percent of the fat from the pot.

Add the onion, celery, and green bell peppers to the pot and cook over medium-low heat, stirring occasionally, until the onion starts to brown, about 10 minutes. Add the tomato paste, stir to coat the vegetables, then deglaze with the beer and reduce by half. Return the short ribs to the pan with any juices from the resting plate and add the thyme and charred jalapeños. Add stock to barely cover the top of the short ribs. Bring to a boil, turn off heat, cover, and transfer to the oven.

Cook until the short ribs are tender, 2 to 2½ hours. Allow the short ribs to rest in their braising liquid until cool enough to handle. Remove the short ribs, pick the meat off the bones, and shred into medium chunks. Take the thyme sprigs out and skim the fat off the braising liquid. Cook the braising liquid on the stovetop over high heat until reduced by half, add the short rib meat to the liquid, and reduce until nicely coated and the sauce is thick. Season with the remaining 1 teaspoon salt and add the Tabasco; keep the short ribs warm.

Make the queso: Assemble a double boiler by filling a large saucepan one-third full with water. Bring to a boil over high heat, then turn down heat to medium to maintain a simmer. Place a stainless-steel bowl on top of that (make sure the bottom of the bowl is not touching the water); now you have a double boiler.

Put the American cheese and milk in the bowl, melt down the American cheese, then add the Cheddar cheese, stir, and repeat with the Monterey Jack and Oaxaca cheeses.

Now that the queso is all yummy and ribbon-y, add the mustard, pickled hot peppers, and hot pepper liquid and season with salt.

Pour the queso into a serving bowl and put a huge scoop of the braised short ribs in the center. Make little piles of white onion, scallions, cilantro, and pickled hot peppers on top. Serve with tortilla chips.

The Inedible
Seven-Layer Dip

You'll break a whole bag of chips with this one. Good luck. It looks better than it eats. It looks ridiculous, but I couldn't help myself. I'm well aware this is impossible to eat and to get a little of every layer on a chip, and I'm well aware that that is the goal of a seven-layer dip. I went off the rails, and now we're in the situation that we're in. Please try to make this the way I did, and post it as much as possible, and for real, you could easily just make it the same way everyone does in a casserole dish and make thin layers so everyone can scoop and get all the layers in one bite. But holy moly, it looks good! Serve with fresh fried tortillas, for family BBQs, Christmas, or any event. It's the best.

FOR THE CREAM CHEESE MIXTURE:

1	pound (450 g) cream cheese, softened
1½	cups (360 ml) sour cream
1	tablespoon Mexican seasoning mix
1	teaspoon ground cumin
1	teaspoon ground coriander
	Kosher salt

FOR THE CORN AND BLACK BEAN SALSA:

1	(15-ounce/450 g) can yellow corn, drained
1	(15-ounce/450 g) can black beans, drained
	Juice of 1 lime
1¼	cups (200 g) finely chopped red onion
3	cups (125 g) finely chopped cilantro
⅔	cup (100 g) seeded and finely chopped jalapeño chiles
¼	cup (60 ml) grapeseed oil
3½	tablespoons (52.5 ml) white wine vinegar
	Kosher salt

FOR THE LAYERS:

½	pound (225 g) ground beef
1	teaspoon Mexican spice powder
1	teaspoon garlic powder
1	teaspoon chili powder
	Kosher salt
2	cups (453 g) Infamous Cheesy Citrus Refried Beans (page 123)
1	pound (450 g) plum tomatoes, cubed
½	pound (225 g) sharp Cheddar cheese, grated
½	pound (225 g) Monterey Jack cheese, grated
1	pound (450 g) cherry belle radishes, julienned

recipe continues

Make the cream cheese mixture: In the bowl of a stand mixer fitted with the paddle attachment, combine the cream cheese, sour cream, Mexican seasoning, cumin, and coriander. Whip on high speed for 2 minutes, then season with salt. Scrape out of the bowl into a container and set aside.

Make the corn and black bean salsa: In a medium bowl, combine the corn, black beans, lime juice, red onion, cilantro, jalapeños, grapeseed oil, and vinegar. Stir the salsa and taste for salt.

Make the layers: In a skillet over medium-high heat, brown the ground beef with the Mexican spice powder, garlic powder, chili powder, and salt to taste. Set aside to cool.

On the bottom of a glass serving bowl, spread the cream cheese mixture in an even layer and smooth it out using a spatula. Layer the ground beef mixture on top of the cream cheese.

Layer the corn and black bean salsa.

Add cheesy citrus refried beans and smooth with spatula.

Pile the diced tomatoes on top of the refried beans, but leave a space in the middle and fill with both cheeses.

Top with lots of julienned radish.

Whipped Goat Cheese with Anchovy Parsley Salad

SERVES:
4

PREP TIME:
20 MINUTES

This may be one of those bites and dishes that changes your life. The anchovy, parsley, and shallot salad, the whipped goat cheese; the creaminess and the acid with the rich, salty anchovy is just something that makes sense, and why would you not love eating anchovies? This reminds me of when I was a kid and we ate smoked oysters out of cans, with Cheddar cheese and hot peppers on Triscuits. This is the elevated version of that, but let's not get it twisted. Smoked oysters on Triscuits with marble cheese is truly world-class. Serve the parsley mixture and the whipped goat cheese with grilled bread, crackers, or as a side to grilled meats.

1	pound (450 g) goat cheese, softened
1	cup (240 ml) sour cream, at room temperature
	Zest of 1 lemon
2	cups (200 g) parsley leaves
½	cup (75 g) sliced (into rings and separated) shallots
8	white anchovy fillets
¼	cup (60 ml) olive oil, plus more for drizzling
2	tablespoons lemon juice
½	teaspoon sea salt, plus more for finishing
1	teaspoon freshly cracked black pepper, plus more for finishing
6	slices of your favorite bread, toasted

Put the goat cheese in the bowl of a stand mixer fitted with the whisk attachment and whip it. Add the sour cream and lemon zest and whip again until light and fluffy. Scrape out of the mixer bowl into a container and set aside.

In a medium bowl, mix the parsley, shallot rings, and anchovy fillets; add the olive oil, lemon juice, salt, and pepper. Transfer to a serving vessel.

Spoon the whipped goat cheese onto the center of a serving plate; using the back of a spoon, spread the goat cheese into a perfect circle, leaving a little space at the edges of the plate. Sprinkle with salt and pepper, and drizzle with olive oil. Serve with a few slices of your favorite toasted bread.

Bone Marrow Tomato Tartine

SERVES:
8 TO 12

PREP TIME:
40 MINUTES, PLUS
12 HOURS INACTIVE TIME

Bone marrow is one of those things that if you love it, you love it. If you don't fuck with it, then I feel sorry for you. Making this dish will make you strong and mighty and fill you with love. Making this dish fills me with joy! When I was making this at home, it really felt real and didn't feel like a cookbook shoot. With the sun shining through our kitchen window, making this dish was a very nice experience. Roasting the bones, grafting the tomato, squeezing the lemon into the parsley–shallot salad. Food like this really makes me happy, and I hope it brings your home the joy it brings mine.

4	(6-inch/15 cm) canoe-cut femur marrow bones (ask your butcher to cut them for you)
	Sea salt
2	beefsteak tomatoes
1	sourdough loaf (best available)
2	tablespoons olive oil
2	garlic cloves, peeled
1	cup (30 g) chopped parsley
1	cup (100 g) sliced shallots
1½	tablespoons lemon juice
1	teaspoon freshly ground black pepper

Note: Be sure to purchase your bone marrow from a place that sources well-raised animals, because toxins are stored in the fatty tissues of animals. Commodity beef is usually filled with antibiotics and hormones. Plus it won't taste like the best beef butter destined for your toast!

A day before serving, pour 6 inches (15 cm) of water into a container big enough to hold the marrow bones. Salt the water generously; slide the bones into the container, cover, and refrigerate for 12 hours. This saltwater soak removes all the blood.

The next day, preheat the oven to 325°F (165°C).

Grate the tomatoes on the largest holes of a box grater into a medium bowl. Drain the tomato pulp in a strainer to remove the juices. Season the pulp with a dash of salt and set aside.

Remove the marrow bones from the water and lay them onto a wire rack set in a baking sheet; throw in the oven and bake for 30 minutes. You are just turning the marrow into molten fat, so do not over-render it; you don't want to lose all that precious beef butter. Pull from the oven and let cool for 1 minute, but don't let it congeal again. Turn the oven to the broil setting.

Split the sourdough loaf in half horizontally (like a big burger bun). Splash it with the olive oil crust to crust. Put the bread cut side up onto a baking sheet lined with parchment paper, place under the broiler, and toast until the bread is nicely golden, allowing it to get a little burnt around the edges. Pull the bread from the broiler.

With the bread still warm and crunchy, scrape the raw garlic cloves up and down both toasted pieces of bread until the garlic has fully broken down and the toast smells of raw garlic. Spread the tomato pulp up and down both pieces of bread, then spoon the bone marrow from the bone all over the bread. Use a knife to dice up the marrow on the bread. Sprinkle with the parsley and shallots and drizzle with the lemon juice. Season with salt and the pepper.

Cut into 8 to 12 pieces and serve still warm and crispy to your pals.

Green Olive Tapenade

You want a great condiment, don't you? Now you have the perfect one in this recipe. Please make this and use it to dress salads, vegetables, grilled meats, cupcakes, pizza, or steamed fish. This olive tapenade will top anything on this planet and make it taste like you're knee-deep in the Aegean Sea, eating olive tapenade.

2¼	pounds (1 kg) Cerignola olives, pitted, 2 tablespoons olive brine reserved
½	pound (250 g) whole shallots, roasted
1	head garlic, roasted
¾	cup (150 g) jalapeño chiles, charred and seeded
¼	cup (60 ml) olive oil, plus more for finishing (optional)
1	cup (65 g) mint leaves
1	cup (65 g) basil leaves
1	cup (65 g) parsley leaves
	Zest of 1 lemon
2	tablespoons lemon juice
	Whole Cerignola olives and mint leaves, for serving (optional)

In the bowl of a food processor, combine the olives, roasted shallots, roasted garlic, and charred jalapeños and pulse until broken down and evenly chopped. Slowly pour in the olive oil through the hole in the top until the tapenade comes together. Scrape out of the machine into a medium bowl.

Gently chop the mint, basil, and parsley separately, then add the chopped herbs to the tapenade base. Fold the olive mixture into the herbs until well combined. Add the lemon zest, lemon juice, and reserved olive brine and mix well. You can add more olive oil to add body and a shine to the tapenade if you like. If not using immediately or if making ahead, store the tapenade in the fridge for up to 2 days. Decorate with whole olives and mint leaves, if you would like.

Romesco Sauce

MAKES:
2 CUPS (480 ML)

PREP TIME:
1 HOUR

Roast nuts, bread, peppers, and tomatoes, then blend—this is such an easy condiment that can be taken in a thousand directions. Almonds, the kingly queen of nuts. Let's all serve this with charred leeks and grilled or plancha-fried squids, okay? Deal? Deal!

2	red bell peppers, cut in half lengthwise, stems, seeds, and membranes removed
2	red serrano chiles, cut in half lengthwise, stems, seeds, and membranes removed
2	Roma tomatoes, cut in half, seeds removed
½	cup (65 g) almonds
1	cup (80 g) bread crumbs
1	cup (110 g) diced onion
3	confit garlic cloves (see Note)
½	cup (120 ml) olive oil, or more if needed
1	tablespoon tomato paste
1	teaspoon smoked paprika
½	teaspoon ground cayenne
2	tablespoons sherry vinegar, or more if needed
1	teaspoon sea salt, or to taste
1	teaspoon freshly ground black pepper
	Whole almonds and cilantro leaves, for serving

Note: To make confit garlic, peel 2 heads' worth of garlic cloves and put them in a small saucepan. Cover with 1 cup (280 ml) grapeseed oil and place over low heat. Cook until the garlic is tender but not browned, about 1 hour. Pour into a clean glass container, let cool, then cover and refrigerate for up to 2 weeks.

Preheat the oven to 450°F (220°C). Line 2 baking sheets with foil.

Place the red peppers, chiles, and tomatoes cut side down on one prepared baking sheet. Place the almonds and bread crumbs on the second sheet. Roast the peppers, chiles, and tomatoes for 15 to 20 minutes, until the skins turn black and they collapse. Remove from the oven. Allow the peppers to cool, then peel off the skin. Toast the almonds and bread crumbs until lightly browned, 3 to 5 minutes

In a skillet, sauté the onion and garlic in the olive oil until soft; add tomato paste and stir until incorporated. Add the toasted almonds and bread crumbs, paprika, and cayenne; cook until fragrant, about 3 minutes. Add the vinegar.

Add the onion mixture to a food processor and pulse until slightly broken down. Chop all the roasted peppers and tomatoes, then fold the peppers and onion mixtures together. Add more oil and vinegar, if needed, and season with salt and black pepper. Decorate with whole almonds and fresh cilantro like I did.

Whipped Goat Cheese with Pea Lardon, Honey, and Bee Pollen

SERVES:
2 TO 4

PREP TIME:
25 MINUTES

I love whipped goat cheese so here's another one. Sweet peas in perfectly rendered lardon in the valley of a little smooth whipped goat cheese mountain. This is a perfect mix of crispy pork and seasoned peas. Pair it with a stewed lamb breast or enjoy it on toast.

½	cup (130 g) soft goat cheese
2	tablespoons honey
¼	cup (30 g) lemon zest
	Kosher salt
⅔	cup (150 g) diced double-smoked bacon
¼	cup (30 g) minced shallot
1	garlic clove, minced
1⅔	cups (350 g) fresh shucked peas, blanched, or frozen peas, defrosted
1	tablespoon lemon juice
	Freshly ground black pepper
3	tablespoons honeycomb
2	tablespoons bee pollen
1	cup (25 g) mixed herbs such as mint, tarragon, chervil, and pea tendrils

Note: Try to make this salad when peas are in season and fresh peas are at the market. Raw peas should be sweet and tender when you taste them.

In a medium bowl, combine the goat cheese, honey, and half of the lemon zest and season with salt. Whip the mixture with a whisk until smooth. Season with more salt and set aside at room temperature.

Place the bacon in a large skillet and add 2 tablespoons water. Turn on heat to high and allow the water to boil and evaporate. Cook the bacon until golden and fully rendered, 5 to 7 minutes, then pour out half the fat. Add the shallot and garlic; cook for 1 minute. Remove from heat and add the peas, remaining lemon zest, and lemon juice and season with salt and pepper.

Spoon several piles of goat cheese onto a flat serving plate. Use the back of a spoon to smear the piles to the side. Quickly warm up the pea and lardon mixture, give it one final toss in the pan, and spoon the mixture all over the goat cheese piles, letting the dressing pool up all over the plate. Tear the honeycomb into pieces and randomly place them onto the plate. Sprinkle the bee pollen and herbs over the entire plate.

CHAPTER 5

Dumplings and Pasta

Who Doesn't Love Sucking on Dumplings and Slurping Up Noodles?

WRITING ABOUT ALL THIS FOOD REALLY MAKES ME FEEL WARM ON THE INSIDE. It makes me think about −16°C (3°F) Toronto winters, walking down Roncesvalles Avenue to my favorite polish restaurant, Café Polonez. I still crave those pork and mushroom dumplings in pork beet broth and pierogis even though I'm two hours away in Fort Erie, so I'll just stay warm by my double-double. That soup was my first taste of a dumpling that was freshly made. I also remember the seafood dumpling in a bowl of golden chicken broth at the Flower Drum in Melbourne, Australia. The seafood was so perfect and fresh, but that's unfair because Australia has the best seafood in the world. Dumplings in broth are an important part of God's plan.

Now pasta is a whole other thing. I'm going to out myself right fucking now: I've never been to Italy. That means I'm still a palate poser. I don't know what a true cacio e pepe, a real Bolognese, or a literal Neapolitan pizza tastes like, ya know. Everything I've eaten in my life is still just an idea of what it should truly taste like.

That's what home cooking is all about. The beauty comes from dreaming about flavors, and the magic of food can take you around the world at any moment. For the cost of ingredients alone you could be making pork and shrimp gyoza that transports you to Harajuku, or eating a clam pasta that makes you feel the breeze coming off the Amalfi Coast. So much of what I make at home is dictated by daydreaming and/or thinking about places I've been that have changed my life.

Enjoy these conjured-up recipes. I hope these dumplings and these pastas inspire you to cook and, maybe one day, travel outside your comfort zone. I'll be out here, daydreaming about the beauty of food and the culinary experiences and places that have inspired me.

Oxtail and Mirepoix Pierogis

SERVES:
6 TO 8

PREP TIME:
4 HOURS

Doughy and fluffy pierogis are what we're looking for. When they are filled with braised oxtail, they are a dream within a dream. The mirepoix and broth are the perfect mix of warmth and texture. Just imagine playing in the snow, throwing snowballs, and getting one right in the face—when it hits your teeth and stings like a whip. You run inside crying and breathing heavy, and Momma and Poppa are boiling fresh oxtail pierogis and broth to warm your fragile soul. This dish was designed specifically for a snowball fight gone wrong for one person.

FOR THE BRAISED OXTAIL:

3	pounds (1.5 g) oxtail, cut crosswise into 2-inch (5 cm) pieces (ask your butcher)
1	teaspoon kosher salt
1	teaspoon freshly cracked black pepper
2	tablespoons vegetable oil
1	yellow onion, diced
1	carrot, peeled and diced
1	rib celery, diced
1	tablespoon tomato paste
1½	cups (360 ml) red wine
1	bouquet garni (8 sprigs thyme, 10 sprigs parsley, and 3 bay leaves tied together with butcher's twine)
4	cups (880 ml) Beef and Bone Marrow Stock (page 55), or store-bought

FOR THE PIEROGI DOUGH (MAKES 30 OR SO PIEROGIS):

4	cups (600 g) all-purpose flour, plus more for rolling
1	teaspoon kosher salt, plus more for cooking
1	tablespoon vegetable oil, plus more for the cooked pierogis
2	eggs
1	cup (240 ml) lukewarm water

FOR THE TOPPING:

1	tablespoon unsalted butter
⅓	cup (50 g) finely diced carrot
⅓	cup (50 g) finely diced onion
⅓	cup (50 g) finely diced celery
⅓	cup (50 g) finely diced leek, white parts only
	Sea salt

Note: You could easily sub high-quality store-bought dumpling wrappers for making your own dough.

recipe continues

Braise the oxtail: Preheat the oven to 350°F (175°C).

Season the oxtail with the salt and pepper. Heat the vegetable oil in a wide-bottom Dutch oven over medium-high heat. Working in 2 batches, brown the oxtail on all sides, about 8 minutes per batch. Transfer the oxtail to a plate and pour out about 70 percent of the fat from the pot.

Add the onion, carrot, and celery to the pot and cook, stirring occasionally, until the onion starts to brown, about 10 minutes. Add the tomato paste and stir to coat the vegetables. Deglaze with the red wine and reduce by half. Return the oxtail to the pot with any juices from the resting plate. Add the bouquet garni to the pot. Add enough stock to barely cover the top of the oxtail. Bring to a boil, then turn off heat; cover the pot and transfer to the oven.

Cook until the oxtail is tender, 2 to 2½ hours. Allow the oxtail to rest in its braising liquid until cool enough to handle. Remove the oxtail from the liquid, pick the meat off the bones, and shred the meat. Strain the braising liquid and set half aside. Cook the other half over medium-high heat until reduced by two-thirds.

In a medium bowl, combine the shredded oxtail with the reduced cooking liquid. Using a spoon, really work the meat so it breaks down a little and emulsifies back into the braising liquid. Immediately cool the oxtail filling in the fridge; the filling needs to be at the temperature of the fridge when filling the pierogis.

While the oxtail is chilling, make the pierogi dough: In a medium bowl, mix the flour and salt and make a well in the middle. Add the oil and eggs to the well; using a fork, stir into the flour. Knead, slowly adding in the lukewarm water as you go, until the dough forms a sticky ball. Transfer the dough to a floured surface and continue to knead until the dough is soft but not sticky, about 5 minutes. Cover the dough with a kitchen towel and allow to rest for 1 hour at room temperature. (You can make the dough a day ahead and store, wrapped in plastic, in the fridge. Just make sure you pull it from the fridge and bring it to room temperature before rolling it out.)

On a floured work surface using a floured rolling pin, roll out the dough ¼ cm (1.5 mm) thick. If you don't have a large enough work surface, roll out the dough in batches. Using a 3- to 4-inch (7.5 to 10 cm) ring or cookie cutter, punch out rounds, cutting out the dough from as close to the edges as possible. Place the cut circles onto a tray lined with a kitchen towel, keeping the top side face up; cover with another kitchen towel, as they can dry out easily.

Fill the pierogis—work in batches and remove from the fridge only a portion of the oxtail filling at a time so the filling stays cold. Place about 1 tablespoon of the filling into a dough circle. Do this by picking up a circle, flipping it over into your hand (the bottom side is better to seal), and placing the filling inside. The dough will stretch as you press the filling in with a spoon; add more filling if necessary. Bring the dough together and seal the edges with your fingers. Make sure no filling is coming out of the edges or on your fingers, or the dough will not close. Repeat until no dough is left. If you have filling left, freeze in a ziplock bag and keep until the next time you make pierogis.

Make the topping: In a medium skillet, melt the butter over medium heat. Add the carrot, onion, celery, and leek and sweat for 10 minutes, or until fork-tender and softened but not colored. Set aside while you cook the pierogis.

Bring a large pot of salted water to a boil. Add 10 pierogis at a time; when they float to the top, cook for 1 more minute. Scoop them out with a slotted spoon into a large bowl and coat lightly with vegetable oil to prevent them from sticking.

To serve, bring the reserved oxtail braising liquid to a simmer and taste for seasoning; add a little water if it is too salty. Place 6 to 8 freshly boiled pierogis into a soup bowl, ladle over some broth, spoon on vegetable topping, and sprinkle with a little sea salt.

Parsnip and Cauliflower Pierogis

SERVES:
6 TO 8

PREP TIME:
2 HOURS AND
20 MINUTES

This dish is for the friend that's visiting during the snowball fight (see page 147). The sweetness of the parsnip and the cauliflower marry till the end of time and space, filling these pierogis with love and commitment.

FOR THE PIEROGI DOUGH (MAKES 30 OR SO PIEROGIS):

- 4 cups (600 g) all-purpose flour, plus more for rolling
- 1 teaspoon kosher salt, plus more for cooking
- 1 tablespoon vegetable oil, plus more for the cooked pierogis
- 2 eggs
- 1 cup (240 ml) lukewarm water

FOR THE BROWN BUTTER CAULIFLOWER:

- 1 head (about 2 pounds/910 g) cauliflower, cored, trimmed, and cut into florets
- ¼ cup (60 ml) brown butter (see page 100)
- ½ teaspoon kosher salt, plus more as needed

FOR THE PARSNIP PUREE:

- 1¼ pounds (500 g) parsnips
- ⅓ cup (85 g) unsalted butter
- ½ teaspoon kosher salt, plus more as needed
- 1 tablespoon lemon juice, plus more as needed
- Maple syrup

FOR SERVING:

- 1 quart (1 L) Pork Stock (page 52), or store-bought
- Sea salt

Note: You could easily sub high-quality store-bought dumpling wrappers for making your own dough.

recipe continues

Make the pierogi dough: In a medium bowl, mix the flour and salt and make a well in the middle. Add the oil and eggs; using a fork, stir into the flour. Knead, slowly adding in the lukewarm water as you go, until the dough forms a sticky ball. Transfer the dough to a floured surface and continue to knead until the dough is soft but not sticky. Cover the dough with a kitchen towel and allow to rest for 1 hour at room temperature. (You can make the dough a day ahead and store, wrapped in plastic, in the fridge. Just make sure you pull it from the fridge and bring it to room temperature before rolling it out.)

On a floured work surface using a floured rolling pin, roll out the dough ¼ cm (1.5 mm) thick. If you don't have a large enough work surface, roll out the dough in batches. Using a 3- to 4-inch (7.5 to 10 cm) ring or cookie cutter, punch out rounds, cutting out the dough from as close to the edges as possible. Place the cut circles onto a tray lined with a kitchen towel, keeping the top side face up; cover with another kitchen towel, as they can dry out easily.

While the pierogi dough is resting, make the brown butter cauliflower: Preheat the oven to 375°F (190°C).

In a large bowl, toss the cauliflower florets in the brown butter and add the salt. Spread evenly onto a baking sheet and bake for about 30 minutes, until nice and charred. Remove from the oven and cool to room temperature.

While the cauliflower is in the oven, make the parsnip puree: Peel and cut the parsnips into ¼-inch (6 mm) coins. Place the parsnips, ⅓ cup (100 ml) water, butter, and salt in a medium saucepan and cover. Cook over high heat to start steaming them quickly, then reduce heat to medium and continue cooking until tender and there is just a little liquid left, about 15 minutes. Put the parsnips and their liquid in a blender and begin blending; add the lemon juice and maple syrup through the hole in the top a little at a time until it is smooth and silky. Pass the puree through a fine chinois or strainer, if the puree is not already extremely smooth. Season with salt and add more lemon juice as needed. Cool to room temperature.

Fold half of the roasted cauliflower into the parsnip puree; check for seasoning. Chill the filling in the fridge.

Then, fill the pierogis; work in batches and remove from the fridge only a portion of the filling at a time so the filling stays cold. Place about 1 tablespoon of the filling into a dough circle. Do this by picking up a circle, flipping it over into your hand (the bottom side is better to seal), and placing the filling inside. The dough will stretch as you press the filling in with a spoon; add more filling if necessary. Bring the dough together and seal the edges with your fingers. Make sure no filling is coming out of the edges or on your fingers, or the dough will not close. Repeat until no dough is left.

Bring a large pot of salted water to a boil. Add 10 pierogis at a time; when they float to the top, cook for 1 more minute. Scoop them out with a slotted spoon into a large bowl and coat lightly with vegetable oil to prevent them from sticking.

To serve: In a medium pot, bring up the pork broth to a simmer and taste for seasoning; add a little water if it is too salty. Place 6 to 8 freshly boiled pierogis into a soup bowl, ladle over some broth, add a few of the remaining cauliflower florets, and sprinkle a little sea salt on top.

Beautiful Shrimp Dumplings

SERVES:
4 TO 6

PREP TIME:
45 MINUTES

Everyone loves these and that's just a fact. Making shrimp dumplings and chicken stock with your family is what life is all about. Also, the photos on the previous spread are my favorites in this book—the fat bubbles and the shimmering broth with the perfectly crafted shrimp dumplings. This came from a trip to Australia, where I was served one giant seafood dumpling in the most perfect chicken broth. The bounce of the shrimp in the dumpling and the dark chicken stock make me so happy I could eat a lot of these. Good thing they take a little bit of work and time, so have some respect and only eat a couple per serving.

2	pounds (880 g) peeled raw shrimp, half whole, half chopped
⅓	cup (30 g) pork lard
2	tablespoons grated ginger
2	tablespoons grated garlic
½	teaspoon kosher salt
30	wonton wrappers
1	quart (1 L) Chicken Stock (page 51), or store-bought, heated
2	tablespoons olive oil

Place 1 pound (440 g) whole shrimp in a high-speed blender and blend on low speed until completely pureed. Add the pork lard and emulsify the shrimp into shrimp mousse. Transfer the shrimp mousse to a medium stainless-steel bowl over another bowl filled with ice to keep the mousse chilled.

Mix 1 pound (440 g) chopped shrimp into the shrimp mousse, keeping the mixture over the ice bowl. Add the ginger, garlic, and salt.

Hold a wonton wrapper in your hand and place the filling off center. Pleat the dumpling by pushing the wonton wrapper with the index finger of one hand and press to secure the pleat with the index finger of the other hand. Keep the cavity a little loose to allow the shrimp mousse to expand during cooking and not explode on you.

Fill a pot with water; bring to a boil. Place the dumplings into a steamer basket and set over the boiling water. Cover and steam the dumplings for 5 to 6 minutes. Remove from the steamer, immediately place into soup bowls, and pour the hot chicken broth and olive oil over the dumplings. Slurp them up!

These dumplings freeze extremely well. Place them on a baking sheet, sitting up and not touching. Place the sheet in the freezer, and once the dumplings are frozen, transfer them to ziplock bags and freeze for up to 3 months.

Frozen King Crab Legs Rangoon

SERVES:
4

PREP TIME:
35 MINUTES

First and foremost, getting under a crabapple tree to make crab Rangoon is the most important part of this whole process. If you don't have a crabapple tree, then don't even try to make these. You can use a different kind of crab, but if you don't have a beautiful orchard to make it in, don't even try. I repeat, don't even try. These could be made in a regular kitchen—maybe, but probably not. So yeah, make sure you're under a crabapple tree.

1	cup (226 g) Newfoundland picked crab, or frozen king crab or canned crab
1¼	cups (300 g) cream cheese, softened
2	tablespoons lemon zest
1	tablespoon snipped chives
1	teaspoon sea salt
	Freshly ground black pepper
1	egg
24	square wonton wrappers
1	quart (1 L) canola oil, for frying
	Lime wedges

In a medium bowl, mix the crabmeat, cream cheese, lemon zest, chives, and salt and season with pepper. Crack the egg into small bowl and whisk; this is your glue for the wonton wrappers.

Open the package of wonton wrappers; cover with a damp kitchen towel as you work to keep them from drying out. Take one wrapper and place it in front of you on a clean work surface (kitchen counter or cutting board). Place a teaspoon of the crab mixture into the center of the wonton. Dip a clean finger into the egg and run your finger along all edges of the wrapper. Pull each corner into the middle of the wonton and smooth all the edges to form a 4-sided pyramid. Repeat until you have used up all the wonton wrappers. Do not overfill the dumplings.

Pour 1 inch (2.5 cm) canola oil into a heavy-bottomed skillet and heat over medium heat to 370°F (190°C). Shallow-fry the dumplings until golden brown on each side, about 4 minutes, spooning the hot oil over the dumplings to get them uniformly golden.

Pull the dumplings out of the pan with a slotted spoon and rest them on a sheet of paper towel for a quick second before plating. Season with salt and a good squeeze of lime juice.

Pork and Shrimp Gyoza

SERVES:
4

PREP TIME:
2 HOURS, PLUS 48 HOURS
INACTIVE TIME

If you've got a party coming up or ever just feel like you wanna make the best snacks for your kids, please make these. Dumplings aren't that hard, and neither is mixing the filling. Making ponzu is like making a salty, sweet, sour cocktail, and everyone loves making cocktails. Mac loves when we make dumplings or gyoza. He doesn't love the sauce, and that's fine. Sometimes he even wants just ketchup, and I actually think that's great. Sometimes I'll even maybe dip a little gyoza into some ketchup and then the ponzu. Don't tell anyone, okay? It may sound disgusting, but a fried pork-and-shrimp dumpling is pretty great with any sauce.

FOR THE PONZU SAUCE:

1	cup (240 ml) soy sauce
2	tablespoons lemon zest
2	tablespoons bonito flakes

FOR THE GYOZA FILLING:

1	pound (450 g) pork belly
1½	teaspoons kosher salt, plus more as needed
1	quart (1 L) pork lard
1	pound (450 g) raw peeled shrimp, chopped
30	round wonton wrappers
4	tablespoons (60 ml) vegetable oil, plus more as needed, for cooking

FOR THE PONZU SAMBAL:

¾	cup (200 ml) ponzu sauce (see above)
½	cup (100 ml) red wine vinegar
½	cup (100 ml) malt vinegar
⅔	cup (150 ml) sambal oelek
¼	cup (30 g) sliced scallions
2	tablespoons julienned ginger

recipe continues

Make the ponzu sauce: In a container, combine the soy sauce, lemon zest, and bonito flakes. Cover and let the mixture sit at room temperature for 48 hours, then strain through a fine chinois or strainer. Store the ponzu sauce in the fridge.

Make the gyoza filling: Season the pork belly on all sides with salt equal to 2 percent of its weight (multiply grams × .02). Let the pork belly sit at room temperature for 1 hour, then wipe off excess salt.

While the pork belly is sitting, preheat the oven to 300°F (150°C).

Melt the pork lard in a medium Dutch oven. Once it's warm, add the pork belly. Cover, place in the oven, and cook for 1 to 1½ hours, until fork-tender. Remove from the oven and let cool in the fat. Once cooled, cut into medium chunks.

Put the chopped pork belly in a food processor and pulse until smooth. Slowly pour in the confit pork oil to emulsify in. Once emulsified, scrape out and transfer to a medium bowl. Add the shrimp, fold it into the pork mixture, and season with a dash of kosher salt. Set in the fridge to chill.

Make the ponzu sambal: In a small bowl, combine the ponzu sauce, red wine vinegar, malt vinegar, 7 tablespoons (100 ml) water, sambal oelek, and scallions. Mix well; add the sliced ginger to garnish. Reserve for dipping.

Wrap the dumplings: Hold a wonton wrapper in your hand and place the filling off center, slightly toward the side closest to you. Pleat the dumpling by pushing the wonton wrapper with the index finger of one hand and press to secure the pleat with the index finger of the other hand.

Cook the dumplings: Heat about 2 tablespoons oil in a large skillet over medium-high heat. Add 8 dumplings at a time, placing them smooth side down, and sear the dumplings for 2 minutes, or until the bottoms turn golden brown. Add a small amount of water to create steam, immediately cover with a lid, and let the dumplings steam for another 3 to 4 minutes. Pull the dumplings out of the pan and rest them on a sheet of paper towel for a quick second before plating. Remove to cook the remaining dumplings.

To serve, place the dumplings on a plate with the ponzu sambal on the side for dipping.

These uncooked dumplings freeze extremely well. Place them on a baking sheet, sitting up and not touching. Place the sheet in the freezer, and once the dumplings are frozen, transfer them to ziplock bags and freeze for up to 3 months.

Ricotta Egg Yolk Raviolo

SERVES:
2

PREP TIME:
1 HOUR AND 15 MINUTES,
PLUS 1 HOUR INACTIVE TIME

Bacon and eggs is such a classic . . . ravioli stuffed with ricotta, timeless . . . all together, forever filled with egg yolk and engulfed in a summer cherry tomato pan sauce . . . BABOOM. The yolk bursting through the pasta, adding to the already perfect tomato sauce; the crispy bacon; the fresh hit of basil—OMG, this dish is perfect, and so are you.

FOR THE PASTA DOUGH:

7   egg yolks

1   cup (150 g) all-purpose flour, plus more for rolling

1   tablespoon olive oil

½   teaspoon kosher salt

FOR THE PASTA FILLING:

1   cup (240 g) ricotta

½   cup (50 g) finely grated Parmesan cheese

½   teaspoon kosher salt, plus more for cooking

1   teaspoon freshly cracked black pepper

6   egg yolks

1   egg, beaten with 1 teaspoon water to make egg wash

FOR THE BACON TOMATO VINAIGRETTE:

1   cup (150 g) diced bacon

4   garlic cloves, thinly sliced

1 ⅓ cups (200 g) cherry tomatoes, cut in half

3   tablespoons honey

5   tablespoons (75 ml) white wine vinegar

1   teaspoon kosher salt

2   stems of basil, for serving

recipe continues

Make the pasta dough: In the bowl of a stand mixer, mix the egg yolks, flour, olive oil, and salt with your hands until a shaggy dough forms. Switch to the machine, fit with a dough hook, and mix until the dough is smooth and elastic, about 10 minutes at medium speed. Cover with plastic wrap and let rest for at least 30 minutes and up to 1 hour.

Make the filling: In a medium bowl, mix the ricotta and Parmesan, the salt, and pepper. Transfer to a resealable plastic bag and refrigerate.

Make the bacon tomato vinaigrette: Place the bacon in a medium skillet and cook over medium heat, stirring occasionally, until rendered and crisp, about 10 minutes. Using a slotted spoon, transfer the bacon to a paper towel–lined plate. Drain and discard about 60 percent of the bacon fat, turn down heat to low, add the garlic, and cook for 5 minutes, or until softened but with no color. Add the tomatoes, increase the heat to medium-high, and blister for 3 minutes. Add the honey and vinegar. Bring to a boil and cook for 2 minutes. Pull from the heat, add the salt, and set aside.

Set a hand-cranked pasta machine to the widest setting and lightly flour your work surface. Using a rolling pin, roll the dough ¼ inch (6 mm) thick. Pass the dough through the machine's rollers.

Continue passing the dough through the pasta machine, adjusting the dial to the next number down each time until you get to the thinnest setting. Run the pasta sheet through the thinnest setting twice. Cut the round edges off.

Lightly flour a baking sheet and set aside. Lay the pasta sheet on a dry, well-floured work surface. Cut out 12 squares. Remove the filling from the fridge, cut a ¾-inch (2 cm) hole in a corner of the bag, and on 6 of the squares pipe a ring of filling that measures about ½ inch (2 cm) high, leaving the center open to hold the egg yolk in place.

Place 1 egg yolk in the center of each piped ring; repeat with the 5 remaining yolks in the remaining piped rings. Using a pastry brush, brush egg wash onto the exposed dry edges of the pasta and carefully cover with the 6 remaining pasta squares, pushing out the air pockets as you go and pressing tightly around the filling and egg yolk to seal. Center a large round cutter around the filling and egg yolk and cut away extra pasta. Repeat with the remaining 5 raviolo. Using a metal spatula, carefully transfer the raviolo to the floured baking sheet. Discard all the trimmings.

Bring a large stockpot with heavily salted water to a boil. Gently drop 3 raviolo at a time into the water and cook for 2½ to 3 minutes (do not overcook, which will fuck up the yolk). Remove from the water with a slotted spoon and place onto a tray. Repeat with the remaining 3 raviolo.

Serve immediately, with a generous amount of vinaigrette and bacon on top and a few leaves of basil.

Le Select Chicken Fusilli

SERVES: 4

PREP TIME: 1 HOURS AND 10 MINUTES

I've made this dish once or twice a year the past fourteen years. Trish craves it for some reason, and I forget about it until I start prepping. It reminds me so much of Le Select and my formative restaurant line cooking years. This dish in no fucking way makes sense in any country, especially France. Italy would have blown off the head of the chef that brought this dish to the pass. It's complete blasphemy, and yet, it's perfect. I love the outcast, and this dish is kinda how I am: I don't make sense to a lot of people, and yet, the second most people meet me, they fall in love. Humble. This dish is the French version of the puttanesca, I guess? Capers, Kalamata olives, pickled red onion, lemon segments, and, LOL, WTF, chicken, chicken stock, and cream—literally the complete opposite of the traditional Roman puttanesca. So if puttanesca is the "whore's pasta," then this is the French cuckold's version? Enjoy! It's my wife's favorite pasta, and when I make it, it reminds us of when we were young and free, living paycheck to paycheck, dreaming of what life would be like.

FOR THE PICKLED ONIONS:

¾ cup (200 g) mandoline-sliced red onion rings

3 tablespoons lemon juice

2 tablespoons granulated sugar

FOR THE CHICKEN:

1¼ pounds (500 g) chicken thighs

1 teaspoon kosher salt, plus more as needed

2 tablespoons vegetable oil

1 quart (1 L) Chicken Stock (page 51), or store-bought

12 ounces (360 g) dried fusilli

¼ cup (60 ml) olive oil, plus more for the cooked pasta

1 cup (150 g) finely chopped white onion

2 tablespoons finely chopped garlic

1⅔ cups (400 ml) whipping cream

⅔ cup (75 g) finely grated Parmesan cheese

Splash of lemon juice

16 small lemon segments

¼ cup (50 g) capers, drained and rinsed

¼ cup (60 g) Kalamata olives, pitted and sliced

Make the pickled onions: Place the red onion rings in a medium bowl. In a small saucepan, combine the lemon juice, ¼ cup (60 ml) water, and sugar; bring to a boil over medium-high heat. Pour over the onions and let cool.

Make the chicken: Season the chicken thighs evenly with the salt. Heat the vegetable oil in a medium Dutch oven over medium-high heat. Once the oil is hot, add the chicken and sear on all sides until golden, about 4 minutes per side. Turn down heat to medium-low and drain excess fat. Add the chicken stock, bring to a simmer, and simmer for 35 minutes, or until the chicken is fork-tender. Turn off heat and allow the chicken to cool in the liquid. Pull the chicken out of the pot and shred it down. Strain the liquid and reserve.

Bring a medium saucepan filled with heavily salted water to a boil. Add the fusilli and boil for 8 minutes, or until al dente. Strain in a colander; return the fusilli to the pot, splash with olive oil, and toss around to prevent the pasta from sticking. Let the noodles hang until the sauce is ready.

In a medium stockpot, heat the olive oil over medium heat. Add the white onion and garlic and sweat until the onion is translucent, about 12 minutes. Deglaze with ¼ cup (60 ml) of the chicken braising liquid and bring to a boil. Add the cream and simmer for 5 minutes, or until it starts to thicken and bubble. Add the shredded chicken and toss to coat the chicken with the sauce. Add the cheese and season with salt and a splash of lemon juice.

Pour the mixture into the pasta pot, stir to coat the pasta with sauce, and spoon into 4 bowls. Garnish with the lemon segments, capers, olives, and pickled onions.

Clams and Hot Italian Sausage Spaghetti

SERVES:
2 TO 4

PREP TIME:
35 MINUTES

This quick and easy dish is rewarding in so many ways. I love one-pan pasta nights for dinner. It's very easy to make. I love how so many great meals can actually be fully ready in thirty minutes or less if you know what you're doing. This is a year-round dish as long as you have clams available; you could use any type of clam, or even canned clams. Cooking should be easy. Please don't stress out if you don't have Manila clams, ya know.

2	tablespoons vegetable oil
1	pound (450 g) hot Italian sausage, casings removed
⅔	cup (75 g) diced white onion
2	tablespoons thinly sliced garlic
⅓	cup (50 g) finely chopped carrot
	Kosher salt
12	ounces (360 g) spaghetti
	Olive oil
⅔	cup (100 ml) dry white wine
30	Manila clams
1	bunch (250 g) broccoli rabe, diced
2	cups (480 ml) Chicken Stock (page 51), or store-bought
1	teaspoon dried red chile flakes
1	tablespoon lemon juice
1	cup (20 g) chopped parsley

In a medium Dutch oven, heat the vegetable oil over high heat. Add the sausage and brown on all sides for 6 to 8 minutes. Turn down heat to medium; add the onion, garlic, carrot, and 1 teaspoon kosher salt and cook until the onion is translucent, about 12 minutes.

Bring a medium stockpot filled with heavily salted water to a boil. Add the spaghetti and boil for 8 minutes, or until al dente. Strain in a colander, reserving ½ cup (120 ml) of the pasta water. Return the noodles to the pot, splash with olive oil, and toss the spaghetti around to prevent it from sticking. Let the noodles hang until the sauce is ready.

Turn up the heat under the Dutch oven to high; deglaze with the wine and reduce the liquid by half. Add the clams, broccoli rabe, and chicken stock; bring to a boil. Cover and cook for 5 minutes, or until the clams have opened up. Discard any clams that haven't opened. Take the lid off, add the cooked spaghetti, and allow the sauce to thicken around the noodles. Adjust the consistency as needed using the reserved pasta water. Add the chile flakes, lemon juice, and parsley and toss one last time.

Use tongs to twirl out the noodles into 2 to 4 plates. Spoon the clams and sauce evenly over noodles.

One-Hour Bolognese

SERVES:
4

PREP TIME:
1 HOUR

As I'm writing this, I'm really feeling how fast you can make great meals around quick pasta, and this one is fast and easy and will make you look like you spent all day working the stoves. Bolognese is a house-to-house dish: every person in every town in Italy has a ragù, sugo, or bolo, and this is my fast and easy one-hour take. You could make it a few different ways, but one thing you should keep constant is that it should be saucy, like sludge in the best kind of way. Using carrot, onion, garlic, tomato paste, beef stock, and browned beef and finishing with milk and egg yolks is my favorite. Use any noodle you love—tagliatelle, pappardelle, bucatini, penne, gnocchi—or serve it on warm buttery and cheesy polenta.

1	pound (450 g) carrots, peeled and finely chopped
1	white onion, finely chopped
1	head garlic, cloves sliced
½	cup (120 ml) olive oil
2	pounds (900 g) ground beef
¼	cup (60 ml) tomato paste
2	quarts (2 L) Beef and Bone Marrow Stock (page 55), or store-bought
1	cup (240 ml) whole milk
4	egg yolks
1	tablespoon freshly cracked black pepper, or to taste
	Kosher salt
12	ounces (360 g) dried spaghetti
1	cup (100 g) grated Parmesan cheese

In a medium Dutch oven, combine the carrot, onion, garlic, and olive oil. Cook over medium-low heat until the onions are translucent but the vegetables do not take on color, about 12 minutes. Add the ground beef, stir to work it up (but do not brown it), and cook for 5 minutes. Add the tomato paste and cook for 5 minutes. Add the beef stock and reduce until sludgy and emulsified. Add the milk, reduce for 5 minutes, then add the egg yolks and stir until glossy. Add the pepper and season with salt.

Fill a large saucepan with heavily salted water; bring to a boil. Throw in the spaghetti and boil for 8 to 10 minutes, or until al dente. Strain in a colander, reserving ½ cup (120 ml) of the pasta water.

Add the cooked pasta to the pot of Bolognese and stir until the spaghetti is coated in sauce. Adjust the consistency as needed using the reserved pasta water. Using tongs, twirl one-quarter of the noodles into a tight bundle and transfer to a serving plate. Repeat 3 more times to make 4 servings. Spoon the remaining sauce evenly onto the plates. Sprinkle with the cheese and boom. ONE-HOUR BOLO!

Braised Rabbit, Cipollini Onions, and Green Olive Bucatini

SERVES:
2 TO 4

PREP TIME:
1 HOUR AND
40 MINUTES

There are two kinds of people: those who eat rabbit and those who don't. The ones who don't often grew up with them as pets, like my wife. I eat them because my pet rabbit, Conan the Barbarian, was a jerk. He walked around our house like a cat. The worst was at night; when you tried to go to the bathroom, he would chase you down and bite you. It was like a Western movie, a duel between you and this crazy little black rabbit. I don't have a problem eating rabbits now because a rabbit used to try to kill me. And let me tell you, this dish is pure Ric Flair "Woo!"

1¼	pounds (500 g) rabbit legs
	Kosher salt
¼	cup (60 ml) vegetable oil
⅓	cup (50 g) diced white onion
⅓	cup (50 g) diced carrot
⅓	cup (50 g) diced celery
½	cup (120 ml) white wine
1	quart (1 L) Chicken Stock (page 51), or store-bought
12	ounces (360 g) dried bucatini pasta
¼	cup (60 ml) olive oil, plus more for the cooked pasta
¼	cup (50 g) unsalted butter
6	garlic cloves, shaved super thin
1	cup (150 g) whole cipollini onions, roasted
½	cup (65 g) Cerignola olives, pitted and sliced
1	tablespoon lemon juice
¼	cup (55 g) grated Parmesan cheese, for serving

Preheat the oven to 325°F (165°C).

Season the rabbit legs evenly with salt. In a medium Dutch oven, heat the vegetable oil over medium-high heat. Once the oil is hot, add the rabbit and sear on all sides, about 4 minutes. Remove the rabbit from the pot and rest on a paper towel–lined plate. Add the onion, carrot, and celery to the pot; reduce heat to medium and cook until the onion is translucent, about 12 minutes. Deglaze with the white wine and reduce the liquid by half. Return the rabbit to the pot, pour on the chicken stock, cover, and braise in the oven for 1 to 1½ hours, until the rabbit is fork-tender. Pull the pot from the oven and allow the rabbit to cool in its liquid. Once cooled, keep the two legs whole and shred the rest of the rabbit off the bones; strain the braising liquid and discard the solids.

Bring a medium stockpot filled with heavily salted water to a boil. Add the bucatini and boil for 8 minutes, or until al dente. Strain in a colander, reserving ½ cup (120 ml) of the pasta water. Return the noodles to the pot, splash with olive oil, and toss the pasta around to prevent it from sticking. Let the noodles hang until the sauce is ready.

In a large skillet over medium heat, melt the butter with the olive oil. Add the shaved garlic and cook for 5 minutes, or until softened but with no color. Add the roasted cipollini, olives, and picked-down rabbit. Stir with a wooden spoon and add ½ cup (120 ml) of the rabbit braising liquid. Add the blanched bucatini and work that together—the sauce should be nice and loose. Adjust the consistency as needed using the reserved pasta water. Add the lemon juice; taste for seasoning.

Use tongs to twirl out the pasta into 2 to 4 bowls and spoon the rabbit sauce over the noodles. Top pasta with the reserved legs. Serve with a bowl of the cheese on the side.

Braised Lamb Neck Ragu Rigatoni

SERVES: 4

PREP TIME: 3 HOURS

This lamb neck is kinda the same as the hour-long bolo (see page 169), but we braise the lamb neck and make a ragù. This isn't fast, but it's still easy. I love braises so much, and this is one of my all-time favorites. You could take this day-old and put it in a casserole dish, cover it with mozzarella, and bake it! You can do that with any day-old pasta, or eat it cold, or make a cold pasta sandwich—buttered bread filled with meat and cold pasta—and wash it all down with a large glass of ice-cold milk.

2	pounds (750 g) lamb necks, cut into 2-inch (5 cm) cross-width pieces (ask your butcher)
1½	tablespoons kosher salt, plus more as needed
1	teaspoon freshly ground black pepper, plus more as needed
4	tablespoons (60 ml) vegetable oil
⅔	cup (100 g) diced white onion
⅓	cup (50 g) diced carrot
⅓	cup (50 g) diced celery
½	cup (120 ml) white wine
1	quart (1 L) Chicken Stock (page 51), or store-bought
6	garlic cloves, thinly sliced
1	tablespoon tomato paste
3	pounds (1.4 kg) crushed tomatoes
12	ounces (360 g) dried rigatoni
	Olive oil
	Finely grated Parmesan cheese, for serving
	Red chile flakes, for serving

Season the lamb necks evenly with the salt and pepper. In a medium Dutch oven, heat 2 tablespoons of the vegetable oil over medium-high heat. Once the oil is hot, add the lamb necks and sear hard on all sides, about 4 minutes. Remove the lamb from the pot and rest on a paper towel–lined plate. Add half of the onion, the carrot, and celery to the pot; reduce heat to medium-low and cook until the onion is translucent, about 12 minutes. Deglaze with the white wine, increase the heat to medium-high, and reduce the liquid by half. Return the lamb necks to the pan, pour on the chicken stock, cover, and braise at a low simmer for 2 to 2½ hours, until the lamb is fork-tender. Turn off heat and allow the lamb to cool in the liquid for 30 minutes. Once cooled, shred the lamb off the bone and strain the braising liquid, discarding the solids.

While the lamb is cooking, in a second medium Dutch oven, heat the remaining 2 tablespoons vegetable oil over medium-high heat. Add the remaining onion and the garlic and cook, stirring occasionally, until the onion is translucent, about 12 minutes. Add the tomato paste and cook for 5 minutes. Add the crushed tomatoes and bring to a boil, using a wooden spoon to break down any big pieces of tomato. Turn down heat to medium-low and simmer for about 45 minutes, stirring occasionally to prevent any sticking on the bottom, until the raw tomato flavor has disappeared. Season with salt and pepper. Cover to keep warm and set aside.

Bring a medium stockpot filled with heavily salted water to a boil. Add the rigatoni and boil for 8 minutes, or al dente. Strain in a colander, reserving ½ cup (120 ml) of the pasta water. Return the noodles to the pan, splash with olive oil, and toss the pasta around to prevent it from sticking.

Add the shredded lamb to the tomato sauce and bring to a simmer. Ladle the hot sauce over the noodles, enough to bring it all together and coat the noodles. Adjust the consistency as needed using the reserved pasta water. Add a splash of olive oil to make it all nice and shiny. Spoon equal amounts into serving bowls. Garnish with a shit-ton of cheese and red chile flakes.

Littleneck Clams Orecchiette

SERVES: 4

PREP TIME: 25 MINUTES

Orecchiette means "little ears," and they kinda look like clams to me, so I thought this would be the perfect chance to make this dish: a cacio e pepe with pasta and clams. Make it extra lemony with the zest and juice, and add so much pepper that it's gray. I love pepper so much. Put even more pepper on it.

	Kosher salt
12	ounces (360 g) dried orecchiette
1	tablespoon freshly cracked black pepper
2	tablespoons olive oil
4	garlic cloves, chopped
30	(155 g) raw littleneck clams, cleaned
2	cups (200 g) grated Parmesan cheese, plus more for serving

Bring a large pot of heavily salted water to a boil over high heat. Add the orecchiette and cook for 8 to 9 minutes, or until al dente. Strain in a colander, reserving ⅔ cup (150 ml) of the pasta water.

In a large skillet, toast the pepper over high heat until fragrant, about 2 minutes. Add the olive oil and garlic and cook for 5 minutes. Throw in 1 teaspoon salt and the clams; cover the pan and allow to steam in their own juices.

Once the clams have opened (discard any that haven't opened), add the orecchiette and cheese; swirl the pan to emulsify the ingredients. Adjust the consistency as needed using the reserved pasta water. Once you achieve a beautiful texture and right melt, you are ready to scoop and serve. Sprinkle with more cheese.

CHAPTER 6

Curries, Soups, and a Stew

"Only the pure in heart can make a good soup." —LvB

YOU ALL KNOW MY SOUL IS MADE OF BONES AND WATER. I AM AS MUCH BROTH AS I AM HUMAN. If you cut me I would bleed coq au vin. I just love soups! All soups! Please: If I die make a stock out of my body; ladle me into cups and raise them up to the galaxy and enjoy me one last time.

After learning about broths and stocks in chapter 2 (pages 36–57), making soups will be easier. It's all about building flavors. Creating soups is such a peaceful place for me. It's making a love potion every time. Remember: You can't ever remove salt after adding it, so be careful when seasoning. It's so easy to throw a handful into the soup; or maybe I'm projecting my salty tendencies.

Why do I love soups so much? Maybe it was the chowders of the Maritimes and the bisques of Christmases past. I love a creamy chowder, thick from flour, even though where I come from thick chowder is looked down on. A Maritime chowder should have a good seafood stock, lots of wine, and just enough heavy cream or whole milk to bring it all together.

The winters are pretty rough in Canada, if you don't know. Stews are a thing of necessity. Growing up, we were a stew family—chicken, beef, rabbit, or moose (when we had it). A stew to me is root vegetables, tomato paste, red wine, stock, and meat, cooked in a pot in the oven for a couple hours until it has transformed into a dark, flavorful mixture. A stew is the older, grumpier grandfather of the food world. It takes a little more time and isn't flashy, but once you know it you'll love it forever, and it'll love you back—just make sure not to burn it!

Making curries and fish in your home is something mostly white people are afraid of, but the smell is worth it. If your house smells fishy you probably started off with gross, nasty-ass fish, so that's on you for not knowing a good fishmonger. People who don't make curry regularly think of curry as that old spice powder that has sat in the back of the cupboard and smelled "bad." I love the smell of the cumin and different spices that combine to make curry one of the most flavorful foods out there. The world would be a better place if we all cooked one another's food and experienced the smells and felt the emotions spices bring to our bodies.

Green Curry Beef Ribs

SERVES:
4 TO 6

PREP TIME:
3 HOURS

Meat and rice is the new meat and potatoes. And braised beef ribs in spicy green curry is great for any meal—breakfast, lunch, or dinner. Real flavor-building, real spice, real tasty meals for the whole family. Building your skills and your palates are very important to keep things exciting in your home life. And guess what, the day after, shred this beef and make little rotis; add some cheese, even. Fuck this shit up.

FOR THE BEEF SHORT RIBS:

4½	pounds (2 kg) beef short ribs, meat removed from the bone and cut into 1½-inch (4 cm) cubes
1	teaspoon kosher salt, plus more as needed
1	teaspoon freshly cracked black pepper
2	tablespoons vegetable oil
1	cup (200 g) diced onion
⅔	cup (100 g) diced celery
2	tablespoons sliced garlic
¼	cup (75 g) seeded and diced jalapeño chile
½	cup (100 g) diced leek, white and green parts only
2	stalks lemongrass, cut in half and smashed with the side of a knife
1	tablespoon grated ginger
1	tablespoon green curry paste
1	tablespoon ground Thai spice (equal parts toasted ground cardamom and toasted ground cumin)
4	cups (880 ml) Beef and Bone Marrow Stock (page 55), or store-bought
1	cup (240 ml) canned unsweetened coconut milk
2	tablespoons lime juice

FOR THE PICKLED GARLIC:

4	garlic cloves, sliced paper-thin
2	bird's eye chiles, sliced
2	tablespoons white vinegar

FOR SERVING:

⅓	cup (30 g) sliced scallions
1½	cups (60 g) cilantro leaves, stems diced
	Steamed jasmine rice, or Grilled Naan (page 30)

Make the short beef ribs: Season the short ribs with the salt and pepper. Heat the vegetable oil in a medium Dutch oven over medium-high heat. Working in 2 batches, brown the short ribs on all sides, about 8 minutes per batch. Transfer the short ribs to a plate and pour out about 70 percent of the fat from the pot.

Add the onion, celery, garlic, jalapeño, leek, and lemongrass to the pot; cook, stirring occasionally, until the onion starts to brown, about 10 minutes. Add the ginger, curry paste, and toasted spice mix and stir to coat the vegetables. Add the short ribs and any juices from the resting plate. Add beef stock to barely cover the top of the short ribs. Bring to a boil, then turn down heat to low; simmer until the short ribs are tender, 2 to 2½ hours. Remove the lemongrass and whisk in the coconut milk. Taste the broth for seasoning. Add the lime juice and salt as needed.

While the beef is cooking, make the pickled garlic: In a small nonreactive bowl, combine the garlic and chiles. Heat the vinegar in a small skillet until bubbling. Pour the hot vinegar over the garlic and chiles and let sit for 1 hour.

To serve: Generously divide the curry into serving bowls. Garnish the bowls with little spoonfuls of pickled garlic and lots of chopped scallion and cilantro leaves. Enjoy with jasmine rice or a big piece of grilled naan.

Green Curry Duck Legs

SERVES:
4

PREP TIME:
2½ HOURS

We ate braised duck leg green curry in a deep country town in New Zealand when we were shooting a show years and years ago. There were zero restaurants in town except for these weird bakeries that are like cafeterias for the public, serving fried chicken and potstickers, ham and cheese sandos, and what have you, like a homemade, bizarre 7-Eleven. The food isn't great and is made in the mornings and sits around, but you could always just say fuck it and have a meat pie! One day, we were driving down this side street, and we found a Thai restaurant. It was unreal, like seeing Valhalla. We ate dinner at this restaurant every night the next three days. I had this duck curry and rotis every night, and they served it with all these pickles, and the jasmine rice was perfectly cooked. This dish is inspired by finding a true gem in the middle of Mordor.

4	duck legs (1 pound/450 g total)
2	teaspoons kosher salt
3	tablespoons canola oil
⅔	cup (100 g) diced onion
⅔	cup (100 g) diced leek, white and green parts only
2	tablespoons sliced garlic
⅓	cup (50 g) diced celery
3	tablespoons grated ginger
2	stalks lemongrass, cut in half and smashed with the side of a knife
1	tablespoon ground turmeric
1	teaspoon ground coriander
1	tablespoon green curry paste
3	cups (700 ml) Chicken Stock (page 51), or store-bought
1	cup (240 ml) canned unsweetened coconut milk
	Zest of 1 lime
¼	cup (60 ml) lime juice
1	cup (30 g) Thai basil leaves
1	cup (40 g) cilantro leaves
1	cup (50 g) sliced scallions
	Mint sprigs
	Steamed jasmine rice
	Lime wedges

Preheat the oven to 400°F (200°C).

Salt the duck legs and place on a baking sheet fitted with a wire rack. Place in the oven and roast until browned, 15 to 20 minutes. Pull from the oven and set aside.

In a medium Dutch oven, heat the oil over medium heat. Add the onion, leek, garlic, celery, ginger, and lemongrass; cook, stirring constantly, until the onion starts to turn golden, about 12 minutes. Add the turmeric and coriander and toast for 4 minutes, then add the curry paste and cook for 5 minutes. Deglaze with the chicken stock, bring to a boil, and scrape the bottom of the pot with a wooden spoon.

Add the roasted duck legs to the broth; bring to a boil, then reduce heat to medium-low. Cover, then simmer for 2 hours, or until the duck is tender and easily comes off the bone. Add the coconut milk, taste for seasoning, and add the lime zest and lime juice.

To serve, place a whole duck leg in the center of each bowl and ladle enough curry to just cover the top of the duck leg. Garnish with the Thai basil, cilantro, scallions, and mint. Serve with rice and lime wedges.

Yellow Curry Clams

You can make a curry as fast it takes to open a clam, and this is another hint for fast dinners or snacks, if you're craving clams in creamy curry. I love the idea of making this in a cabin, obviously, 'cause that's where we shot the photo on the opposite page. So make sure you get a cabin, and make some clams in a yellow creamy curry, and eat that while playing gin rummy, smoking smokes, and talking about ice fishing when the winter rolls in.

36	hard-shell clams, such as cherrystone or Manila
2	quarts (2 L) cold water (if using wild clams)
⅔	cup (100 g) cornmeal (if using wild clams)
1	tablespoon canola oil
1	cup (150 g) diced onion
¾	cup (100 g) diced leek, white and green parts only
1	teaspoon diced garlic
1	tablespoon peeled and minced ginger
	Kosher salt
1	tablespoon yellow curry powder
⅔	cup (150 ml) Chicken Stock (page 51), or store-bought
1¼	cups (300 ml) heavy cream
2	tablespoons lime juice
	Freshly ground black pepper
½	cup (10 g) basil leaves, torn
	Roti (page 29), sticky rice, or crusty bread, for serving

If you've purchased farm-raised clams, they are usually flushed out and are ready to eat. For wild fresh clams, you'll need to soak them in the cold water with the cornmeal sprinkled in for 20 minutes, so the clams spit out any sand sitting in their bellies.

In a medium Dutch oven, heat the oil over medium heat until the oil is hot and makes a splatter noise when it comes into contact with a drip of water. Add the onion, leek, garlic, and ginger. Cook the vegetables for 20 minutes, or until lightly golden. Add a pinch of salt.

Add the curry powder and toast it for 2 minutes. Deglaze with the chicken stock and reduce by half. Add the cream, bring to a simmer, and simmer for 5 minutes. Add the clams and stir so they are all coated. Cover and cook until all the clams are open; discard any clams that do not open.

Season the clams with the lime juice, salt, and pepper. Garnish with torn basil and serve with roti, sticky rice, or crusty bread.

Lamb Neck Dizi Sangi

SERVES: 6

PREP TIME: 4 HOURS, PLUS 2 HOURS INACTIVE TIME

Although this is called "dizi sangi," we aren't cooking these in *dizis*—the traditional stone pots that it is cooked and served in. I have only had this soup at a restaurant once in my life, and I loved it so much but have not gone back to where I had it because we had to sit on the floor pretty much, and unfortunately, the big dog eating some interactive soup on the floor isn't the greatest. So, make this in your home. Yes, it's a lot of work. Some recipes are easy, and some are hard. Let's get to work and build out a beautiful soup that's gonna make your tongue explode in joy!

3	pounds (1.3 kg) lamb necks
1	tablespoon ground turmeric
1	teaspoon kosher salt, plus more as needed
1	teaspoon freshly cracked black pepper
1½	cups (300 g) diced white onions
¼	cup (60 ml) tomato paste
2	quarts (2 L) Lamb Stock (page 56), or water
4	Yukon Gold potatoes, peeled and quartered
1	cup (150 g) canned chickpeas, drained
1	cup (150 g) canned white beans, drained
¼	cup (60 ml) lemon juice, plus more as needed
⅓	cup (50 g) garlic, thinly sliced
¼	cup (60 ml) white vinegar
2	tablespoons sugar
6	Roti (page 29), or store-bought flatbreads
¾	cup (180 ml) plain Greek yogurt
1½	cups (40 g) mint leaves
1½	cups (60 g) tarragon leaves

Note: I have returned to Takht-e Tavoos and ate this at a table. It was glorious.

Place the lamb necks in a shallow container and season with the turmeric, salt, and pepper. Keep in the refrigerator for 3 hours.

Preheat the oven to 400°F (200°C).

Place the lamb necks on a baking sheet fitted with a wire rack. Brown them in the oven for 30 minutes, then remove from the oven and transfer them to large Dutch oven, reserving the rendered lamb fat from the bottom of the baking sheet. Add the onions, tomato paste, and lamb stock. Bring to a boil over high heat, stirring to dissolve the tomato paste. Cover the pot, reduce heat to low, and simmer for 2 hours.

Add the potatoes, chickpeas, white beans, and lemon juice; simmer until the meat and potatoes are fork-tender, about 1 hour. Taste for seasoning; the broth should be tangy and bright. Remove from heat and let rest for 10 minutes.

Put the garlic in a small bowl. In a small saucepan, combine the vinegar, ¼ cup (60 ml) water, and sugar and bring to a boil; pour over the garlic. Cool and reserve for the soup.

Use a slotted spoon to remove the meat, beans, and potatoes from the broth and transfer them to a large bowl. Use a fork to pull the meat off the bones; discard the bones. With a potato masher, mash the meat, beans, and potatoes into a soft uniform paste. If it's a little dry, add broth and continue mashing until fully broken down and emulsified.

Strain the stock through a fine chinois or strainer and heat it back up in the pan. Season with salt and lemon juice. This is a two-part meal: the broth and the meat paste. Serve the broth in soup bowls drizzled with rendered lamb fat and sprinkled with the pickled garlic. Put the meat paste in a serving bowl, spread it on the roti, dollop yogurt over it, and top with the herbs. Eat the little meat breads with your hands.

Phở Gà

Phở gà means "chicken phở," if you didn't know, and it is my ultimate breakfast. If I could eat this every morning, I would. I love phở gà, and I'm kinda mad at myself that I never even looked for phở gà or knew it existed for as long as I did. I was the same as most people that go to a phở restaurant: I get the chef's special—ya know, tripe, tendon, brisket, rare beef, and beef ball. Then, I started getting into chicken phở, and it changed my whole life. In the past ten years I think I've only had beef phở a handful of times, and I eat phở a lot. I love phở, it is my favorite soup. It is my true soup love; it is my everything. I'm sure I would have found phở without Rang, but still, every time I eat phở, I think of him. Love you, Rang.

5	pounds (5 kg) chicken feet
5½	pounds (2.6 kg) whole chicken (1 large or 2 small chickens)
1	cup (60 g) halved and sliced scallions
1	(3-inch/7.5 cm) knob ginger, peeled
1	white onion quarter, plus ½ cup (75 g) thinly sliced
4	stalks lemongrass
2	cups (50 g) whole cilantro leaves, plus 1 cup (45 g) chopped
1	tablespoon coriander seeds, toasted
1	teaspoon whole white peppercorns
2	tablespoons paper-thin sliced garlic
2	green bird's eye chiles, thinly sliced
2	tablespoons white vinegar
	Kosher salt
1	(14-ounce/400 g) pack vermicelli noodles

Place the chicken feet in a large stockpot and cover with water. Bring to a simmer over medium heat, then turn down heat to super low and keep it at a bare simmer for 24 hours. Strain through a fine chinois or strainer. Discard the feet, clean the pot, and pour the chicken feet stock back into the pot.

On a cutting board, break down the whole chickens into parts: breast, wings, legs, and thighs; place them into the chicken feet stock. Heat over medium heat, gently skimming away any scum. Once the stock comes up to a light boil, skim again and turn down heat to medium-low.

Add the scallions, ginger, onion quarter, lemongrass, cilantro, coriander seeds, and peppercorns to the broth and cook for 3 hours. Turn off heat and steep the broth for 1 hour.

Put the garlic and chiles in a small nonreactive bowl. In a small skillet, heat the vinegar until bubbling; pour over the garlic and chiles. Let sit for 1 hour.

Pull the chickens out, save 2 breasts and 2 thighs for slicing. Shred the meat off the rest of the bones and mix all the shredded meat together. Pull the breast and thigh meat off the bones and slice the meat. Strain the broth through a fine chinois or strainer; return it to the pot and add salt for desired saltiness.

Bring a medium stockpot of water to a boil. Add the vermicelli noodles and cook according to the directions on the package, then drain in a colander.

Divide the vermicelli noodles among serving bowls; place the shredded and sliced chicken in the center of the noodles and ladle broth over the chicken to fill the bowl. Garnish with the sliced onion and chopped cilantro and spoon on garlic–chile vinegar for a spicy kick.

Master Rang's Sister's Vietnamese Fish Ball Soup

SERVES:
6

PREP TIME:
1 HOUR AND
15 MINUTES

This recipe is an ode to Chi Hai, who is Rang's older sister. When we first met in Vietnam, she served us shrimp cakes that were like large fried pancakes sliced into small wedges like a pie. We ate them, and Rang smoked, and they drank cans of cold beer and talked for hours. I just sat and watched a brother and sister catch up from not seeing each other for fifteen years. She told me to go to this one food stall and have their fried seafood ball soup. We met the next morning and had a bowl. Fried seafood balls filled with shrimp, scallop, and white fish (probably snapper) with coriander, chile, and some fish sauce. The broth was so light yet so flavorful. It was made of grouper head and onions and herbs. When served, you got some udon-like noodles, some whittled napa cabbage, and four seafood balls. They offered white pepper and extra chopped coriander. I miss Vietnam.

2¼	pounds (960 g) shrimp, peeled and deveined
¼	cup (25 g) pork lard
¼	cup (60 ml) fish sauce
½	teaspoon ground white pepper
1	teaspoon kosher salt, plus more as needed
2	tablespoons seeded and diced Anaheim chiles
1	cup (30 g) chopped cilantro stems
1	teaspoon finely chopped ginger
1	teaspoon finely chopped garlic
	Canola oil
1½	quarts (1.5 L) Fish Fumet (page 48)
2	packed cups (200 g) sliced napa cabbage
2	packed cups (200 g) sliced bok choy
¼	cup (60 ml) lime juice
2	cups (40 g) sliced scallions

Put the shrimp in a high-speed blender and pulse until smooth. Add the pork lard and blend until emulsified. Scrape the mixture out of the blender into a medium bowl set over a larger bowl filled with ice. Add the fish sauce, white pepper, salt, chiles, cilantro stems, ginger, and garlic and fold until fully mixed. Cover and chill in the refrigerator for 20 minutes.

Line a baking sheet with parchment paper and brush with canola oil. Pull the shrimp from the fridge. Using 2 spoons, scoop 1-tablespoon (25 to 30 g) piles of shrimp paste and put them on the your baking sheet, just like you are making cookies, 36 to 48 balls total.

Bring a pot of water to a boil. Oil your hands and roll the shrimp paste piles into nice little balls. Now poach the shrimp balls until cooked through, 3 to 5 minutes, then drain very well and pat dry. Return to the fridge to cool.

Heat 1 cup (240 ml) of canola oil to 350°F (175°C). Drop in all the balls and fry for 4 minutes or until lightly golden. Set aside.

In a large saucepan over medium-high heat, bring the fish fumet up to a light simmer, add the napa cabbage and bok choy, and cook for 2 minutes. Add the fried shrimp balls and bring to a simmer, about 2 minutes. Taste for salt. Divide the shrimp balls, vegetables, and broth into bowls and finish with the lime juice and scallions.

Smoked Ham Hock and Split Pea Soup

SERVES:
8

PREP TIME:
3 HOURS, PLUS 48 HOURS
INACTIVE TIME

There's two feet of snow on the ground right now, and I'm trying to think of something clever to write about a split pea soup filled with crispy ham hock, and all I got is, I wish I had some right now. There is something about thick soups or purees, like a cauliflower or butternut squash soup. And the split pea soup seems like a great-grandfather kind of soup, from the time of having last year's dried pea haul up in the rafters, hanging in some cloth bag, and slaughtering the last animal and using its bones to make broth to cook the peas. Yeah, split pea soup is for old people, but it's still good.

2	tablespoons kosher salt, plus more as needed
2	pounds (900 g) fresh ham hocks, cut 2 inches (5 cm) thick (ask your butcher)
1½	quarts (1.5 L) pork lard
4	whole garlic cloves
2	bay leaves
1	tablespoon black peppercorns
4	sprigs thyme
1	cup (25 g) chopped parsley
8	ounces (250 g) double smoked bacon, cut into ½-inch (1 cm) squares
1	carrot, peeled and chopped
½	onion, chopped
4	ribs celery, chopped
¼	cup (60 ml) olive oil
¼	cup (50 g) plus 2 tablespoons unsalted butter
2¼	pounds (1 kg) dried yellow split peas, rinsed
⅔	cup (150 ml) dry white wine
2	quarts (2 L) Pork Stock (page 52), or store-bought
2	quarts (2 L) Chicken Stock (page 51), or store-bought, plus more as needed
1	tablespoon chopped garlic
2	teaspoons freshly cracked black pepper

In a large container, whisk the salt into 2 quarts (2 L) water. Place the ham hocks in the salt brine, cover, and refrigerate for 24 hours. Take the hocks out of the brine and pat dry.

In a medium Dutch oven, heat the pork lard over medium-high heat. Add the whole garlic, bay leaves, peppercorns, thyme, parsley, and ham hocks; bring the fat up to 300°F (150°C). Turn down heat to medium-low and cook for 2 to 2½ hours, until fork-tender.

Turn on your smoker to 300°F (150°C). Remove ham hocks from the fat; place in the smoker for 2 hours until golden brown.

In a large Dutch oven, cook the bacon over medium-high heat until rendered down and golden brown, about 8 minutes.

Meanwhile, put the carrot in a high-speed blender or food processor and blend until broken down into small chunks. Scoop out the carrots and set aside in a bowl. Repeat the blending process with the onion and celery.

Once the bacon is cooked, add the olive oil and ¼ cup (50 g) of the butter and let the fat get all bubbly and frothy. Add the pureed vegetables and cook for 12 minutes, stirring occasionally. Add the split peas and cook for 5 minutes. Deglaze with the white wine and reduce the liquid for a minute. Add both stocks and bring to a boil, skimming off any scum that comes to the top. Cook until the split peas are tender, about 25 minutes, then remove from heat.

Working in 3 batches, ladle the soup into a blender and blend until smooth, then transfer the soup back into the pot. Whisk in additional warm chicken stock if needed—you want the soup buttery smooth. Season with the pepper and more salt, if needed. Keep warm.

Pull your hocks from the smoker and shred all the meat from the bone.

Divide the soup into serving bowls and top with the smoked ham hock. Serve to friends in the colder months.

Double Rib Chili

SERVES:
8 TO 10

PREP TIME:
3½ HOURS

This is totally inspired by the Sunday gravy that Carol, my mother-in-law, makes—but I made it into a chili! How smart am I, and how smart are you gonna look when you make this on game day and show the whole family and whoever else was invited over to consume the greatest chili on the planet? Everyone always talks such a big game on who makes the best chili, and now you have the magic key to destroy everyone's egos and set yourself up for chili world domination. Big chili energy.

1½	pounds (700 g) boneless beef short ribs, cut into 1-inch (3 cm) cubes
2	teaspoons kosher salt, plus more as needed
1	tablespoon freshly ground black pepper
1½	pounds (700 g) pork ribs, cut into 2-bone pieces
1	white onion, quartered, plus ½ cup (100 g) grated
⅔	cup (100 g) diced red bell peppers
⅔	cup (100 g) diced green bell peppers
⅓	cup (75 g) chopped celery
4	garlic cloves, peeled
1	poblano chile, cut lengthwise and seeded
2	jalapeño chiles, cut lengthwise and seeded
1	tablespoon ground cumin
1	tablespoon ground paprika
1	tablespoon ground coriander
1	tablespoon ground mace
1	tablespoon ground cayenne
1	tablespoon Mexican chili powder
¼	cup (60 ml) canola oil
1	pound (450 g) ground beef
1	pound (450 g) ground pork
¼	cup (60 ml) tomato paste
1½	cups (360 ml) Mexican lager beer
2	(14.5-ounce/411 g) cans crushed tomatoes
2	(15-ounce/425 g) cans red kidney beans
1	quart (1 L) Beef and Bone Marrow Stock (page 55), or store-bought
1	bouquet garni (6 sprigs cilantro, 6 sprigs parsley, and 2 bay leaves tied together with butcher's twine)
⅓	cup (70 ml) Tabasco sauce
⅓	cup (70 ml) Worcestershire sauce
1	cup (160 g) grated Cheddar cheese
3	tablespoons sour cream
2	cups (55 g) sliced whole scallions

recipe continues

Place the cubed beef short ribs in a medium bowl and season with some of the salt and pepper. Place on a baking sheet until ready to cook. In the same bowl, season the pork ribs with salt and pepper and place them on the sheet with the short ribs.

In a large bowl, combine the quartered onion, red peppers, green peppers, celery, garlic, poblano, and jalapeños. Working in batches in the blender, blend the vegetable mixture into fine chunks, almost a puree. Set aside.

In a medium bowl, combine the cumin, paprika, mace, coriander, cayenne, and Mexican chili powder and stir to form your spice powder.

Heat a large Dutch oven over high heat and add 2 tablespoons of the canola oil. Once the oil is hot, add the beef short ribs in batches and brown all sides until caramelized, about 8 minutes. Pull the short ribs out and rest on a baking sheet. Repeat with the pork ribs, browning both sides for about 6 minutes. Pull the pork ribs out and rest them on the same sheet.

In a large bowl, combine the ground beef and ground pork and mix together with your hands. Carefully place chunks of the ground meat in the hot Dutch oven and sear it in batches until all the meat is browned and caramelized. Scoop it out and set aside.

In a clean large Dutch oven, heat the remaining 2 tablespoons canola oil over medium heat. Add the vegetable puree and cook, stirring occasionally, for 12 minutes. Add the chili spice mixture and toast the spices for 4 minutes. Add the tomato paste and cook for 5 minutes. Deglaze with the beer and reduce by half. Add all the proteins back into the pot, stirring to coat the meat with the tomato mixture. Add the crushed tomatoes and kidney beans. Pour in the beef stock so it covers the meat and beans by ¾ inch (2 cm). Add the bouquet garni, Tabasco sauce, and Worcestershire sauce and bring to a boil, then turn down heat to medium-low and simmer for 2 to 2½ hours, stirring the bottom frequently to prevent sticking until the meat is fork-tender. Taste the chili for seasoning and add salt if needed.

Portion the chili into serving bowls, sprinkle the top with cheese, add a big dollop of sour cream, scallions, and grated white onion and serve yourself a big old dawg bowl of chili.

Beef Cheek Risotto

SERVES:
6

PREP TIME:
3 HOURS AND
20 MINUTES

Beef cheeks are so buttery, OMG, everyone at dinner is gonna be over the moon. Making risotto is one of the most fun cooking techniques. Cooking the shallots just right, getting the rice perfectly opaque before you hit it with the wine, working it all with a wooden spoon, and ladling in the hot chicken stock is really such a peaceful process. Finally adding in the butter, Parm, and mascarpone, spooning that into a shallow bowl, then puting the braised beef cheek, all glazed up, right in the bull's-eye, and adding fresh thyme leaves and some nice sea salt—baboom, you guys are lucky for picking this recipe to cook tonight.

2	tablespoons canola oil
2	pounds (900 g) beef cheeks, trimmed and cut in half
1	teaspoon kosher salt, plus more as needed
1	teaspoon freshly ground black pepper, plus more for finishing
⅔	cup (100 g) diced white onions
⅔	cup (100 g) diced carrots
⅔	cup (100 g) diced celery
2	tablespoons tomato paste
1¼	cups (300 ml) red wine
1	quart (1 L) Beef and Bone Marrow Stock (page 55), or store-bought
1	bouquet garni (5 sprigs thyme, 5 sprigs parsley, and 2 bay leaves tied together with butcher's twine)
⅓	cup (70 ml) olive oil
½	cup (70 g) finely chopped shallots
3	tablespoons finely chopped garlic
3½	cups (750 g) Arborio rice
1¼	cups (300 ml) dry white wine
3	tablespoons thyme leaves
2	quarts (2 L) Chicken Stock (page 51), or store-bought, heated, plus more as needed
¼	cup (50 g) unsalted butter
⅓	cup (75 g) Mascarpone cheese
	Zest of 1 lemon
2	tablespoons lemon juice
¼	cup (50 g) grated Pecorino cheese

recipe continues

Preheat the oven to 300°F (150°C).

Heat the canola oil in a medium Dutch oven over high heat. Season the beef cheeks with the salt and pepper and sear on all sides until golden brown, 4 to 5 minutes per side. Remove from the pot to a plate. Discard about 70 percent of the fat from the pot. Reduce heat to medium, add the onions, carrots, and celery, and cook for 10 minutes, or until the onions are translucent. Add the tomato paste and cook for 4 minutes, then deglaze with the red wine and reduce by half. Add the beef cheeks back in, cover with the beef stock, and add the bouquet garni. Bring to a boil, then turn off heat; cover and place in the oven. Cook for 2 to 2½ hours, until the beef cheeks are fork-tender. Take out of the oven and let cool in the liquid, about 30 minutes.

Once the beef cheeks are cooled, remove them from the liquid, strain the liquid through a fine chinois or strainer, and cook the liquid over high heat until reduced to a sauce consistency. Set the meat and sauce aside.

In a wide stockpot, heat the olive oil over low heat. Add the shallots and garlic and cook, stirring constantly, for 15 minutes. You don't want to burn them here, just a slow mellow sweat. Add the rice, turn up heat, and stir with a wooden spoon to evenly toast the rice grains, about 5 minutes. Deglaze with the white wine and stir until all the wine is absorbed, then add 2 tablespoons of the thyme leaves.

Ladle in some hot chicken stock to cover the rice, turn down heat to medium, and keep stirring until all the stock is absorbed into the rice. Repeat, adding more stock, until the rice is cooked to al dente, 20 to 25 minutes.

Warm the beef cheeks in the reduced braising liquid, cover, and keep warm.

Add the butter to the risotto and stir until completely melted. Add the Mascarpone one spoonful at a time and keep stirring until the risotto is nice and creamy. Add the lemon zest and juice, taste for seasoning, and add more salt and chicken stock as needed.

Spoon the risotto into serving bowls, tapping the bottom of the bowls to even it out. For each serving, spoon one beef cheek on top and sprinkle with the remaining 1 tablespoon thyme leaves, some pepper, and the Pecorino.

Sichuan Preferably Newfoundland Cod

Sichuan is killing it right now: I'm so in love with the spice, and I think the biggest misunderstanding is that it's too spicy, and that's not right. Good Sichuan should be balanced. Some cooks pour in the spice, but a good spot is spiced enough to get a little sweat on the brow, the nose running, and the senses cleared; not just numb your mouth so bad that it turns water into a nuclear warfare bomb. This dish is something you need to make, and please make the effort to get good fish. Newfoundland cod is maybe the best fish in the world, so have at it.

1½	cups (300 g) jasmine rice
	Kosher salt
⅔	cup (150 ml) canola oil
¼	cup (60 g) minced garlic
¼	cup (40 g) dried red chile flakes
1	tablespoon Szechuan peppercorns
1	teaspoon paprika
1½	cups (360 ml) Fish Fumet (page 48)
1½	cups (360 ml) Chicken Stock (page 51), or store-bought
1½	cups (200 g) chopped (1½-inch/3.8 cm pieces) napa cabbage
1½	cups (200 g) chopped (1½-inch/3.8 cm pieces) bok choy
1½	pounds (600 g) cod, preferably Newfoundland, scaled, filleted, and portioned into 4 to 6 pieces
1	cup (30 g) cilantro leaves and chopped stems
	Lime wedges

Rinse the rice in cold water for 10 minutes and drain. Transfer the drained rice to a rice cooker, add water according to the manufacturer's instructions, stir in a pinch of salt, and turn the machine on.

In a medium stockpot, combine the oil and garlic and cook garlic over low heat until golden brown, about 10 minutes. Add the chile flakes, Sichuan peppercorns, and paprika and infuse in the hot oil 10 minutes, stirring the oil to prevent sticking on the bottom.

Pour the fish fumet and chicken stock into the stockpot and bring to a boil over high heat. Turn down heat to medium, add the napa cabbage and bok choy, and simmer for 2 minutes, then add the fish fillets and gently poach for 8 minutes. Turn off heat and let rest for 2 minutes.

Open the rice cooker, fluff the rice with a fork, check the seasoning for salt, and scoop out and pack into a serving bowl.

Gently scoop out the cooked vegetables from the poaching liquid and plate, then scoop out cod and place on top of the vegetables. Ladle the broth over the fish until covered. Serve family-style with the rice, cilantro, and lime wedges.

Turkey Neck Stew

SERVES:
6

PREP TIME:
1 HOUR AND
40 MINUTES

This photo makes me laugh so much; it looks like a couple of logs, ya know? But let me tell you, turkey neck is the new oxtail and I have zero idea why it hasn't caught on yet. I really don't. One of the last meals I cooked for my grandmother was turkey neck stew, and she loved it. You will love this stew, and you will find turkey necks, and you could totally cut them into 3-inch (7.5 cm) pieces or smaller so they don't look like turds. I love you guys.

FOR THE TURKEY NECK STEW:

2	tablespoons canola oil
2	pounds (900 g) turkey necks (ask your butcher to cut them into 5-inch/12.7 cm pieces)
	Kosher salt and freshly cracked black pepper
1	cup (150 g) diced white onion
⅔	cup (100 g) diced carrot
⅔	cup (100 g) sliced celery
¼	cup (60 ml) tomato paste
¾	cup (200 ml) red wine
3½	cups (800 ml) Chicken Stock (page 51), or store-bought
½	cup (1 stick/115 g) unsalted butter
⅔	cup (150 g) all-purpose flour
½	pound (200 g) Tokyo turnips, cut in half, edges turned (means rounded edges)
½	pound (200 g) rutabaga, peeled, cut into wedges, edges turned
½	pound (200 g) butternut squash, peeled, cut into 1-inch (3 cm) wedges, edges turned
6	ounces (150 g) whole pearl onions, peeled
½	pound (200 g) Yukon Gold potatoes, peeled, cut into 1-inch (3 cm) wedges, edges turned
2	tablespoons olive oil
	Sea salt and lemon juice

FOR THE MASHED POTATOES:

5	pounds (2.2 kg) Yukon Gold potatoes, peeled and quartered
1¼	pounds (570 g) unsalted butter, at room temperature, cut into pieces
	Kosher salt

Make the turkey neck stew: Heat the canola oil in a large Dutch oven over high heat. Season the turkey necks with 1 teaspoon each kosher salt and pepper and brown them on all sides, about 6 minutes; remove from the pot and rest on a plate. Discard about 70 percent of the fat from the pot. Lower heat to medium, add the onion, carrot, and celery, and cook for 12 minutes, or until the onion is translucent. Add the tomato paste and cook for 4 minutes, then deglaze with the red wine and reduce the liquid by half. Return the necks to the pot and cover with the chicken stock. Bring to a boil, then turn down heat to medium-low and simmer for 1 hour, or until the necks start to come apart. Take the necks out, strain the liquid through a fine chinois or strainer, and return the liquid to the pot; cook to reduce the liquid by two-thirds.

In a medium bowl, mix ½ cup (1 stick/115 g) of the butter and the flour together; slowly whisk the mixture into the liquid. Cook for 20 minutes to cook out the raw flour flavor and thicken the stew.

Meanwhile, make the mashed potatoes: Put the potatoes in a medium stockpot and cover with water; place the pot on the stove. Over high heat, bring potatoes to a boil; add salt until the water tastes like the sea. Turn down heat to medium-low. Cook the potatoes at a light simmer for 15 to 20 minutes until fork-tender; strain in a colander. Let the potatoes stand for 5 minutes.

Place a potato ricer over another pot; mill the cooked potatoes into the pot. Start adding the tempered, cubed butter to the potatoes; fold until butter is absorbed. Taste for seasoning, then cover with lid and keep warm.

Working in batches, in a large skillet over medium heat sauté the turnips, rutabaga, squash, pearl onions, and potatoes in the olive oil until fork-tender; add a little water and cover the pan if they brown too quickly, 12 to 15 minutes. Transfer the cooked vegetables to a large stockpot, add the turkey necks, and ladle the reduced braising liquid over the top until you reach your desired stew consistency. Bring to a light simmer and add the sea salt and lemon juice.

Serve the stew family-style with your mash.

CHAPTER 7

Sandwiches

No One Ever Eats a Sandwich for Dinner. Why?

I HATE WHEN PEOPLE ASK ME IF A HOT DOG IS A SANDWICH. It's one of those stupid food questions I get asked a lot, like "What's your death row meal?" or "What's your favorite ingredient?" Death row meal? It is such a morose question. Why the fuck would I even be in jail? I've spent the last six years changing everything in my life to get me the farthest place from jail. When people ask me that, it blows my mind. I guess I'd like to have a balanced sandwich and a hot chocolate, or an extravagant meal with lobster and caviar for one last flourish. It's just all so wild.

I'm sorry for being fully triggered. I don't even know why I'm thinking about this. It makes me mad to think about it but not mad enough to not waste time writing in this book about why a hot dog is not a sandwich. First off, it's just a hot dog, plain and simple, the same way a cheeseburger is a cheeseburger. A hot dog deserves its own lane. Don't belittle it. A peanut butter sandwich isn't a hot dog, for fuck's sake. But what if you put peanut butter and jam in a hot dog bun—is that a PB&J dog? I don't judge. Freak what you feel.

Bread and fillings can be divided into so many dimensions: shawarmas, patty melts, or hamburgers. Even submarines are called so many different things, from hoagies and grinders to twisters. I believe that what a sandwich is called is dictated more by the filling. A hot dog is a hot dog because it's a hot dog, and a shawarma is a shawarma because it's a chicken-filled naan or pita. A katsu in Japan is fried pork, fish, or beef placed on milk bread with bulldog sauce and cabbage. The world of sandwiches is vast and colorful. I'm not a dictator, so if you think a hot dog is a sandwich then maybe you need to get out of the house, or maybe people who think like that are just trolls who should live under bridges eating hot dogs covered in peanut butter topped with pickled beets and sauerkraut.

Making sandwiches at home is all about the setup. It's crucial for building a great one. If one ingredient is not prepped and placed into a container and waiting like a soldier, then the sandwich could crumble and die quickly. Always get your sauces, mayos, vinaigrettes, dry garnishes, pickles, lettuces, tomatoes, and breads ready before you begin. Setting yourself up for success is key with cooking. Obviously that's why you're reading this book. I'm the shepherd in this vicious food world, guiding you to safer and tastier pastures. Once you have your mise en place ready, start getting your frying pan ready for searing or braising. With Mac we always play restaurant and make it fun. I'll give him one job and get him to place the final toothpick with an olive into a patty melt or a sprinkle of sea salt on a fried pork katsu. He feels like he's a champion. It is fun to make sandwiches if you set yourself up properly. The more you do something, the better it will get. You will learn from your mistakes and quickly become the technician that a sub shop could only wish for.

One last thing: Please don't feel like you need to make all the bread at home. I don't even make all my breads at home. I would never, ever do that. Cooking is heavy lifting, and making twelve sesame rolls from scratch is something you can build up to. Just go buy the bread for now.

Double Beef Patty Melt with Gruyère and Molasses Bread

SERVES:
4

PREP TIME:
45 MINUTES

There really isn't a patty melt culture in Canada. It might be because we don't have a lot of diners. Regardless, I love a patty melt so much, and I don't think there's a more Canadian patty melt than this one. Homemade molasses bread butter-fried in a cast-iron pan, melting cheese covered in onions, and two juicy beef patties. It's okay if you want just one patty or no patty; just cheese and onions is pretty perfect.

1¾ pounds (800 g) ground brisket
¼ cup (50 g) unsalted butter, plus softened butter for the bread
¼ cup (60 ml) olive oil
1 pound (450 g) yellow onions, sliced into half rings
3 tablespoons maple syrup
   Kosher salt
2 teaspoons sherry vinegar
2 tablespoons vegetable oil
   Freshly ground black pepper
2 cups (400 g) grated Gruyère cheese
1 loaf Molasses Bread in an Apple Juice Can (page 25)
¼ cup (60 g) yellow mustard

Portion the ground brisket into eight 3½-ounce (100 g) balls. Place the balls between two squares of parchment and squish them super flat with a flat plate or the bottom of a pan.

In a medium stockpot, melt the butter in the olive oil over medium heat. Add the onions and cook low and slow until they start to caramelize and get creamy, about 20 minutes. Deglaze with the maple syrup. Season with salt and add the vinegar. Reserve warm until it's time to build the melts.

Heat the vegetable oil in a large cast-iron skillet over high heat. Once the oil is hot, throw in the smashed beef patties, season with salt and pepper, then flatten them out with a spatula. Cook on one side 95 percent of the way through, flip with a spatula, then spoon on the cheese and flatten the cheese out. Add a splash of water to the pan, cover, and let the cheese melt.

Butter both sides of the molasses bread and toast the slices in a dry skillet over medium-high heat. Add more butter to the pan when you flip the bread. Transfer to a plate, place a patty on the bottom slice of bread, then add another patty on top of that. Spoon a big scoop of caramelized onions on the top patty, add mustard, and throw on the top slice of bread. Repeat until you have the desired number of patty melts for your friends.

Eggplant Parmesan and Italian Sesame Seed Bun

SERVES:
4

PREP TIME:
1 HOUR AND
20 MINUTES

I usually make a full eggplant Parm casserole and scoop it out like a lasagna, but for this sandwich I love frying rounds and building nice, tall leaning towers of Pisa. The best part is smooshing it down, so all the cheese, sauce, and fried eggplant become one. The onion and pepper salad is so crucial, just for that extra crunch and acid and flavor-build.

2	pounds (900 g) eggplant, peeled and sliced into 1-inch (2.5 cm) rounds
3	eggs
2	cups (300 g) panko (Japanese bread crumbs)
⅔	cup (100 g) all-purpose flour
	Olive oil
4	garlic cloves, sliced
2	pounds (1 kg) canned tomatoes (preferably Bianco)
	Kosher salt and freshly ground black pepper
⅔	cup (150 ml) canola oil
⅔	cup (100 g) sliced roasted red peppers
⅓	cup (50 g) sliced pickled hot peppers
½	cup (65 g) sliced white onion
1	teaspoon dried oregano
1	tablespoon white vinegar
1	cup (240 g) sliced mozzarella cheese
1	tablespoon unsalted butter, softened
4	sesame seed buns
	Leaves from 2 sprigs basil

Put the eggplant on a baking sheet. In a medium bowl, lightly beat together the eggs and a splash of water. Put the panko and the flour in two other medium bowls.

Dredge 1 piece of eggplant in the flour bowl, then dip it into the egg wash bowl, and then, using the same hand every time (wet vs. dry), take the eggplant out of the egg wash and place in the panko bowl, tossing it around a little to coat evenly. Remove from the panko and place on a baking sheet. Repeat with the remaining eggplant.

In a medium stockpot, heat 2 tablespoons olive oil over medium-high heat. Add the garlic and cook until golden, about 2 minutes; watch so it does not burn. Add the tomatoes and stir with a wooden spoon, breaking down big chunks of tomatoes. Bring to a simmer, then reduce heat to medium-low; cook for 45 minutes to 1 hour, until thickened and sauce-like. Season with salt and pepper.

In a large Dutch oven, heat ¼ cup (60 ml) olive oil and the canola oil to 225°F (110°C). Adding 2 or 3 breaded eggplant slices at a time, shallow-fry for 3 to 4 minutes per side, until golden and crunchy. Remove from the oil with a slotted spoon and place on a paper towel–lined sheet. Season with kosher salt. Repeat with the remaining breaded eggplant.

In a medium bowl, combine the roasted red peppers, pickled hot peppers, onion, oregano, vinegar, and 1 teaspoon olive oil. Reserve for building the sandwiches.

Set an oven rack to the middle position and preheat the broiler to high. Line a baking sheet with parchment paper.

Place 6 fried eggplant disks on the prepared baking sheet. Top with a spoonful of tomato sauce, then place a nice big slice of mozzarella on top of that. Put the baking sheet in the oven; once the cheese starts to melt, 3 to 5 minutes, take it out of the oven.

Butter the inside of the sesame buns and toast in a hot skillet. Add the first eggplant Parmesan, then spoon the pepper mixture over it and add a couple of basil leaves; repeat for the next two stacks and finish with the top bun. Serve with extra tomato sauce on the side.

Beef and Cheddar

I'll say it in this book so it's forever, and if you have a problem maybe you're the problem . . . but Arby's rules. Here's my beef with people who don't like Arby's: People always say it's paste and what is it and you don't know what's in it. Let me tell you, it's just beef mortadella. Everyone loves mortadella. Everyone loves it thin or thick, sliced, piled high between crunchy olive oil–soaked focaccia, or cubed with a cherry tomato on a toothpick stuck through it. People hate on bologna and hot dogs 'cause they're emulsified sausage, and maybe they're not studded with beautiful back fat or fresh-picked pistachios from some tropical island, but I think hot dogs and bologna are great and so is Arby's. If you don't love what I'm talking about, then make your own Arby's with this top sirloin and you'll be the real king. I'm a sucker for high-low food. Wagyu brisket smothered with warm, dripping Cheez Whiz on a King's Hawaiian sweet roll would be the greatest sandwich of all time.

5	pounds (2.25 kg) beef top sirloin
1	cup (225 g) freshly cracked pepper
⅓	cup (75 g) kosher salt
1	cup (240 g) Cheez Whiz
¼	cup (60 ml) yellow mustard
½	cup (120 ml) prepared horseradish
½	cup (120 ml) sour cream
½	cup (120 ml) mayonnaise
¼	cup (50 g) unsalted butter
10	potato rolls (preferably Martin's)

Clean the sirloin, taking off all silver skin and heavy fat pockets. Place the sirloin on a baking sheet. Mix the pepper and salt together and season the sirloin super heavy to create a crust. Let the sirloin sit out for 1 hour to bring the meat to room temperature.

When the sirloin is nearly at room temperature, preheat the oven to 325°F (165°C).

Place the sirloin in the oven and cook to 115°F (46°C). Pull from the oven, wrap in plastic wrap, and let rest for 1 hour.

In a medium saucepan, combine the Cheez Whiz and ½ cup (120 ml) water and let melt on medium-low heat. Whisk the cheese sauce until emulsified and runny. Whisk in the mustard and reserve, covered, to keep warm.

In a medium bowl, combine the horseradish, sour cream, and mayonnaise. Whisk together until combined. If not using right away, cover and reserve in the fridge.

In a skillet over medium heat, melt some of the butter; toast one of the buns on the cut sides. Repeat the process with the remaining buns.

Thinly slice the sirloin. Pile about 3½ ounces (100 g) of the meat onto each bottom bun, spoon the cheese sauce over the meat to cover it, then add a dollop of horseradish cream. Finish with the top bun, toasted side up. Serve this at any gathering, subbing out for burgers.

Italian Beef

SERVES:
4 TO 6

PREP TIME:
4 HOURS, PLUS 24
HOURS INACTIVE
TIME

I love Chicago so much because it's a lot like Toronto except it has restaurants that rule and have been around longer than ten years. Italian beef done right is a sandwich designed by some nonna secret circle. I don't get it wet because by the time you unwrap the juicy beef, the oily giardiniera has done its job and that puppy is a wet ol' dirty dog. You can eat it pretty quick: Just think of those hot dog–eating champs smashing dogs by dipping them in Kool-Aid or whatever the fuck they dip those dogs in to make the bun pretty much nonexistent. Halfway through I always think, Fuck, I should have gotten two. But by the end, and within three minutes after eating, I'm so thankful I didn't get two. I love these sandwiches so much. Thank you, Chicago. For real, though, Chicago might have the best sandwich game in the USA.

FOR THE GIARDINIERA:

1	quart (1 L) white vinegar
1	cup (250 g) granulated sugar
2	teaspoons kosher salt
1	cup (200 g) red pearl onions, peeled and cut in half
1⅓	cups (200 g) chopped celery
1⅓	cups (200 g) sliced carrots
1	cup (150 g) cauliflower florets
¼	cup (50 g) sliced garlic
½	cup (100 g) seeded and sliced serrano chiles
½	cup (100 g) seeded and sliced jalapeño chiles
1	teaspoon dried oregano
1	teaspoon dried basil
1⅓	cups (300 ml) olive oil

FOR THE BEEF:

3	quarts (3 L) Beef and Bone Marrow Stock (page 55), or store-bought
2	teaspoons kosher salt, plus more to taste
1	teaspoon black peppercorns, toasted, plus freshly ground black pepper to taste
3	pounds (1.3 kg) boneless beef roast chuck
1	pound (450 g) white onions, cut in half

4 to 6 Sesame Seed Rolls (page 21)

Make the giardiniera: In a large saucepan, combine the vinegar, 2 cups (500 ml) of water, sugar, and salt. Place over high heat and bring to a boil.

In a nonreactive container, combine the pearl onions, celery, carrots, cauliflower, garlic, and serrano and jalapeño chiles. Pour the boiling hot pickling liquid over the top and let sit at room temperature, covered, for 24 hours.

Strain the pickled vegetables and reserve half of the pickling liquid. In a medium bowl, combine the pickled vegetables, the pickling liquid, the oregano, and basil. Add olive oil to just barely cover pickled vegetables.

Make the beef: Pour the beef stock into a large Dutch oven and add the salt and peppercorns. Add the chuck roast and onions and bring to a boil, skimming the scum that rises to the top. Turn down heat to low, cover, and braise for 3 to 4 hours, until the meat is tender and the connective tissue and fat is broken down. Allow the roast to rest in the liquid until it cools down to room temperature. Remove the beef from the liquid and shred it in a large bowl. Strain the liquid through a fine chinois or strainer, then add just enough liquid to the braised meat to moisten it, so it's super juicy. Season the braised meat with salt and pepper and keep warm.

Cut the sesame seed rolls down the middle, add a big pile of braised meat, and spoon the giardiniera over the meat. Serve with a hot cup of the remaining beef broth for all your sandwich dipping needs.

Fried Mortadella with American Cheese Sauce and Savory Focaccia

SERVES:
2

PREP TIME:
20 MINUTES

Layering gently fried mortadella with American cheese is a real Italian nightmare and a Canadian chef's miracle. It's like a mille-feuille of pure love. It's a slippery little guy once you cut it. This photo was just holding on by a thread. There's even a technique where you could just layer your pan with the mortadella, cover with cheese, then fold it into itself like an envelop or crepe. This is a mortadella cheese crepe sandwich.

1	recipe Focaccia (page 34)
¼	cup (60 ml) olive oil
8	thin slices (150 g) mortadella
6	slices American Kraft Singles (preferably)
¼	cup (60 ml) mayonnaise (preferably Hellmann's)
¼	cup (60 ml) yellow mustard
½	cup (40 g) thinly shaved iceberg lettuce
⅓	cup (40 g) very thinly shaved white onion
1	large dill pickle (see page 70 for homemade), cut in half

Cut the focaccia into quarters and reserve three-fourths for more sandwiches later. Cut your piece of focaccia down the middle on the bias, split it open, and drizzle olive oil all over the inside of both sides of bread.

Heat a large skillet and add olive oil to the pan. Once the oil is hot, add one-half of the focaccia and toast until golden and nice and crunchy. Just toast the one side, then remove to a plate, crispy side facing up. Repeat with the other half.

Take 1 slice of mortadella, then add 1 slice of cheese. Then add another mortadella slice and a slice of cheese on top of that. Repeat until you have a stack of 4 slices of mortadella and 3 slices of cheese in between. Heat the meat pancake over medium heat until the cheese starts to melt. Leave warm and melty in the pan.

Spread mayo over both sides of the toasted focaccia, followed by the mustard. Place the lettuce on the bun bottom and top that with the onion. Place the cheesy mortadella on top and finish with the bun top, then slice down the middle, exposing the layered cheesy goodness. Spear a dill pickle with a toothpick, then spear the top of a sandwich half. Repeat with the other sandwich.

Chicago-Style Pork Chops

SERVES:
2

PREP TIME:
15 MINUTES

Half of these sandwiches are inspired by my trips to Chicago, it seems, and this pork chop is a perfect piece of history. A bone-in pork chop sandwich may seem weird or even troublesome, but I feel it's a challenge and I'm always up for it. Whenever I go to get one of these, I can smell the onions from down the street—piles of caramelized onions covering seared pork chops, keeping them warm like the belly of a mama bear. I love the kind of spots that can hand you a sandwich in less than a minute flat, and the whole family instantly has food that's eaten on the hood of the car, eating and chewing away at an American classic that now can be made at home. You could buy good pork, maybe, or buy those frozen bone-in quarter-inch-thick guys that we all remember growing up.

2   bone-in pork chops (the thinnest pork chops available, about 4 ounces/115 g per chop)

1   teaspoon kosher salt, plus more for the onion

1   teaspoon freshly ground black pepper

2   tablespoons vegetable oil

1   white onion, julienned

4   slices toast

2   tablespoons yellow mustard

2   pickled jalapeño chiles

Season the pork chops with the salt and pepper.

Heat the vegetable oil in a large cast-iron skillet over high heat. Once the oil is smoking hot, add the pork chops and sear hard on the first side, about 2 minutes. Flip and repeat on the other side. Take out of the skillet and rest on wire rack.

Heat the vegetable oil in the hot pan. Throw the onion into the pan, stir it up, and hard-sear for 2 to 3 minutes. Put a lid on the pan and let the onion steam for a minute. You want those onions a little caramelized and burnt. Season with salt. Remove from heat and let rest.

Spread 1 tablespoon of the mustard on one side of both the top and bottom pieces of toast. Place the pork chops on the bottom toast, cover with onions, and finish with the top toast, mustard side down. Serve with a pickled jalapeño.

Nashville Hot Halibut

SERVES: 6   PREP TIME: 1 HOUR

Who doesn't love a fried fish sandwich, and who doesn't love spicy heat?! I love Nashville hot chicken. It's so addicting. It's so lovely. It's so HOT! Hot fried fish doesn't get as much love as the chicken, but as with the beef phở and the chicken phở, everyone knows about one and really not the other. I love this sandwich fresh or even a couple hours later. Wrap it up in wax paper and eat it under the shade of a maple tree with some unsweetened iced tea. That's my favorite place to eat: under trees in the late summers with my kids, eating spicy fish sandwiches.

5	cups (1.25 L) canola oil
⅓	cup (75 g) roughly chopped Scotch bonnet chiles
¼	cup (50 g) roughly chopped bird's eye chiles
⅓	cup (75 g) roughly chopped jalapeño chiles
1	pound (480 g) unsalted butter
⅓	cup (50 g) ground cayenne
⅓	cup (50 g) smoked paprika
1	cup (150 g) all-purpose flour
1	teaspoon kosher salt, plus more for seasoning the fish
6	eggs
2	cups (300 g) panko bread crumbs
1½	pounds (680 g) halibut fillets, cut into 4-ounce (115 g) portions
12	slices Japanese milk bread
½	cup (120 ml) mayonnaise (preferably Duke's)
¾	cup (180 g) Bread and Butter Pickles (page 71)
6	slices American Kraft Singles
⅓	cup (120 g) sliced white onion

In a large pot over high heat, combine 1 cup (240 ml) of the canola oil and the Scotch bonnet, bird's eye, and jalapeño chiles and cook until a deep-fry thermometer reaches 350°F (175°C). Turn off the heat and let steep for 30 minutes. Working in 2 batches, pour into a blender and blend until smooth. Pass through a fine chinois or strainer into a medium pot. Heat again, then add the butter, cayenne, and paprika and stir with a whisk. Set aside and keep warm.

In a large Dutch oven, heat the remaining 4 cups (800 ml) canola oil over medium-low heat to 320°F (160°C).

Mix the flour and salt in a medium bowl, whisk the eggs in another medium bowl, and put the panko in a third medium bowl. Dust a piece of fish in the flour, then dip in the eggs, then coat in the panko. Place on a wire rack set over a baking sheet. Repeat with the remaining halibut.

Once the oil has come up to temperature, use a spider to carefully lower 2 pieces of the breaded halibut into the oil. Cook until golden and the internal temperature is 275°F (135°C), 4 to 6 minutes. Scoop out the fish and rest on a baking sheet with a rack set on it. Repeat with the remaining halibut and spoon the hot chile oil over it until the fish is covered and glossy.

Build your sandwiches: Lay out the bottom bread, mayo, then pickles, the halibut, followed by the cheese and onion slices. Slather mayo on the top bread and squish the sando down.

Submarine

SERVES: 2   PREP TIME: 15 MINUTES

I'm not trying to completely shit on Toronto, but holy cow, they can't make a sub. It's so wild that you cannot get just a normal submarine sandwich that's fire in the largest city in Canada. Until we opened Maker Pizza. Then, BABOOM, I made a sub that's called the Bodega 'cause literally anywhere in NYC or most of America you can get a fire sub, hoagie, grinder—whatever you wanna call it. Every corner store has a sandwich that's better than anything in Toronto. We called it the Bodega as an ode to these great establishments. This is just a perfect assorted sub: couple of cold cuts, couple of cheeses, a lot of shaved onions, iceberg, some peppers, and oil and vinegar—the way it should be; the way it should stay. Please, any Canadians reading this, please make this so you know that what you've been raised on is not the reality; it's the problem. Take the blue pill and escape the submarine sandwich matrix! AWAKE AND RISE, MY SWEET LITTLE FREAKS!

1	tablespoon garlic powder
1	tablespoon dried basil
1	tablespoon dried oregano
⅓	cup (75 ml) white vinegar
2	tablespoons olive oil
⅔	cup (100 g) sliced lengthwise roasted red peppers
	Kosher salt
⅓	cup (75 g) thinly sliced white onion
¼	cup (60 g) thinly sliced roasted jalapeño chile
¼	cup (60 g) pickled hot peppers
1	cup (150 g) shredded iceberg lettuce
2	Sesame Seed Rolls (page 21)
7	ounces (200 g) mortadella, thinly sliced
7	ounces (200 g) soppressata, thinly sliced
7	ounces (200 g) capicola, thinly sliced
6	ounces (100 g) sliced mozzarella cheese
1	hothouse tomato, thinly sliced
1	teaspoon kosher salt
1	teaspoon freshly cracked black pepper

In a small bowl, combine the garlic powder, basil, oregano, and vinegar and aggressively whisk in the olive oil.

In a medium bowl, combine the roasted red peppers, white onion, jalapeño, and pickled hot peppers. Add the vinaigrette and stir until completely incorporated. Taste for seasoning and add salt. Then toss with the shredded iceberg lettuce.

Place the sesame seed rolls on a baking sheet and cut the top center out. In the bottom part of the bun, lay out a layer of mortadella, then a layer of soppressata, then a layer of capicola. Repeat with another layer of all three. Place the cheese over the meat. Season the tomatoes with salt and pepper and place them on top of the cheese. Add the onion/lettuce salad on top of the tomatoes, then cut in half. Perfect sandwich.

222   Home Style Cookery

CHAPTER 8

Fried Foods and
Cast-Iron Cookery

Everything in Moderation Is Good for You

FRIED CHICKEN IS A PERFECT FOOD. MAKING IT AT YOUR HOUSE IS THE BEST AND THE WORST.
Flour will get everywhere in your kitchen, but you'll have piping hot and perfectly crispy fried chicken. Nothing is better than fried chicken.

It pairs perfectly with honey and hot sauce. For some that might mean Tabasco; for others it's Louisiana's or Crystal's, depending on where you are from. Because where I'm from is right across the border from Buffalo, New York, Frank's is my nostalgic choice. The sweet, spicy vinegar with the crispy, moist, fatty chicken thigh is a special pair. Wash it all down with a dill pickle or a bread-and-butter crisp. Fried foods get a bad rap. I'm no scientist, but if done well with nice clean oils, then maybe they are kind of good for you.

From Chicken Cutlets (page 230) to Pork Shoulder Schnitzel (page 235) to the greatest Fish Sticks with Kewpie Tartar Sauce (page 239) you've ever tasted, this chapter will allow you to make food for your kids without serving them frozen meat paste with shitty crumbs covering it. My kids love it when I make fried chicken or a crunchy minute steak cooked in my grandmother's cast-iron pan.

Cast-iron cooking is as real as it gets for me. Making pan-fried chicken or liver and onions creates a positive cooking culture in the home. Please throw out your nonstick pans and shitty Teflon that you shredded while washing it with a green scrubby. Cast-iron pans are traditional and timeless. They can do a lot of things in the kitchen, from making bread, to making breakfast, to making a stew. I have so many different cast-iron pans and pots that Trish says I'm not allowed to have any more. For me it's like seeing a sick animal. If I see a dusty, dry-ass cast-iron pan in the back of some antique store, I have to save it! I have to take it home, give it a deep clean, oil it, and love it the way it deserves.

I'm so excited to share the tradition of cast-iron cooking with you. If you already fuck with it, forgive me.

Fried Chicken

SERVES:
4

PREP TIME:
1 HOUR, PLUS
OVERNIGHT BRINE
AND 2 HOURS
CHILLING

This fried chicken is an honest recollection of my fried chicken adventures in America. I love making fried chicken at home. It's not that messy, and who doesn't love fresh fried chicken? You'd have to be a serial killer or one of those people who only eats food for fuel. Fried chicken should be served in the home to your loved ones.

2	cups (480 ml) warm water
⅓	cup (100 g) plus 1 teaspoon kosher salt, plus more for finishing
2	cups (200 g) ice
1	(2-pound/900 g) whole chicken
3	cups (450 g) all-purpose flour
2	tablespoons onion powder
2	tablespoons garlic powder
2	tablespoons ground cayenne
1	tablespoon paprika
2	teaspoons ground fennel
1	teaspoon freshly cracked black pepper
	Canola oil
	Zest of 1 lemon

In a small pot, combine the water and ⅓ cup (100 g) of the salt; bring to a boil over high heat. Cover, remove from heat, and let sit for 10 minutes. Put the ice in a large container, pour the brine over the ice, and stir until melted. Allow the brine to cool to room temperature.

Break down the chicken on a secure work surface. Flip the bird on its breast side and, using a good pair of kitchen scissors, run the scissors up from the tail end to the neck on both sides of the spine, then discard the spine. On a cutting board, use a large knife to cut off the legs, then slice in between the thigh and drumstick, separating them. Flip the bird over so the breasts are facing up and cut the bird in half, then cut each breast in half. A whole chicken will give you 10 pieces: 4 breast halves, 2 thighs, 2 drumsticks, and 2 wings. Place the chicken into the brine, cover, and refrigerate overnight.

In a large bowl, combine the flour, onion powder, garlic powder, cayenne, paprika, fennel, the remaining 1 teaspoon salt, and the pepper and mix well. Remove the chicken from the brine (discard the brine) and pat dry with paper towels. Rinse and dry the container, then put the chicken back in the container. Add the flour mixture, coat the chicken in it, and place in the fridge for 2 hours. Reserve the flour mixture.

Pour canola oil into a large Dutch oven halfway up the pot. Place a candy thermometer in the oil and heat on medium-high until the temperature reaches 325°F (165°C).

Take the chicken out of the flour mixture and place on a wire rack. Knock off as much excess flour as you can, then re-dredge the chicken, covering up any wet spots on the chicken. Place the chicken back on the rack.

Fry half of the chicken at a time—2 breast halves, 1 thigh, 1 drumstick, and 1 wing—for 13 to 16 minutes, until golden brown and it reaches an internal temperature of 150°F (65°C). Using a slotted spoon, pull the chicken out of the hot oil onto a clean rack to rest. Allow the oil to get back up to temperature over medium heat, then repeat with the remaining chicken. Zest the lemon over the chicken, sprinkle with a dash of salt, and eat!

Chicken Cutlets

SERVES:
4

PREP TIME:
1 HOUR

If you look closely and see a heart in this photo, I love you! Chicken cutlets fried in the basement kitchens all over New Jersey: I love you, too. This cutlet is for you!

1¼	pounds (500 g) boneless, skinless chicken breast
1	cup (150 g) all-purpose flour
1	teaspoon kosher salt, plus more for finishing
1	teaspoon freshly cracked pepper
3	eggs
2	cups (200 g) unseasoned bread crumbs
2	cups (480 ml) canola oil, plus more as needed
	Zest of 1 lemon
2	tablespoons lemon juice
1	lemon, quartered, for garnish

Butterfly the chicken breast: Put the chicken breast on a cutting board. Place your hand on top of the chicken breast and start slicing into the thickest part of the breast. Keep making thin slices all the way in to the thinnest point. Be careful not to cut all the way through to the other side. Open the breast up so it resembles a butterfly.

Pull a large piece of plastic wrap out from its container and fold it back onto itself so you have a double layer of wrap that is the size of your large cast-iron skillet. Make a second plastic wrap sheet.

Place a butterflied chicken breast onto the center of the plastic wrap, place the second sheet of plastic wrap on top, and using a meat mallet, pound the chicken, working from the center and pounding out to the edges until the chicken is super thin. Repeat with the remaining cutlets.

Place the flour in a shallow bowl and season with the salt and pepper. Put the eggs in another shallow bowl and whisk. Put the bread crumbs in a third shallow bowl. Season the flattened chicken with salt and pepper and dredge in the flour. Remove and shake off any excess flour.

Submerge one chicken cutlet at a time in the egg wash, hold them above the wash to let some egg wash drain off, then dip them into the bread crumbs and toss lightly to evenly coat the chicken.

Heat the canola oil in a large cast-iron skillet over medium heat, to 350°F (175°C). Fry one chicken cutlet until golden brown on each side, 2 to 2½ minutes per side. Make sure the oil doesn't get too hot—it should not be smoking at any point. Remove the chicken from the oil and onto a paper towel–lined plate. Add more oil to the pan if needed, bring the oil up to temperature, and repeat with the remaining chicken.

Finish the chicken with lemon zest, lemon juice, and salt as soon as they come out of the oil. Garnish with the lemon quarters.

Master Rang's Wok-Fried Red Snapper

SERVES:
2 TO 4

PREP TIME:
35 MINUTES

When we worked together at Le Select, Master Rang would buy a fresh snapper from Chinatown every Saturday for his staff meal. He would fry it and eat it, without sharing it with anybody. Eventually, I earned his trust, and he would break off a tiny piece and hand it to me like it was a special gem. Everyone thought this was really funny, and that the fish was prepared in a particular way, but it was just salted. Then one Saturday Rang brought in two snappers, one for me and one for him. My heart soared. It was like Christmas and all the holidays combined into one. I got to the final test, like some fucking karate guy in training—and passed. But now I had to cook both of them. I realized quickly he did this because he wanted to have a smoke break while I cooked him lunch. Rang got the fat boy to cook for him by buying some cheap snapper out of a tank in Chinatown.

1	teaspoon kosher salt, plus more for finishing
1	(1½-pound/680 g) whole snapper, gutted and cleaned
2	cups (480 ml) canola oil
4	garlic cloves, peeled
7	ounces (200 g) Chinese broccoli
	Dash of lemon juice
	Scallion slices, for finishing
	Julienned daikon, for finishing
2	cups (400 g) steamed rice
2	tablespoons chili oil

Salt the fish inside and out, then let rest on a wire rack for 15 minutes.

Heat the canola oil and garlic cloves in a large cast-iron skillet over medium-high heat. Once the garlic starts to brown, add the snapper and cook for 5 to 7 minutes, until golden on the first side. Gently flip the fish away from you to prevent oil from splashing up. Fry until golden on the second side and the fish is cooked through. There's a fine line between overcooking and undercooking, so really pay attention.

Bring a steamer up to a boil, place the Chinese broccoli in the perforated basket, cover, and cook for 4 minutes, until vibrant green.

Pull the fish from the oil onto a paper towel–lined plate; season both sides with salt and a dash of lemon juice. Finish with the scallion and daikon. Serve with steamed rice, the steamed Chinese broccoli, and chili oil.

Pork Shoulder Schnitzel

SERVES:
4

PREP TIME:
1 HOUR

Café Polonez is my favorited restaurant in Toronto. I always order the pork and mushroom dumpling soup. Yes! You can do half pork and half mushroom. Then, for my entrée I always get the polonez schnitzel, which is a pork schnitzel, obviously, with seared mushrooms, and a side of pork gravy, which is something like a stew. It's one of the best things ever. They use that gravy with the pork goulash, which is a mind bender as well. It's def the best restaurant. This is just the beginning for you, though. This recipe is the perfect schnitzel, okay?

1¼ pounds (560 g) boneless pork shoulder, cut into 4 steaks

1⅔ cups (240 g) all-purpose flour

Kosher salt and freshly cracked black pepper

3 eggs

6 cups (300 g) unseasoned bread crumbs

2 cups (480 ml) canola oil, plus more as needed

Zest of 1 lemon

2 tablespoons lemon juice

Lemon, quartered, or clementine, cut in half, for garnish

Pull a large piece of plastic wrap out from its container and fold it back onto itself so you have a double layer of wrap that is the size of your large cast-iron skillet. Make a second plastic wrap sheet.

Place a pork steak onto the center of the plastic wrap, place the second sheet of plastic wrap on top of that one, and using a meat mallet, pound the steak, working from the center and pounding out to the edges until the pork is super thin. Repeat with the remaining steaks.

Place the flour in a shallow bowl and season with salt and pepper. Put the eggs in another shallow bowl and whisk. Put the bread crumbs in a third shallow bowl. Season the flattened steaks with salt and pepper and dredge them in the flour. Remove and shake off any excess flour.

Submerge one steak at a time in the egg wash, hold them above the wash to let some egg wash drain off, then dip them into the bread crumbs and toss lightly to evenly coat the pork.

Heat the canola oil in a large cast-iron skillet over medium heat until it reaches 350°F (175°C). Fry one pork cutlet until golden brown on each side. Make sure the oil doesn't get too hot—it should not be smoking at any point. Remove the schnitzel from the oil and let drain onto a paper towel–lined plate. Add more oil to the pan if needed, bring the oil up to temperature, and repeat with the remaining schnitzels.

Finish the schnitzels with lemon zest, lemon juice, and salt as soon as they come out of the oil. Garnish with lemon or clementine.

Chicken Fried Steak

SERVES:
4

PREP TIME:
1 HOUR

My love for chicken fried steaks really clicked when we started traveling with my dad in the States and going to Cracker Barrel. Once again, Canadians do not have soul food or classic diner culture really, so even a mass-produced Walmart-type restaurant like CB would be a heaven for tourists like us, driving to Florida. We'd be full on sweet tea and chicken fried steaks, listening to rented books on tapes about Navy SEALs or hobbits or sci-fi (our choices). I recently went back to a CB and loved it just as much. I was in Oklahoma with Brad Leone shooting that noodlin' video. The sides could use some work, but the fried chicken and the chicken fried steak are winners. And I love that it's a dry and 100 percent family restaurant. No drunk losers around is a paradise in sawmill gravy heaven.

FOR THE CHICKEN FRIED STEAK:

1¼   pounds (520 g) top sirloin, cut into 4 steaks
1   cup (150 g) all-purpose flour
      Kosher salt and freshly cracked black pepper
3   eggs
2   cups (200 g) unseasoned bread crumbs
2   cups (480 ml) canola oil

FOR THE GRAVY:

2   tablespoons unsalted butter
2   tablespoons all-purpose flour
1   cup (240 ml) Chicken Stock (page 51), or store-bought, at room temperature
½   cup (120 ml) whole milk

      Zest of 1 lemon
2   tablespoons lemon juice
1   lemon, quartered, for garnish

Make the chicken fried steak: Pull a large piece of plastic wrap out from its container and fold it back onto itself so you have a double layer of wrap that is the size of your cast-iron skillet. Make a second plastic wrap sheet the exact same way.

Place a portion of steak onto the center of the plastic wrap, place the second sheet of plastic wrap on top of that one, and using a meat mallet, pound the steak, working from the center and pounding out to the edges until the steak is super thin. Repeat with the remaining portions of steak.

Place the flour in a shallow bowl and season with salt and pepper. Put the eggs in another shallow bowl and whisk. Put the bread crumbs in a third shallow bowl. Season the flattened steak with salt and pepper and dredge in the flour. Remove and shake off any excess flour.

Submerge one portion of steak at a time in the egg wash, holding them above the wash to let some egg wash drain off, then dipping them into the bread crumbs and tossing lightly to evenly coat the steak.

Heat the canola oil in a large cast-iron skillet over medium heat. Fry one portion of steak until browned, 3 to 5 minutes on each side. Make sure the oil doesn't get too hot—it should not be smoking at any point. Remove the steak from the oil and onto a paper towel–lined plate. Add more oil to the pan if needed, bring the oil up to temperature, and repeat with the remaining steak.

As the steak is cooking, make the gravy: Melt the butter in a medium saucepan over medium heat. Stir in the flour and cook, stirring constantly with a whisk and scraping up the browned bits of flour until the mixture is light golden brown, about 4 minutes. Gradually stir in the chicken stock, then add the milk. Bring to a boil, stirring constantly with a whisk, and cook until the gravy thickens, about 5 minutes. Season with salt and pepper and adjust the gravy with more stock until desired consistency.

Finish the steaks with lemon zest, a squeeze of lemon, and salt as soon as they come out of the oil and serve with the gravy and lemon quarters.

Fish Sticks with Kewpie Tartar Sauce

SERVES:
2

PREP TIME:
45 MINUTES

This is me helping every family who eats fish sticks. If your kid hates them, you're in luck. Well, actually, who even makes fish sticks or eats fish sticks, or is this literally from the microwaved vortex of the past? Do people even know what these are? Are forty-five-year-old parents gonna be so triggered that they rip this page out? Homemade fish sticks are good for you, for sure—a healthy alternative to maybe eating store-bought frozen trash.

FOR THE KEWPIE TARTAR:

5	eggs, hard-boiled and chopped
1	cup (30 g) finely chopped dill pickle
⅓	cup (40 g) finely chopped red onion
2	tablespoons chopped capers
½	cup (15 g) chopped parsley
½	cup (20 g) chopped dill
1	tablespoon Dijon mustard
1	tablespoon grated garlic
1	teaspoon freshly cracked black pepper
¼	cup (60 ml) mayonnaise (preferably Kewpie)
	Kosher salt

FOR THE HALIBUT:

1	pound (450 g) halibut fillets, cut into 6 symmetrical batons (stick shapes)
	Kosher salt
1	quart (1 L) canola oil
2	cups (300 g) all-purpose flour
4	eggs
5	cups (400 g) panko bread crumbs, blitzed into finer crumbs
	Sea salt
	Zest of 1 lemon

Make the Kewpie tartar: In a medium bowl, combine the hard-boiled eggs, dill pickle, red onion, capers, parsley, dill, mustard, garlic, and pepper. Add the mayo one spoonful at a time until the mixture is lightly bound together and has a chunky-creamy consistency. Season with salt.

Make the halibut: Season the halibut with salt on all sides and place on a wire rack. Let the halibut sit on the rack for 30 minutes to come to room temperature.

Heat the canola oil in a large Dutch oven over medium-high heat to 350°F (175°C).

Put the flour in a shallow bowl and season with 1 teaspoon salt. Beat the eggs in a second shallow bowl and put the panko in a third shallow bowl. One piece at a time, drench the halibut in the flour, then dip into the egg wash to completely cover the halibut. Scoop the halibut out, pausing for a second to allow excess egg wash to drip off. Place the halibut into the bowl with the panko and give it a quick toss to coat the fish.

When the oil comes up to temperature, add the halibut and deep-fry until golden brown, about 5 minutes. To test for doneness, use a cake tester to check that the halibut is hot in the middle. Take out the fish sticks using a metal spider and place on a wire rack or paper towel–lined plate; sprinkle with sea salt and the lemon zest.

Stack the fish sticks in log cabin formation on a piece of butcher paper and add a dollop of Kewpie tartar.

Minute Steak and Onions with House of Parliament Sauce

SERVES:
2

PREP TIME:
30 MINUTES

Minute steak is the new 4,647-hour reverse-sear sous vide. Get a thin slice of top sirloin, sear it on a pan, then eat it like a real human. I'm gonna sound like a real boomer idiot, but do we need to make this more complicated or can we just understand that you don't have to have a $500 immersion circulator to make a steak, however fat it is? In the Commonwealth, we use HP sauce; in America, there's A.1. Sauce. Guess what, America? HP destroys A.1. Send the check, HP! A steak is good with ketchup, caviar-spiked bearnaise, or au poivre. Let's not get this shit twisted. Steak is good, but it's best dipped in something—even A5 Wagyu is dipped in sukiyaki all day. So get to dippin' this minute steak in store-bought HP dip dippy-dippers.

½	pound (225 g) top sirloin (½ inch/1.25 cm thick, nice and long, with a little fat)
1	teaspoon kosher salt
1	teaspoon freshly ground black pepper
2	tablespoons canola oil
1	white onion, cut in 1-inch (2.5 cm) rounds
2	tablespoons unsalted butter
	Sea salt
¼	cup (60 ml) HP Sauce

Season the steak on both sides with the kosher salt and black pepper and bring to room temperature for 30 minutes.

Heat half of the canola oil in a large cast-iron skillet over medium-high heat until it reaches the smoking point. Add the steak and cook hard on the first side until golden brown and crispy, 4 to 5 minutes. Flip the steak and repeat on other side, then remove from the skillet to a cutting board. Don't worry about the color on the inside of the steak; it's going to be medium-well.

Drain out the hot oil and use a paper towel to wipe out any burnt bits left over from the steak. Add the remaining canola oil and bring it up to temperature, at the smoking point. Add the onions and cook them until half burnt, about 3 minutes; turn down heat to medium-low, add the butter, and cook until the onions are softened, about 10 minutes.

Lay the steak on a serving plate and season with sea salt. Spoon the charred onions on top and serve the HP sauce on the side.

Toad in a Hole: Pig Cheek, Sausage, Giant Yorkshire Pudding, and Frozen Vegetable Gravy

SERVES:
4

PREP TIME:
3½ HOURS,
PLUS 2 HOURS
INACTIVE TIME

Yorkshire puddings are the best puddings. I love that in England, pudding is pretty much anything made with eggs and cream. I love making a giant cast-iron Yorkshire pudding filled with different meats and then roasting it over high heat so the Yorkie fills in and bubbles and darkens and becomes a landscape for demi-glace (or the gravy on page 236). I love food that is self-contained and meant for gravy. Let's add some vegetables like peas and carrots as well so we have balance and some composure. Toad in the hole is a landscape made from love and can be carved into, like, a bleeding heart.

10½	ounces (300 g) pork cheek (ask your butcher to order)
	Kosher salt
2	teaspoons granulated sugar
2	quarts (2 L) duck fat
1	whole lemon's worth of peel
3	sprigs thyme
2	bay leaves
2	tablespoons canola oil
2	(½-pound/200 g) sausages (any type, preferably pork-based)
4	eggs
1½	cups (360 ml) whole milk
1¼	cups (187 g) all-purpose flour
¾	cup (200 ml) beef demi-glace
	Leaves from 1 sprig rosemary, chopped
1	teaspoon sherry vinegar
2	tablespoons unsalted butter
2	cups (255 g) frozen peas
6	heirloom carrots, roasted and cut into small cubes
1	cup (240 ml) Dijon mustard

On a clean work surface, trim any excess fat and silver skin off the pork cheek. In a small bowl, mix 1 tablespoon salt and the sugar and rub the pork with the mixture. Let cure in the refrigerator, covered, for 2 hours.

In a large saucepan, bring the duck fat up to a light simmer over medium heat. Add the lemon peel, thyme, and bay leaves Wipe the cure mixture off the pork cheek with a paper towel and place into the seasoned duck fat. Bring back to a simmer, then reduce heat to low and cook for 2 to 2½ hours, until the cheeks are fork-tender but not falling apart. Turn off heat and let the cheeks cool in the fat to room temperature.

Heat a large cast-iron skillet over medium heat. Add the canola oil, and once the oil is hot, add the sausages and sear for 6 minutes, or until golden brown on the bottom. Flip the whole sausages and repeat on other side. Turn down heat to medium-low, cover with a lid, and cook until the sausages are cooked through, about 5 minutes. Take the sausages out and allow to cool to room temperature.

Wipe the oil from the sausages out of the skillet and set aside.

Preheat the oven to 450°F (230°C).

In a blender, combine the eggs, milk, flour, and 1 teaspoon salt. Blend until well combined, then pour into a container and place in the fridge for 30 minutes to rest, or until you are ready to use it.

In a small skillet, gently heat the beef demi-glace over low heat. Add the rosemary and bring to a light simmer, add the vinegar, and season with salt. Set aside, covered to keep warm.

Slice the sausages into bite-size pieces and place on a tray. Remove pork cheeks from the duck fat, leave one pork cheek whole, and slice the other pork cheek in half down the middle. Place on the tray with the sausages. Reserve the fat.

Now you are ready to build. Preheat the large skillet. Place the sausages into the skillet in their original sausage shape. Arrange the pork cheek slices around the sausages and place the other pork cheek in the center. Heat the pan in the oven with the reserved fat, then pull out and pour in the batter to come three-quarters of the way up the sides of the skillet. The batter should sizzle. Immediately put back in the oven.

While your Yorkie is cooking, heat the butter, peas, and carrots for 3 minutes in a medium skillet over medium heat, then season with salt to taste.

Bake until the pudding is well risen, golden brown, and crisp, 15 to 20 minutes. Do not open your oven until the end, or it might collapse. Serve with the demi-glace sauce and a big old bowl of Dijon mustard.

Joanie's Liver and Onions

SERVES:
2

PREP TIME:
35 MINUTES,
PLUS 2 HOURS
INACTIVE TIME

I'm calling this Joanie's Liver and Onions 'cause one time, just one time, she said she loved liver and onions and I was like, We've never had liver and onions ever. I was working at Southsides and we had frozen slices of beef liver, and we would cook everything on one flat-top using clarified butter. My mom ordered it once and it blew my mind. Neither she nor my dad ever cooked liver and onions, but I wish they had. If they did actually cook them, this would be how they would have done it, for sure. People should cook liver and onions at home more often.

2	pounds (905 g) veal liver, sliced lengthwise into 4 pieces
2	cups (480 ml) 2% milk
½	cup (75 g) plus 2 tablespoons all-purpose flour
	Kosher salt and freshly ground black pepper
¼	cup (60 ml) canola oil
1	onion, cut into 6 rings
4	tablespoons (55 g) unsalted butter
1	tablespoon sherry vinegar
½	cup (120 ml) Chicken Stock (page 51), or store-bought
1	teaspoon soy sauce
1	teaspoon Worcestershire sauce
½	teaspoon lemon juice

Put the liver in a medium container and cover with the milk. Allow the liver to sit for 2 hours to draw out any blood from inside the liver.

Place ½ cup (75 g) of the flour in a shallow bowl. Take the liver out of the milk and pat dry with paper towels. Season with salt and pepper and dredge in the flour in the shallow bowl.

Heat the canola oil in a large cast-iron skillet over medium-high heat. Add the liver, dropping it away from you to prevent hot oil from splattering. Cook until the first side is caramelized, about 3 minutes. Flip the liver, add the onion rings and 2 tablespoons of the butter, and cook for about another 3 minutes, basting the liver with the frothy butter, until the liver is cooked medium-rare to medium, then remove to a plate. Continue to brown the onions for 7 to 10 minutes more, then remove from the pan to a plate.

Deglaze the pan with the vinegar. Sprinkle the remaining 2 tablespoons flour into the pan and stir with a wooden spoon, mixing the flour and the remaining 2 tablespoons butter in the pan to create a roux. Add the chicken stock and continually stir to absorb the flour and thicken the stock into a gravy. Let the gravy come to a boil, then turn down heat to medium-low and add the soy sauce, Worcestershire sauce, and lemon juice.

Serve the liver with the onions spooned on top and piping hot gravy.

Fried Catfish Taco Night

SERVES:
4 TO 6

PREP TIME:
1 HOUR AND
20 MINUTES

We would do this dish at Parts & Labour. It's easy enough to make at home. Buy a catfish, score it, season it, cover it in flour, and fry it in a large Dutch oven. This dish is so fire, and the kids will love it, and your friends will love it. Scoring will allow you to rip off the catfish nuggets and make tacos, and it's super fun and tastes amazing. You can serve with guacamole and the Infamous Cheesy Citrus Refried Beans (page 123), if you like. I wish you the best in every recipe, and I hope you make all these dishes one day 'cause besides looking beautiful in photos and being really strong recipes, they taste so good!

FOR THE PICO DE GALLO:

½   cup (75 g) finely chopped white onion

½   cup (75 g) finely chopped tomato

⅓   cup (45 g) seeded and finely chopped jalapeño chiles

2   tablespoons lime juice

½   teaspoon kosher salt

3   tablespoons olive oil

FOR THE CREMA:

⅔   cup (165 ml) sour cream

½   cup (50 g) finely grated Parmesan cheese

    Zest of 1 lime

1   tablespoon lime juice

FOR THE DRY SLAW:

2   cups (250 g) thinly sliced green cabbage

1   cup (150 g) thinly sliced white onion

1   serrano chile, thinly sliced

2   cups (50 g) chopped cilantro leaves and stems

1   teaspoon kosher salt

FOR THE TORTILLAS:

2⅓   cups (360 g) masa harina, plus more as needed

½   cup (100 g) pork lard, melted

½   teaspoon kosher salt

½   cup (120 ml) water, plus more as needed

1   tablespoon canola oil, for brushing

FOR THE FISH:

2   quarts (2 L) canola oil

1   pound (450 g) whole catfish, gutted and cleaned

1   cup (150 g) all-purpose flour

1   teaspoon kosher salt

1   teaspoon freshly cracked black pepper

recipe continues

Make the pico de gallo: In a medium bowl, combine the onion, tomato, cilantro, jalapeños, lime juice, and salt and stir, adding olive oil to bind the mixture together. Set aside until serving time.

Make the crema: In a small bowl, combine the sour cream, cheese, and lime juice and season with salt. Set in the fridge until ready to serve.

Make the dry slaw: In a medium bowl, combine the cabbage, onions, and serrano chile and season with salt. Set aside until ready to serve.

Make the tortillas: In a medium bowl, whisk the masa harina, pork lard, and salt. Stir in the water and knead the dough until a ball forms. The dough should feel firm, like Play-Doh. If it's too wet, add more masa; if it's too crumbly, add more water.

Measure 1 heaping tablespoon of dough and roll into a ball. Flatten on a tortilla press lined with a plastic bag. If the tortilla crumbles, the dough is too dry; if it sticks, it's too wet. Repeat until all the dough is pressed.

Brush a large cast-iron skillet with vegetable oil and heat over medium-high heat. Cook 1 or 2 tortillas at a time (or as many as the skillet will hold) until charred in spots and the edges start to curl, 1 to 2 minutes. Flip and cook through until the tortillas puff. Transfer to a kitchen towel and fold them over to keep warm. Repeat with the remaining dough.

Cook the fish: Fill a large Dutch oven halfway with canola oil and heat over medium-high heat to 350°F (175°C). You can start heating the oil as you are cooking the tortillas.

On a secure cutting board, lay the catfish down, belly facing away from you. Using a sharp knife, score the flesh deep, almost to the bone, into ¾-inch (2 cm) diamond shapes from the collar to the tail. Repeat on the other side of the fish.

While the oil is coming up to temperature, in a large bowl, whisk the flour, salt, and pepper and dredge the catfish into the flour mixture.

Once the oil is hot, very carefully lower the whole fish using a spider. The oil should bubble to the top of the pot; be careful it doesn't boil over on you. Fry until golden brown and cooked through, about 7 to 10 minutes. Pull the catfish out of the hot oil using the spider and place on a baking sheet with a wire rack set on it. Immediately season the fish with salt.

Serve the tacos family-style: Keep the catfish whole, and have everyone rip off golden crunchy squares as they build their tacos with fresh warm tortillas, the dry cabbage slaw, pico de gallo, and punchy crema.

CHAPTER 9

Roasts, Bakes, and a Pie

Easy to Start,
Hellish to Clean Up

ROASTS ARE TRICKY 'CAUSE SO MANY PEOPLE LIKE THEIR MEATS COOKED DIFFERENTLY.

Let's clear something up right now: Your roast can be rare. How do we make everyone happy? How do we make people not afraid to cook? I want everyone who buys this book to salt bake a leg of lamb (see page 257). I hope you do, because we did, and it's way easier than I thought. The lamb was so perfect. It was cooked medium and it had that perfect melt in your mouth, that fatty lamb taste we all love. The salt bake allowed it to be purely salty lamb, like it was cooked at the side of the ocean.

What's better than tuna casserole or a giant Yorkshire pudding filled with pigs' cheeks and sausages covered in peas and carrots then pooled with chicken gravy?! Holy cow, roasting is the best. One-pot cooking in an oven is the dream. Just throw a whole fish on a baking tray in the oven and hit it with a squeezed lemon, some sea salt, and a drizzle of some good olive oil. That's literally perfection. I feel baking or roasting is always less messy. You will have fewer dishes to clean, so that's a plus, because doing the dishes is always such a chore. But if you're cooking, hopefully you don't have to do the dishes as well.

Obviously, I cook because I hate doing the dishes. Trish always says I'm not good at doing them and that I make more of a mess because I clean the kitchen like when I'm working at a restaurant, with a huge bucket filled with hot, soapy water. I scrub and move everything around. Trish gets stressed 'cause she is literally the best cleaner ever. All I'm saying is that I hope you guys have the dishes situated.

The techniques in this chapter are pretty far-ranging. You'll have to combine a few you've already learned in this book with some new ones. For example, you get crispy skin from roasting by making cuts in the skin. This allows the fat to bubble up and literally turn itself into chicharrón. Drying out the skin of any piece of meat will help you achieve a juicier and crispier piece. I bet you did think if you took a dry-looking bird and roasted it, it would come out even better than some water-bleached chicken from your local supermarket. Using the wrapping technique while cooking a perfect top sirloin and prime rib is so crucial. I learned it from Adam Perry Lang. It helps the meats cool in a more controlled way and at the same time keeps the moisture in and assists in breaking down the tendons and collagens. It will give you the most delicate beef you've ever had. I'm pretty sure you have not had the patience to rest your meats for more than an hour.

Roasted Salt Crust
Leg of Lamb

SERVES:
6 TO 8

PREP TIME:
2 HOURS AND
20 MINUTES,
PLUS 12 HOURS
INACTIVE TIME

Family dinner just got incredibly exciting. Bake an entire bone-in leg of lamb encapsulated in salt and egg whites, then get your kids to smash it open to reveal one of the greatest meals of all time. You won't have that crispness, but you'll have the softest textures you've ever come across with lamb. There's a lot of trust in this one as well. You'll need one of those instant-read thermometers so you don't overcook this beautiful lamb leg. This is the kind of cooking that families and friends will remember during their lifetimes. If you don't want to cook a lamb, use the same technique with a celeriac root, butternut squash, or even a cabbage. Salt life bro, *shaka*!

FOR THE POTATOES:

5	pounds (2.25 kg) Yukon Gold potatoes
3	tablespoons kosher salt
½	cup (120 ml) duck fat
	Sea salt

FOR THE LAMB:

3	(3-pound/1.36 kg) boxes kosher salt
15	egg whites
1	(5- to 6-pound/2.25 to 2.75 kg) bone-in leg of lamb
	Canola oil
2	teaspoons freshly ground black pepper
2	cups (50 g) sprigs rosemary
6	garlic cloves, crushed

FOR THE LAMB SAUCE:

2	quarts (2 L) Lamb Stock (page 56)
1	tablespoon unsalted butter
¼	cup (50 g) finely chopped shallots
2	tablespoons green peppercorns
2	tablespoons bourbon
¼	cup (60 ml) heavy cream

FOR THE CREAMED SPINACH:

	Kosher salt and freshly ground black pepper
3	(10-ounce/300 g) bags spinach
2	tablespoons unsalted butter
2	tablespoons all-purpose flour
1½	cups (360 ml) whole milk
2	tablespoons cream cheese
1	tablespoon ground nutmeg

recipe continues

The day before cooking your lamb leg, par-cook the potatoes: Peel the potatoes, then cut them in half on the bias, so they are two fatties. Place in a medium stockpot and cover with cold water by a few inches. Place over high heat and bring to a boil; turn down heat to medium-low heat, add the kosher salt, and simmer until the potatoes are about 90 percent cooked. Drain the potatoes, place on a baking sheet, and refrigerate uncovered overnight. This works to dry out the outer layer of the potatoes so they get nice and crispy. Remove the potatoes from the refrigerator 30 minutes before roasting.

Roast the lamb: Preheat the oven to 350°F (175°C). Line a rimmed baking sheet with parchment paper.

Pour the salt into a large bowl. Mix in the egg whites ⅓ cup (70 ml) at a time until you achieve a wet sand consistency. Take one-third of the salt mixture and, on the prepared baking sheet, build a bottom platform ½ inch (1.25 cm) thick in the shape of the lamb leg.

Coat the lamb leg with a thin layer of canola oil and the black pepper. Place a few sprigs of rosemary on the layer of salt along with 3 crushed garlic cloves. Place the lamb leg on top of the salt and add the remaining rosemary and garlic to the top of the leg. Mold the remaining salt all over the lamb until completely encrusted and ½ inch (12 mm) thick all the way around.

Roast for about 1½ hours, until an instant-read thermometer inserted into the thickest part of the lamb leg (without touching the bone) reads 130°F (54°C). Remove from the oven and allow the lamb to rest in the salt crust for 45 minutes. Increase the oven temperature to 400°F (205°C).

Roast the potatoes: Place the par-cooked potatoes in a nonstick casserole pan, drizzle the melted duck fat over the potatoes, and roast until golden brown and super crispy, 35 to 45 minutes, shaking the pan every 15 minutes to unstick any stuck potatoes. Season with sea salt.

Make the lamb sauce: While the potatoes are roasting, in a medium saucepan, reduce the lamb stock over high heat by two-thirds, until it's at a demi-glace consistency. In a separate saucepan, melt the butter over medium heat, add the shallots, and cook for about 3 minutes, until translucent. Add the green peppercorns and cook 30 seconds, then deglaze with the bourbon. Watch carefully to avoid setting it ablaze. Add the reduced lamb stock and cream, bring to a boil, and let reduce for 3 minutes. Cover and set aside.

Make the creamed spinach: While the potatoes are finishing up in the oven, bring a large stockpot full of salty water to a boil. Blanch the spinach in 3 batches, quickly dipping the spinach into the water until wilted, then scoop the spinach out and place in a colander to drain excess water. Place the spinach in a clean dish towel, squeeze out any excess liquid, then roughly chop.

Melt the butter in a medium saucepan over medium heat. Add the flour and slowly whisk in the milk. When the milk has all been incorporated, cook, stirring, for 5 minutes, or until the sauce thickens. Add the cooked spinach to the milk sauce, stir, then stir in the cream cheese until incorporated and season with salt, pepper, and the nutmeg. Keep warm with the lid on until ready for serving.

To reveal the lamb and serve: Crack the lamb out of its salt crust and wipe off any excess salt. Carve the lamb and arrange it on a platter. Pour the sauce over the lamb until it pools the entire plate to the rim. Serve the creamed spinach in a side bowl along with the crispy potatoes in their own separate bowl.

Crispiest Pork Belly

SERVES:
6 TO 8

PREP TIME:
3 HOURS AND
20 MINUTES,
PLUS 48 HOURS
INACTIVE TIME

Crispy pork belly is pretty easy to make. You could literally do nothing but throw it in the oven, and you'd have to be a pretty horrible cook for it to not come out crispy and juicy. Pork belly is the ultimate part of pork. When you cook a larger piece, there are more lean parts and everything isn't just fat. Follow this technique and you'll be rewarded with perfect skin: spike the skin before and during roasting to allow the fat to rise through the skin and shallow fry—that's the move to the perfect chicharrón.

5	pounds (2.25 kg) skin-on pork belly (square shape)
1	cup (220 g) kosher salt
½	cup (110 g) granulated sugar
1	tablespoon baking soda

Place the pork belly on a large cutting board skin side up. Using a Jaccard (a handheld skin-piercing device that punctures dozens of small holes on the surface of a piece of meat), puncture holes all over the skin side of the belly. Alternatively, use a very sharp knife to score the skin every ½ inch (12 mm).

In a small bowl, mix together the salt and sugar and evenly sprinkle the cure on all sides of the belly. Place the belly on a rimmed baking sheet and transfer to the fridge to cure, uncovered, overnight.

The next day, pull the belly out and rinse briefly to remove the cure. Pat super dry with paper towels.

Boil 1 quart (960 ml) water. Remove from heat and dissolve the baking soda in the water. Grasp one corner of the pork belly with tongs, and holding the pork belly over the sink, slowly pour the baking soda mixture in a thin stream over the pork skin to scald it. Return the pork to the baking sheet, pat dry, and chill in the fridge overnight again.

Preheat the oven to 375°F (190°C) and pull the pork belly out of the fridge to come to room temperature.

Place the pork belly in the oven and roast until super crispy and golden brown, 2 to 3 hours. If the skin is browning too quickly, lower the oven temperature or cover loosely with foil. Once the belly is ready, remove from the oven, carefully pierce the skin again with the tip of a sharp paring knife, then return to the oven and set the oven to broil; don't walk away. Broil until the skin bubbles; do not let the skin get black.

Pull the belly from the oven and place it on a cutting board. Cut the belly into 3 pieces, then carve it into thin slices. Turn it onto the skin side, if necessary, for easier slicing.

Beef Tourtière

SERVES:
6 TO 8

PREP TIME:
1 HOUR AND 20 MINUTES,
PLUS 30 MINUTES
INACTIVE TIME

Meat pies are all I think about during winter months and making them is my favorite thing to do, ever. It's so funny 'cause I'm not a huge fan of fruit pies, but I love custard pies and cream pies. I think I'm not that into hot jams or something. I like hot jam on bread with a slab of cold salted butter, but that's it, maybe. Meat pies are special, and making them can take two days. It's smart to make your dough and filling ahead of time, then assemble the pie so there's no heat from the filling to warm the dough, making it soggy. You could easily make this with a variety of game meats such as moose, venison, squab, boar, rabbit, or hare. I hate homemade ketchup, but I love ketchup with this dish. I love it so much. It just makes sense to me. I don't love ketchup with a lot of dishes, but for me this one has just enough ketchup—every other bite is the perfect amount.

FOR THE PÂTE BRISÉE:

3⅓	cups (425 g) all-purpose flour, plus more for rolling
2	teaspoons kosher salt
1⅔	cups (375 g) cold unsalted butter
½	cup (120 ml) ice water, plus more as needed

FOR THE BEEF:

2	tablespoons unsalted butter
2	tablespoons canola oil
1	cup (150 g) finely chopped onions
1	cup (150 g) finely chopped celery
1	cup (150 g) finely chopped leeks
3	pounds (1.3 kg) lean ground beef
1½	teaspoons ground cloves
1½	teaspoons ground cardamom
1½	teaspoons ground cinnamon
½	teaspoon ground mace
½	teaspoon ground star anise
½	cup (75 g) all-purpose flour
1	egg, beaten with 1 teaspoon water to make egg wash
2	cups (480 ml) Heinz ketchup, for serving

Make the pâte brisée: In a food processor, combine the flour and salt. Add the butter and pulse for a few seconds at a time until the butter is the size of peas. Add the cold water and pulse again until a dough just begins to form, adding more water as needed. Remove the dough from the food processor and form 2 disks; wrap with plastic wrap and let rest for 30 minutes. You can make the dough a day ahead and store in the fridge. Pull out 1 hour before making your pie crust.

Set an oven rack to the middle position and preheat the oven to 375°F (190°C).

Make the beef: While the dough is resting and the oven is preheating, in a large Dutch oven, melt the butter in the oil over medium heat. Add the onions, celery, and leeks and cook until the onions are translucent with no color, about 10 minutes. Add the ground beef and cook for 8 minutes. Add the cloves, cardamom, cinnamon, mace, and star anise. Once the spices are toasted, sprinkle in the flour to thicken the fat in the pan and bring the meat mixture together, cooking for 3 to 5 minutes. Cool completely. It is really important that the meat is cool or your tourtiere will leak when it is being baked.

Prepare the dough: Roll out half of the dough on a floured work surface to a ⅛-inch (3 mm) thick sheet, about 13 inches (33 cm) long, and set it into a 9-inch (23 cm) pie pan. Roll out the second half of the dough. Fill the crust with the meat mixture, place the second crust on top, and seal the edges by pinching the lid and base together with your thumb and index finger, creating a pleated look. Cut an X to make a steam hole in the top center of the tourtière.

Brush the top of the tourtière with egg wash and bake for 45 minutes, or until the crust is golden and beautiful. Let the tourtière cool for 5 to 10 minutes, cut a big old slice, and serve with a large dollop of Heinz ketchup on the side.

Broiler Pork Chops

SERVES:
6

PREP TIME:
50 MINUTES

Meat doesn't have to be browned perfectly or seared hard all the fucking time. Sometimes, just throw everything in a pan and roast it, and let it be, and it'll turn out great. This dish is a Hail Mary for timing, and there's nothing better than an oven pan dinner that's even a little burnt sometimes. This one's for all the one-pan people out there!

1	tablespoon paprika
1	tablespoon onion salt
2	teaspoons kosher salt
½	teaspoon ground cayenne
6	pork chops (about 6 ounces/170 g each)
2	teaspoons canola oil
1	(28-ounce/794 g) can whole tomatoes
1	tablespoon fennel seeds
4	garlic cloves, thinly sliced
1	onion, cut into ½-inch (1.25 cm) wedges
2	small jalapeños, seeded and diced
2	red bell peppers, seeded and diced
2	banana peppers, seeded and diced
	Sea salt
2	tablespoons lemon juice
1	cup (25 g) chopped parsley
	Green Olive Tapenade (page 136; optional)

Preheat the oven 380°F (195°C).

In a small bowl, combine the paprika, onion salt, kosher salt, and cayenne. Place the pork chops on a large plate or baking sheet. Rub the canola oil over the pork chops to lightly coat all sides, then rub the spice mix all over the chops. Set aside until ready to cook.

Drain the tomatoes, reserving ½ cup (120 ml) of the juices. Put the tomatoes in a medium bowl and lightly break them up with your hands. Add the fennel seeds, garlic, onion, jalapeños, red peppers, and banana peppers and drizzle on the reserved tomato juice as you stir the mixture together.

Spread the tomato and pepper mixture in the bottom of a large casserole, place in the oven, and roast until the vegetables start to soften and brown, about 35 minutes. Put the pork chops on top of the roasted vegetables, then turn the broiler on and blast the pork chops for about 5 minutes per side, until nicely browned on both sides.

Remove the pork chops to a plate and season the tomato mixture with sea salt, lemon juice, and parsley. To serve, pile the 6 chops on top of each other with the tomato mixture spooned between each layer and on top. Serve with tapenade, if desired.

Macaroni and Tuna Casserole

SERVES:
6

PREP TIME:
1 HOUR

The very first time I had this dish, it was at the house of my very first friend, who I'd met when I was new in town. We met playing basketball at the schoolyard across the street from our houses. We played for hours and hours. It was a really nice moment, looking back. Just kids being kids. He lived across from the park, and we became best friends. The first time I ever ate dinner at his house, it blew my mind. It was a casserole of macaroni and cheese with canned tuna. Remember eating at other people's houses as a kid and everything just tasted so different? It was wild. This is one of those dishes brought back to life through years of pondering where Cliff went after high school. He never had social media, so we lost touch. This tuna casserole is for all the kids who've lost their best friends but know that if they were to see each other again, it would be like nothing ever changed. This is way more dramatic than I thought it would be, LOL. Cliff is probably doing great in a small town minutes from where I live now.

	Kosher salt
1½	pounds (680 g) dried elbow macaroni
2	tablespoons canola oil
3	tablespoons unsalted butter
3	tablespoons all-purpose flour
1	quart (1 L) whole milk
1	cup (100 g) grated sharp white Cheddar cheese
1	cup (100 g) grated Monterey Jack cheese
1	cup (100 g) cream cheese
1	cup (100 g) American cheese
2	tablespoons yellow mustard
1	tablespoon lemon juice
4	(5-ounce/142 g) cans tuna packed in water
2	cups (160 g) panko bread crumbs

Bring a large stockpot of water to a boil over high heat and add ½ cup salt. Add the elbows and cook to al dente, about 85 percent cooked. Drain, then toss with the canola oil so it doesn't stick. Set the pasta aside.

Preheat the oven to 350°F (175°C).

In a medium saucepan, melt the butter over medium-low heat. Add the flour and cook, stirring constantly, for 2 minutes without coloring the flour to make a white roux. Whisk in the milk, bring up to a light simmer, and cook for 10 minutes. Add the Cheddar cheese and cook, stirring, until melted. Repeat with the Monterey Jack, cream cheese, and American cheese until all are melted. Add the mustard and lemon juice and season with salt as needed.

Strain and press out all the water from the 4 cans of tuna, place in a medium bowl, and use a fork to flake the tuna into bite-size pieces.

Spoon a layer of macaroni into a large casserole dish and cover that with a layer of flaked tuna. Follow by ladling cheese sauce over everything, then take a spatula and mix everything together. Repeat until the casserole is filled to the top. (You can also bake this in individual serving-size ramekins.)

Sprinkle the panko to cover the top of the casserole, place the casserole in the oven, and bake for 35 to 40 minutes (20 to 25 minutes if you're using ramekins), until the top is golden brown. Pull out of the oven and serve right away.

Whole Turbot with Peas and Bacon

SERVES:
4 TO 6

PREP TIME:
1 HOUR

Roasting a whole fish is the best, and it's so easy. If you can get your hands on a small turbot, you're in for a great supper. You could also use any white fish. Making food can be intimidating, especially a whole fish, so just take your time. There's no rush. When you make fish, understand that you should allow it to rest the same as meat. You don't want to start ripping and taking apart a whole fish the second it comes out of the oven or off the grill. Making a white wine, cream, and bacon sauce and not adding peas is just criminal. This dish is ideal for those cooler summer months, or winter, or really anytime you want to eat fish. That belly tastes like bone marrow, and make sure to have good bread for sopping up all the sauce and fishy goodness.

1	(1½-pound/680 g) whole turbot
	Canola oil
1	tablespoon kosher salt, plus more as needed
1	cup (150 g) double-smoked bacon, cut into ¾-inch (2 cm) squares
¼	cup (75 g) diced shallot
3	garlic cloves, grated
1	tablespoon thyme leaves
⅓	cup (70 ml) white wine
2	tablespoons Dijon mustard
½	pound (225 g) cold unsalted butter, cubed
½	cup (15 g) chopped parsley
½	cup (15 g) chopped chervil
½	cup (15 g) chopped tarragon
	Juice of ½ lemon
½	cup (100 g) sweet peas, fresh shucked if in season, or frozen
1	teaspoon ground white pepper

recipe continues

Preheat the oven to 350°F (175°C). Line a baking sheet with foil.

Pat the fish dry with paper towel, drizzle a little canola oil all over the fish, and rub the oil into the skin. Heavily season with salt on both sides and allow the fish to come to room temperature, about 30 minutes.

Meanwhile, place the bacon in a large skillet and add about ½ cup (120 ml) water to cover. Bring to a boil over high heat. Let all the water evaporate and allow the bacon to render down and get all crispy and golden. Drain all but 2 tablespoons of the fat and place the bacon on a paper towel–lined plate.

Reduce heat to medium, add the shallot, garlic, and thyme, and sweat for 4 to 5 minutes, or until the shallot is tender. Deglaze with the white wine and reduce the liquid by half. Turn down heat to low and whisk in the mustard. Whisk in the butter one cube at a time until it is melted and emulsified. If it starts to get too hot, take it off the heat. Keep adding butter until all the butter is used and the sauce is nice and creamy. Add the parsley, chervil, and tarragon and season with salt and a little of the lemon juice. Cover and keep in a warm spot but not over direct heat, because that will cause the sauce to split.

Bring a medium pot of water to a boil over high heat and salt it. Blanch the peas for 2 minutes, or until bright vibrant green. Strain the peas, allow them to cool to room temperature, then add them to the butter sauce.

Place the turbot on the prepared baking sheet belly side down, place in the oven, and bake for 20 minutes, or until the edges of the fillet start to release from the side fins. Switch the oven to the broiler setting and do not walk away. Broil until the skin is golden brown, bubbly, and a little burnt around the edges. Pull the turbot out and slide the fish onto a platter. Season with salt and white pepper and a splash of lemon juice.

Spoon half of the butter and pea sauce all over the fish. Using a spoon and knife, release the fillet from the bone and portion the fish into 4 to 6 fillets. Spoon the remaining sauce and peas over the fillets.

Sunday Roast Beef

SERVES:
6

PREP TIME:
3 HOURS AND
30 MINUTES,
PLUS 2 HOURS
INACTIVE TIME

Simple is best. That's why slow-roasted meats are the best. People always think you have to crank up the oven and burn meats on high heat. I'm not sure how that came into play but low and slow is best for cooking larger pieces for roasts. I love seasoning a large roast with just salt and pepper. You don't have to smother it with herbs and garlic that will burn and make it taste bitter. Keep it simple and be patient.

FOR THE SIRLOIN:

1	(5-pound/2.25 kg) top sirloin
¼	cup (60 g) kosher salt
1	cup (130 g) freshly cracked black pepper
¼	cup (60 ml) canola oil

FOR THE ROASTED CARROTS AND BEETS:

3	pounds (1.3 kg) large carrots
6	tablespoons canola oil
2	teaspoons kosher salt, or more if needed
1	bunch rosemary
3	pounds (1.3 kg) large red beets
½	bunch thyme

FOR THE BONE MARROW JUS:

1	(6-inch/15 cm) marrow bone
¾	cup (200 ml) beef demi-glace
	Leaves if 1 sprig rosemary, chopped
1	teaspoon sherry vinegar
	Kosher salt

FOR THE MASHED POTATOES:

5	pounds (2.25 kg) Yukon Gold potatoes
	Kosher salt
1¼	pounds (570 g) unsalted butter

recipe continues

Make the sirloin: Clean the whole top sirloin, taking off all silver skin and heavy fat pockets. Mix the salt and pepper together, rub the meat with the oil, and season the sirloin super heavy with the mixture to create a crust. Let the sirloin sit out for 1 hour to come to room temperature.

While the sirloin is resting, preheat the oven to 325°F (165°C).

Put the sirloin in a roasting pan in the oven and cook to 115°F (46°C), about 2½ to 3 hours. Once it is fully cooked, remove from the oven and wrap the sirloin in plastic wrap, then wrap in a kitchen towel and let rest for 1 hour. Put the sirloin in a portable cooler if you have one.

Increase the oven temperature to 400°F (205°C) for roasting the carrots and beets.

Prep your carrots and beets as your sirloin is roasting: Wash and peel the carrots and cut them in half lengthwise. Toss in a large bowl with 3 tablespoons of the canola oil, 1 teaspoon of the salt, and the rosemary. Line up the carrots on a baking sheet lined with parchment paper, resting them on the bunch of rosemary. Wash and peel the beets, then quarter them. Toss in a large bowl with the remaining 3 tablespoons canola oil, remaining 1 teaspoon salt, and the thyme. Line up the beets on a second baking sheet lined with parchment paper, resting them on the half bunch of thyme.

Put both the carrots and beets in the oven and roast for 15 minutes, then turn the oven temperature down to 350°F (175°F) and continue to roast for 30 minutes, until carrots and beets are fork-tender.

Roast the bone marrow: Place the bone marrow on a rimmed baking sheet with a wire rack set on it. Roast for 15 minutes at 350°F (175°F), or until the marrow has rendered out but there still is some marrow in the bone. Take the marrow out of the oven and reserve the fat that's on the bottom of the sheet.

Make the mashed potatoes: While everything is roasting, peel the potatoes, then quarter them, put them in a medium stockpot, and cover with cold water. Place over high heat and bring to a boil. Add salt until the water tastes like the sea. Turn down heat to medium-low and cook at a light simmer until the potatoes are fork-tender, about 25 minutes. Strain in a colander and let the potatoes stand for 5 minutes. Place a potato ricer over the pot you cooked the potatoes in and mill the potatoes into the pot. Melt the butter in a medium saucepan and pour the butter in as you fold the potatoes. Keep going until all the butter is used and the potatoes have absorbed the fat and are buttery as hell. Taste for seasoning and add more salt if you like, cover, and keep warm.

Make the marrow jus: In a small saucepan, gently heat the beef demi-glace over low heat, add the rosemary, and scoop out any marrow nuggets that are left in the roasted marrow bone. Bring to a light simmer, add the vinegar, and season with salt. Add the reserved rendered marrow fat, cover, and keep warm.

Cook the sirloin and finish the dish: Turn the oven temperature up to 500°F (260°C). Place the sirloin on a deep sheet pan on the middle rack of the oven and blast for 5 to 10 minutes, until a crunchy crust forms. Remove from the oven to a cutting board and allow to rest for 5 minutes. Slice the sirloin up and place on a serving platter; plate the roasted carrots and beets, buttery mashed potatoes, and rosemary marrow jus all separately, and serve family-style.

CHAPTER 10

Smoked

Smoke Meat, Vegetables, and Fish, Not Cigs

SMOKING AT HOME IS VERY DIFFICULT, ESPECIALLY IF YOU DON'T HAVE A SMOKER OR A FIRE ESCAPE OR A PATIO OR A YARD. So if you don't have any of those things, then befriend someone who does and barter for a delicious meal. I never, ever smoked anything until I moved out of the city, so I hope you have this figured out.

When I was a kid, my dad was always into smoking. He was always buying different smokers, mostly propane with chip assist or electric smokers. Steve always loved smoking ribs, prime ribs, and chickens; then one Christmas I was like, let's smoke some ducks, glaze the fuck out of them, and have smoked duck instead of some lame-ass turkey. We took all the shelves out of the refrigerator except the top rack and hung them inside after drying them in the fridge for forty-eight hours. I made a glaze with orange juice, Cognac, hoisin, five spice, and maple syrup and poured it into a spray bottle. We started the smoker kinda high, at 350°F (175°C) for the first 30 minutes to get the fat running. Then we sprayed the ducks and turned them down to 325°F (165°C) for an hour, spraying every 20 minutes. Near the end we cranked the smoker to 450°F (230°C) and sprayed them every 5 minutes. At the end, they were like glowing orbs. That was the first real collaboration with my dad where we both contributed equally and didn't really argue about times or temperatures. And, the best part, we delivered a perfect Christmas smoked duck to our family. It was a beautiful moment. Not like me and my dad argue a lot, but you know, a smoker, a dad, and a kid trying to tell the dad what's up might not be the best idea, lol.

I fell in love with smoking after that moment. My next smoking memory is the first time I went to Texas. Somehow I had lived my life for thirty-six years and never made it to the big ol' state of beef and smoke. And now in the last year I've been to Austin three times, Houston once, Dallas once, and Wichita Falls once. I still have a lot to learn about the craft. Also, I still don't understand why, in the hottest place in America, they cook enormous pieces of meat in giant hot metal drums filled with fire. I would think they would just be eating light salads and cooled shellfish. Have you ever stood in Aaron Franklin's pit room in August? It's hotter than hell! They use beautiful machines run by a steadfast crew that changed history, but holy fuck, it's hot in there.

It's everyone's dream to cook a perfect brisket or beef rib, but I think there is a lot more to smoking than just cooking those big boys. Smoking can be delicate and light. I love the idea of smoking fish and shellfish. Use whatever smoker you want—if it's an electric with Wi-Fi and Bluetooth and you're happy with that, for fuck's sake keep going. If it's a Big Green Egg, keep going. Even if it's an offset, live fire, giant gas drum welded together that looks like a post-apocalyptic spaceship, then have at it. If you can get an end product that you're genuinely happy with, then that's the one for you. I have used almost every type of smoker in the world, and at home I swear by my Traeger (send the check). For real, it's the easiest smoker I've ever used, and it gives me a product that I'm always happy with. My family is blown away, but remember, it's still miles and miles away from anything going on in Austin or Lexington or any of the small rural towns in central Texas.

After reading this book, just promise me to be true to yourself and don't let any barbecue snobs or bullies push you around and make fun of your electric or propane smoker, okay?

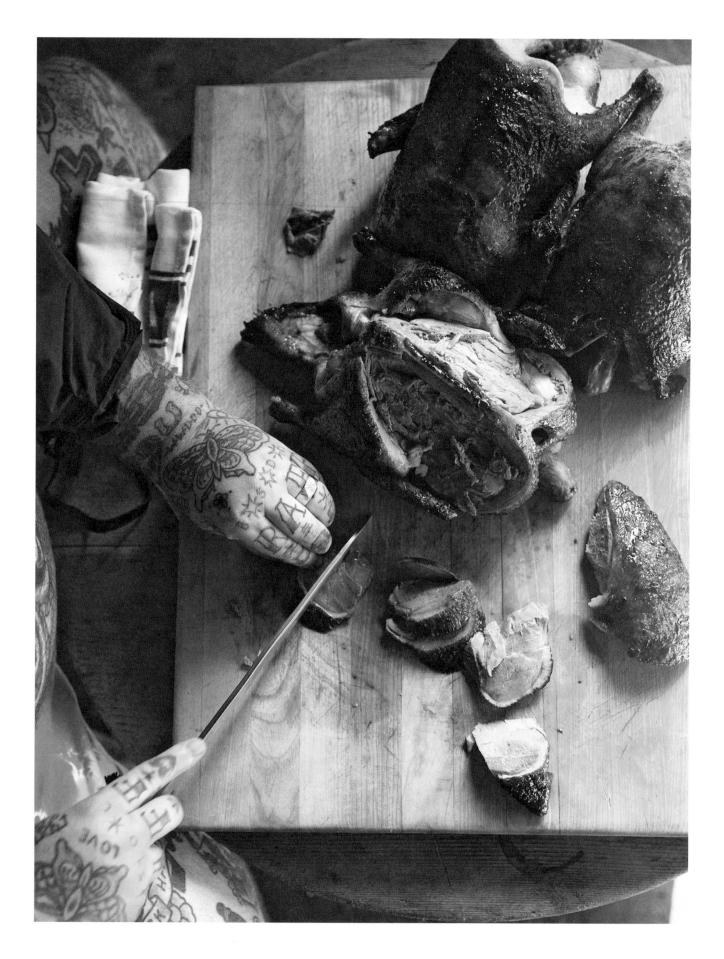

Christmas Ducks with Orange, Whiskey, and Hoisin Glaze

SERVES:
8 TO 12

PREP TIME:
1½ HOURS, PLUS 12 HOURS
INACTIVE TIME AND 2 HOURS
TO GET THE COAL BED READY

A couple Christmases ago we smoked duck and it was truly such a great day. My dad loves smoking and grilling so much, like most dads, and it was the best duck I think I've ever made, even to this day. If you're not smoking, you can still make this in your oven, so don't get stressed out. Christmas turkey can be so boring. We always do one traditional Christmas, then a weird one every other year, ya know? Couple years ago we made laap and curries. Christmas should be about family being together, not just eating turkey and butter-soaked stuffing.

2   whole Peking or Muscovy ducks (4 to 5 pounds per duck)

1   cup plus 2 tablespoons (265 ml) hoisin sauce

¼   cup (60 ml) whiskey or Cognac

½   cup (120 ml) orange juice

⅓   cup (70 ml) maple syrup

1   tablespoon Chinese five spice, plus more for serving

1   tablespoon pureed garlic (see Note)

1   tablespoon pureed ginger (see Note)

        Sea salt

        Freshly ground black pepper

        Orange zest

FOR SERVING:

        Roti (page 29)

        Hoisin sauce

        Julienned leeks

        Cilantro leaves

        Lime quarters

Note: Cook minced garlic or ginger in oil over low heat until tender, then puree.

recipe continues

Bring a large stockpot of water to a boil. Trim off the tips of the duck wings where they meet at the elbow joint. One at a time, plunge the ducks into the boiling water for 4 seconds to render the skin. Pat the ducks dry inside and out with paper towels. Place on a baking sheet and refrigerate uncovered overnight to continue to air dry. This will enhance crispiness during cooking.

Build your coal bed 2 hours before cooking. In the center of your grill, stack newspaper and kindling in a teepee formation and light on all sides with a lighter. Once the fire is lit, keep feeding the fire with 2 to 3 more pieces of wood until you've built a medium-size fire. Let the wood burn down to form your coal bed, about 1 hour. This is where I start my second fire in my Green Egg to supply the rotisserie with coal throughout the cooking process.

In a medium saucepan, combine the hoisin sauce, whiskey, orange juice, maple syrup, Chinese five spice, garlic puree, and ginger puree and bring to a boil over medium heat. Turn down heat to low and simmer for 5 minutes, or until all the ingredients are incorporated and the glaze coats the back of a spoon. Take off heat and let the glaze cool to room temperature. Pour the glaze through a funnel into a spray bottle.

Pull the ducks from the fridge and let them come to room temperature for 1 hour. Next, you are going to skewer the ducks. Set a fork on a skewer off center to the left and skewer duck 1 all the way to the left and puncture the breast with the fork to keep the duck spinning at the speed of the rotisserie. Skewer duck 2's breast to the ass of duck 1. Tighten the second fork into the ass of duck 2 so both ducks are now locked into place.

Build the coal bed around the ducks on all 4 sides, about a foot and a half from the birds. Turn on the rotisserie and let the birds fly. At this point, it's a good idea to use your hand to identify all the hot spots in the BBQ, adjusting the coals so you have a consistent heat source all around the ducks. Now you can start to spray the marinade all over the ducks as they turn, using a brush to help even out the glaze. It's really important to keep the heat source at medium so you don't burn your ducks in the first 30 minutes. Once the ducks are looking nice and lacquered, continue to apply the glaze and stoke the coals for 30 more minutes. Once the ducks have reached 130°F (54°C), remove all the coals and let the ducks carry over to 135°F (57°C) for medium-rare. Place on cutting boards and allow the ducks to rest for 15 to 20 minutes.

Carve the duck breasts off the crown. Remove the 4 legs and set on a large platter. Slice the duck breasts across the width of the breast in ¾-inch- (2 cm) thick pieces. Fan the breasts meat evenly over a large serving platter and season the breast with sea salt, pepper, five spice, and orange zest. Serve the ducks with roti, hoisin sauce, julienned leeks, cilantro leaves, and lime quarters.

If you don't have a rotisserie BBQ: You can roast the ducks in a preheated 425°F (220°C) oven. Roast the ducks breast side up for 45 minutes, glazing the ducks every 20 minutes. Remove the ducks, turn over, and roast for another 45 minutes, then turn one last time, still adding glaze and cooking the ducks to 135°F (54°C). Pull the ducks and let rest for 20 minutes.

Hard Smoked Merguez Sausage and Polenta

SERVES:
4 TO 6

PREP TIME:
1½ HOURS, PLUS
TIME FOR HEATING
UP THE GRILL

Mergeuz sausage is my favorite sausage. Usually, it's in a long and skinny casing, but a sausage is a sausage is a sausage, and these smoked little wrinklers are perfect for eating with creamy cheesy polenta. If you wanted to add a little salad that would be nice too. This is a lot like the sausage and potatoes recipe in my first book. I guess I love sausages and starches.

1	lamb rack with fat cap attached
1	cup (240 ml) red wine
⅓	cup (70 ml) pomegranate juice
2	tablespoons ground cumin
2	teaspoons ground cayenne
2	teaspoons kosher salt
	Freshly cracked black pepper
1	tablespoon garlic powder
	Lamb casings
1	quart (1 L) whole milk
3	tablespoons unsalted butter
2	cups (500 g) instant cornmeal (polenta)
½	cup (60 g) grated Parmesan cheese
	Lemon juice
	Sea salt
	Canola oil

recipe continues

Set up your meat grinder with a medium-size die hole.

Remove the lamb bones from the back of the rack using a sharp fillet knife and clean all the meat between the bones. Dice the whole lamb loin plus the fat cap into medium pieces that will fit through your grinder. Grind the lamb into a large stainless-steel bowl over another bowl of ice; it's important to keep the meat as cold as possible.

Add the red wine, pomegranate juice, cumin, cayenne, kosher salt, black pepper, and garlic powder and mix well. Chill in the fridge for 20 minutes, then grind the lamb mixture through the grinder again, back into your bowl, and chill in the fridge until you are ready to case your sausage.

Give your lamb casings a good rinse and let them sit in a bowl of water for 20 minutes before using.

Set up your stuffing station atop a wet work surface; you'll need the wet surface later, so keep a bowl of water near in case it dries up.

Pull the lamb mixture from the fridge, mix it with your hands and form it into a large ball. Add the sausage to the sausage stuffer and push down on the mixture, removing all the air pockets. Press down on the sausage stuffer until the mixture starts to come out the tube's end.

Grab the casings from the water, place them over the end of the tube, and push the casing down all the way until the end of the casing is the only thing left off the tube. Pull a thumb length of casing back off the tube and tie a knot. Then push down on the lever of the sausage stuffer and begin to fill the casing with the lamb mixture. As the casing fills, slowly swirl the stuffed sausage into a spiral on the wet surface. Make sure to twist each link every 4 inches; first twist toward you, then away on the next 4 inches, and so on. Repeat this process until you have built your coil.

Once the coil is the size of two hands, pull off the casing a couple inches and use scissors to cut the casing neatly, and tie another knot to lock in the sausage. Continue to fill casings until you've used all the meat.

Use a pin to prick a few tiny holes into the sausage to help prevent it from exploding during cooking.

Turn your smoker on and heat to 360°F (180°C) with the lid closed.

In a medium saucepan, combine the milk and butter and bring up to a light simmer over medium heat. Whisk in the cornmeal and keep whisking until it thickens, then change out the whisk for a wooden spoon, scraping the bottom of the pot to prevent it from sticking to the bottom. Turn heat down to medium-low and cook for 15 minutes, or until the polenta has a soft, creamy texture. Add the cheese and stir until incorporated. Season with lemon juice and sea salt. Cover and set aside until serving.

Once your smoker is up to temperature, rub the sausages with canola oil, place them in the smoker, and hot smoke for 35 to 45 minutes, until cooked through.

Spoon a heaping spoonful of the polenta onto each serving plate and add 4 sausage links on top. Season with sea salt and pepper.

Curry Spiced Whole Lamb Rack

SERVES:
6 TO 8

PREP TIME:
1 HOUR AND 10 MINUTES, PLUS
TIME TO FIRE UP THE SMOKER

Smoking curried lamb makes me happy, and eating it outside in a casual way like this just makes sense. This was an idea I had from loving curried lamb or stewed lamb, and smoking is just dry stewing, ya know?—cooking something for a while to break down the tendons and collagens and letting the muscles become happy and tender. So why not a curry dry rub, and why not eat it with your hands in a garden? I would serve this lamb with All the Tomatoes Tomato Salad (page 87), Pickled Hot Peppers (page 67), Grilled Naan (page 30), or labneh. Get some, you freaks!

2	tablespoons ground cumin
2	tablespoons ground coriander
2	tablespoons yellow curry powder
2	tablespoons smoked paprika
1	tablespoon ground cayenne
1	tablespoon ground cloves
1	tablespoon ground cardamom
1	tablespoon ground nutmeg
1	tablespoon ground fennel
2	pounds (1 kg) Frenched lamb rack (8-bone rack)
3	tablespoons canola oil
1	teaspoon sea salt, for finishing
1	teaspoon freshly ground black pepper

Turn an electric smoker to 325°F (165°C) and allow the chamber to fill with smoke.

In a medium bowl, combine the cumin, coriander, yellow curry powder, paprika, cayenne, cloves, cardamom, nutmeg, and fennel and mix well.

Place the lamb on a baking sheet and rub the canola oil evenly over whole rack. Coat the lamb rack with the curry spice mixture to cover all sides. Place the lamb rack on the center rack of the smoker with the fat cap facing up and bones down.

Smoke the lamb rack until it reaches an internal temperature of 120°F (49°C), 45 to 50 minutes. Pull the lamb out of the smoker and allow to rest uncovered for 10 minutes.

Carve the lamb between each rib bone and sprinkle with the sea salt and pepper.

Texas-Style Prime Rib

SERVES:
6 TO 12

PREP TIME:
3 HOURS, PLUS 1 HOUR
INACTIVE TIME AND TIME
TO FIRE UP THE SMOKER

This recipe is dedicated to Adam Perry Lang, who was my gatekeeper into the barbecue world and introduced me to some living legends. He was the one who taught me a little bit about barbecue but a lot about beef. The technique of wrapping the meat with plastic wrap instead of butcher's paper is GENIUS. We're using the heat and the steam of the beef to control and finish the cooking. If you have a small cooler, that would help; if not, you can just wrap and place it in a Dutch oven with a lid. When you unwrap this prime rib, make sure to reserve all the juices and pour them into a gravy or a jus or something. It's pretty special stuff. The resting allows for all the collagen to break down and become butter-like, as it should be. You can serve this with so many different sides from this book, like Green Olive Tapenade (page 136), Black Radish Kraut (page 65), Kombu-Steamed Fingerling Potatoes (page 91), or Roasted Cauliflower and Hazelnuts (page 99). I love you, Adam, and I love this prime rib 'cause it works every time, in any oven, and I think the wrapping has leveled the playing field for home cooks and professionals.

1	(14-pound/6.3 kg) whole prime rib roast with 6 bones attached
3	cups (360 g) freshly cracked black pepper
1	cup (130 g) kosher salt
½	cup (120 ml) canola oil
	Sea salt

Turn your smoker to 275°F (135°C) and allow the chamber to fill with smoke.

On a secure cutting board, trim any silver skin that's left on the outside of the prime rib. If your electric smoker can't fit a whole prime rib, cut it in half.

Mix together the pepper and kosher salt in a medium bowl; rub down the prime rib with a thin layer of canola oil. Heavily season the outside of the roast with the pepper mixture until completely covered and a nice crust has formed. Allow the meat to come to room temperature as the smoker heats up.

Place the roast on the center rack of the smoker; cook until it reaches an internal temperature of 115°F (46°C), 3 to 4 hours. Remove from the smoker.

Wrap the roast in plastic wrap, then wrap in a kitchen towel. Place in a cooler and allow to rest for 1 hour.

Preheat the oven to 500°F (270°C).

Once the meat is rested, place it on a baking sheet with a wire rack set in it. Blast the roast in the crazy-hot oven to form a quick crust, 5 to 8 minutes. Pull it out and allow it to rest for 5 minutes. Slice down the back to remove all the bones, then slice in half and slice both halves again down the middle. Thinly slice and place on platters. Season with sea salt and serve family-style.

Burnt-Ends Hot Dogs

SERVES:
6

PREP TIME:
3½ HOURS, PLUS TIME
TO FIRE UP THE SMOKER

You wanna hear something funny? When we were making this recipe for the book, my chef, Coulson, did something very, very funny. He literally took two slices of bologna and covered them in pepper, and I was like, Noooooooooo. And he was like, I thought it was weird too. Why would we put two slices of bologna in a smoker for hours and baste them with a sticky barbecue sauce? And I told him to cut hot dog shapes out of one of those large bologna tubes, ya know; then it clicked for me: I'm just making hot dogs—like, fuck! I'm such an idiot. But smoked hot dogs rule, and so do burnt ends, so make these and make sure to enjoy them with kids and neighbors, and give one to the mail person if they happen to come by at that perfect moment, when these bologna burnt-end dogs come out of the smoker.

2½	pounds (1.3 kg) whole bologna
¼	cup (40 g) freshly cracked black pepper
2	tablespoons kosher salt
1	can cola
1	cup (240 ml) yellow mustard, plus more for serving
1	cup (240 ml) ketchup
1	cup (240 ml) apple cider vinegar
½	cup (120 ml) molasses
1	tablespoon ground cumin
1	tablespoon ground cayenne
1	tablespoon mustard powder
1	tablespoon smoked paprika
2	tablespoons garlic powder
6	hot dog potato rolls (preferably Martin's)
1	cup (150 g) grated white onion

Turn an electric smoker to 325°F (165°C), and allow the chamber to fill with smoke.

Cut the bologna into 6 pieces, shaped like hot dogs.

Mix the black pepper and salt in a small bowl. Season the bologna pieces with the pepper mixture and place them on a baking sheet with a rack set on it. Place it in the smoker and smoke for 3 hours.

In a medium saucepan, combine the cola, yellow mustard, ketchup, vinegar, molasses, cumin, cayenne, mustard powder, smoked paprika, and garlic powder. Whisk until the ingredients are incorporated, then bring to a boil over high heat. Turn down heat to medium-low and simmer for 30 minutes, then cool to room temperature.

Pull the bologna from the smoker, dip it in glaze, and place back in the smoker for about 30 minutes, until all sticky and glazed. Pull from the smoker.

Fill the hot dog buns with the glazed bologna, squeeze yellow mustard on them, and add a couple tablespoons of grated raw onion.

Smoked Seven Seafood Chowder

SERVES:
6 TO 8

PREP TIME: 1 HOUR AND
45 MINUTES, PLUS 12 HOURS
INACTIVE TIME AND TIME TO
FIRE UP THE SMOKER

Smoking the seafood for a creamy chowder is perfect—a subtle smoky flavor once the cream washes over the golden hue of the scallops, mussels, and white fish; the clams just kissed with the smoke. I love this idea, and I love chowder. As a reminder, please don't ever put red peppers in a chowder, and make sure to never add flour because I hate it. So promise me you won't, okay? Thanks!

2	pounds (980 g) mussels, scrubbed and debearded
3	pounds (1.4 kg) littleneck clams, scrubbed
1	cup (180 g) cornmeal
2	mackerel fillets, cleaned, pin bones removed
2	trout fillets, cleaned, pin bones removed
	Kosher salt and freshly ground black pepper
½	cup (120 ml) canola oil
4	onions, diced
4	ribs celery, diced
2	carrots, peeled and diced
2	leeks, cleaned and diced
2	garlic cloves, thinly sliced
2	tablespoons unsalted butter
2	cups (480 ml) dry white wine
1½	quarts (1.5 L) Fish Fumet (page 48)
2	pounds (980 g) Yukon Gold potatoes, peeled and diced
1	bouquet garni (3 sprigs each thyme, tarragon, and parsley tied together with butcher's twine)
2	lobster tails
1	pound (450 g) scallops
2	pounds (980 g) shrimp, peeled and deveined
4	cups (1 L) heavy cream
¼	cup (60 ml) brown butter (see page 100)
1	sleeve saltines

recipe continues

Clean the mussels and clams the night before by rinsing with cold water in buckets in the sink. Place the clams and mussels in a container with water and add the cornmeal. Refrigerate overnight. The cornmeal makes the clams spit out the sand from their bellies. Dry the mackerel and trout fillets with paper towels, season with salt and pepper, place on a plate, and allow to air dry uncovered in the fridge overnight.

Turn an electric smoker to 225°F (110°C) and allow the chamber to fill with smoke.

While the smoker is coming up to temperature, start your chowder base. In a large heavy-bottomed pot, heat the canola oil over medium heat. Add the onions, celery, carrots, leeks, and garlic and cook until translucent, about 10 minutes. Add the butter and allow to bubble and froth. Deglaze with the white wine and reduce the liquid by half. Add the fish fumet, potatoes, and bouquet garni, bring to a simmer, then reduce the heat and cook for 1 hour.

Cook the lobster: Fill a large pot three-quarters full with water, add ¼ cup (48 g) salt, and bring to a boil over high heat. Fill a large bowl with ice and water to make an ice water bath.

Add the lobster tails to the boiling water and boil for 5 minutes to cook it 80 percent of the way through. This works to release the shell from the meat. Take the lobster out of the water, place it in the ice bath, and allow to chill through. Once the lobster is chilled, remove the shell using sharp kitchen scissors, cutting up the back of the spine and then peeling off the shell, exposing the beautiful meat inside. Place the lobsters on one of the smoker's racks and set aside.

Gather all your seafood and place it in separate perforated pans or directly on the smoker racks: Place the trout and mackerel at the top of the smoker; the scallops, shrimp, and lobster in the middle; and the clams and mussels on the lower racks. Set a tray on the bottom of the smoker to catch any liquid that drips down. Smoke for 30 minutes.

Remove the seafood from the smoker to a tray and allow to rest for 10 minutes. Pick the shellfish from the shells, collecting any liquor and placing all of the meat into a large bowl. Flake up the trout and mackerel into bite-size pieces and place into a bowl. Slice the lobster, shrimp, and scallops into large coins, or you can leave the shrimp whole. It's up to you how you want those shellfish to look in the chowder.

When the chowder base is cooked, add the cream and bring to a boil. Turn down heat to medium-low, add the seafood, and cook for 5 minutes.

Ladle into bowls and hit the smoked chowder with a drizzle of brown butter and a few cranks of pepper. Serve with the saltines.

Smoked Mackerel

SERVES:
6 TO 8

PREP TIME:
30 MINUTES, PLUS 1 HOUR
INACTIVE TIME AND TIME
TO FIRE UP THE SMOKER

Smoked whole fish is a beautiful thing. And surfing out on a paddleboard and fishing for mackies to smoke, like my good ol' buddy Den does out in Cow Bay, Nova Scotia, is the best. Imagine drinking a cup of coffee in the morning, then going surfing, then paddling out and dropping a line, then paddling in fresh mackies to a homemade smoker that looks like a barn door and an old wood-burning oven. That's the good life right there, and that's what mackerels will give you . . . that's right, they will give you a better life, so make sure to smoke lots mackerel. Surfing in cold water then eating hot-smoked fish—there's nothing better.

4	whole mackerel, spatchcocked, spines out, heads on (ask your fishmonger to do this)
½	cup (112 g) granulated sugar
½	cup (175 g) sea salt

FOR SERVING:
Pickled Onions (see page 165)
Seeded Rye Bread (page 22)
Sour cream
Sea salt

On a secure board, wipe dry the mackerel with a paper towel. Using a sharp fillet knife, remove the spines from the mackerel. Place mackerel on a rimmed baking sheet.

Mix the sugar and salt together in a small bowl. Cover both sides of the fish with the mixture and allow to cure at room temperature for 1 hour.

Turn an electric smoker to 310°F (155°C) and allow the chamber to fill with smoke.

Wipe the cure off the fish with a damp paper towel. Place the mackerel on the smoking rack, flesh side down, and in the smoker and smoke hard for 30 minutes, or until the skin is golden brown all over. Pull the fish from the smoker and allow to rest for 5 minutes.

Serve smoked mackerel with pickled onions, rye bread, sour cream, and sea salt.

Smoked Trout Almondine

SERVES:
4

PREP TIME:
2 HOURS, PLUS 5 HOURS
INACTIVE TIME AND TIME
TO FIRE UP THE SMOKER

Eating hot-smoked trout is god's plan for all of us. Add almondine and green beans and lots of butter and it's the greatest light lunch of all time. Make this dish for all your friends, and make some nice tea and have a talk about life, and you're in the running for the greatest lunch of your life.

1	quart (1 L) water
1	cup (240 g) kosher salt
¼	cup (104 g) brown sugar
2	pounds (980 g) trout fillets, cleaned, scaled, pin bones removed
1	pound (450 g) green beans, trimmed
½	cup (120 g) unsalted butter
1	garlic clove, thinly sliced
¾	cup (75 g) sliced almonds
3	tablespoons lemon juice, plus more for finishing
¼	cup (20 g) chopped parsley
¼	cup (20 g) chopped tarragon
¼	cup (20 g) chopped chervil
	Sea salt

Combine the water, ½ cup (120 g) of the kosher salt, and the brown sugar in a 4-quart (4 L) container and stir until the salt and sugar dissolve, about 2 minutes. Add the cleaned trout fillets, making sure they are completely submerged. Cover and put in the fridge for 3 hours.

Remove the trout from the brine and pat dry. Place the trout on plates and place back into the fridge, uncovered, for 2 hours to dry the skin out.

Turn an electric smoker to 310°F (155°C) and allow the chamber to fill with smoke.

Place the trout onto smoking racks, skin side down. Smoke for 30 to 45 minutes, or until they are a deep golden hue and desired level of smoke flavor is reached.

While the trout is smoking, bring a large pot of water to a boil over high heat and add the remaining ½ cup (120 g) salt. Make an ice bath by filling a large bowl with ice and cold water.

Working in batches, add the green beans to the boiling water, making sure the water remains at a rolling boil the entire time. Cook the green beans until they just become tender, 3 to 4 minutes. Transfer to the ice bath to stop the cooking process. Repeat with the remaining green beans, then drain all the blanched green beans in a colander.

Melt the butter in a large skillet over medium heat. When the butter is foamy, add the garlic and cook until fragrant, about 1 minute, then add the almonds and cook until they start to brown and the butter starts to develop a nutty aroma, about 5 minutes. Add the green beans and stir to coat in the brown butter. Add the lemon juice, parsley, tarragon, and chervil.

Remove the trout fillets from the smoker and place on serving plates. Spoon the green bean almondine all over the smoked trout and season with sea salt and a dash of lemon juice.

CHAPTER 11

Grilled

Hope Y'all Got (or Know Someone Who Has) a Grill

THIS WAS ONE OF THE TOUGHEST CHAPTERS TO WRITE. I KEPT THINKING: HOLD THE FUCK UP, THERE'S NO FUCKING WAY PEOPLE ARE COOKING AND GRILLING LIKE THIS AT HOME. But maybe, just maybe, they have a gas grill or a little backyard where they have a Weber or the luxury of having a giant wood-burning grill. You could make all these recipes on anything, even on one of those piece-of-shit gas grills with the broken lids like my in-laws have.

Do you want to talk about a crazy grill situation? Ol' Bill and Carol had two of the wildest natural-gas barbecues, one in the front yard and one in the backyard by the lake. Now, listen to me, these grills literally were installed in 1982, the year I was born! WTF, Bill, how the fuck you trying to blow up the block?! I love that people would rather fix and tinker with a broken grill than just buy a $600 natural-gas grill from the local Canada Tire. Bill's barbecue was a bomb! Every time I wanted to cook on it was a death wish. Even at Trish's sister's wedding, someone left the gas on and the lid down, and when we lit it from the bottom it fucking sounded like World War III was about to start inside. Gas grills freak me out—especially thirty-year-old ones—like, c'mon, guys. But let's not forget that you can make great food with shitty grills. Some people love cooking on the grills that only have one hot spot. You know those grills that you have to use when you are cooking for twenty-seven friends? The results are so many half-cooked half-burnt gray portobellos dripping with shitty soy sauce. I love and hate those grill people so much.

That was a lot, sorry, guys. Now let's talk about grilling some seafood, okay? This takes a little bit of care, and a key thing is that you make sure you aren't buying frozen, waterlogged fish and seafood. You can get away with that bullshit if you're making a stew or a soup, maybe, but please always buy fresh. Grilling and water don't really go together—you want your product to be dry before you start grilling. Remember that your grill needs to be hot and well oiled. I get it ready by using a rag dabbed in oil to brush the grill with tongs to season the cooking surface. And most importantly, don't move the fish or seafood once you place it on the grill. It's very bad to fuck around and move it. If you do, it will tear. Be patient.

Grilling should be fun, and like most things worthwhile, it takes a little time. Choppin' wood, building fires, and waiting for the coals to become the perfect temperature is hard work. Maybe invest in a nice little hand fan to flame the coals to raise the temperature. That will help you get the perfect sear on the whole squid. Grilling a whole lobster is the only way I eat a hot lobster. If I'm blanching it, I want it to be ice cold, but grilling a lobster brings to it such an amazing flavor—but overcooking it should be punishable by death. That's why it's so important to get your coals hot for all seafood. It will give you the mouth orgasm you've been searching for your whole life.

Take your time. All will be good, and don't blow up your in-laws' house!

T-bone Steak and Fine Herb Chimichurri

SERVES:
4 TO 6

PREP TIME:
3 HOURS, PLUS 2½ HOURS
INACTIVE TIME AND TIME
FOR FIRING UP THE GRILL

Cooking these over maple wood coals in the woods from which the trees were harvested is a true kind of cooking. Cooking larger pieces of steaks can be broken down into two techniques that are pretty much the same but flipped on their heads: (1) hard sear or grill first, then raise up the grill grate and cook slowly; (2) cook slowly, then sear on a grill over high heat. It all depends on what you wanna do, and I don't think either is better or worse. If you get color on your steak and let it temper properly, or temper your steak then sear, I feel there's no real difference. The T-bone is a little different because you can stand it up with the bone and let the bone warm through and cook from the bone, which is nice. Also, trying to tell a "man" how to cook a steak is like trying to tell me to not yell in my videos: It's literally impossible. Everyone knows how to cook a steak, and everyone thinks they are pros, and everyone thinks they know what rare and medium-rare are, but most of the time they just sear the outsides and leave the steak raw on the inside, and they think they are kings when it is that black and blue. You can't even taste the beef. In my older age, I'm leaning toward medium to get a full taste of the beef. If you think you can taste the beef better rare, you're an idiot, but hey, keep grilling, boys!

FOR THE STEAK:

1	(2-pound/900 g) T-bone steak, 2½ inches (6 cm) thick (contains less tenderloin than a porterhouse)
¼	cup (60 g) sea salt, plus more for finishing
1	cup (250 g) unsalted butter, melted
½	bunch rosemary, tied with butcher's twine to create a brush
	Freshly ground black pepper

FOR THE CHIMICHURRI:

2	tablespoons garlic
2	shallots, chopped
¾	cup (180 ml) olive oil
3	tablespoons sherry vinegar
3	tablespoons lemon juice
1	teaspoon sea salt, plus more as needed
½	teaspoon freshly ground black pepper
3	cups (150 g) parsley leaves
2	cups (100 g) cilantro leaves
1	cup (50 g) mint leaves

recipe continues

Prepare the grill: Build your coal bed, starting the fire about 90 minutes before cooking. It's really important to have a large coal bed to feed your ember bed as you are cooking. You don't want to be cooking over burning logs; you want to burn the wood down until you have glowing embers in order to impart a clean charcoal flavor to the steak.

Grill the steak: Take your steak out of the refrigerator 1 hour before cooking and season with the salt on all sides, especially the nice fat cap.

To cook the steak, use the reverse sear method: Don't put the steak right over the embers at the start, but instead, start the steak in one of the other zones about a foot and a half over the coals, rotating the steak on all sides until the internal temperature reaches 115 to 120°F (46 to 49°C).

Next, build the coal bed back up and lower your grill to 1 inch (2.5 cm) from the embers. As the steak starts to sear, with the rosemary brush, baste the steak with melted butter. After a nice crust has formed, 4 to 6 minutes, flip the steak and repeat searing and basting on the other side. Once the internal temperature reaches 130°F (54°C), pull the steak off the grill and put it on a cutting board. Let the steak continue to cook and as it rests for 20 minutes.

Make the chimichurri: While the steak is resting, combine the garlic, shallots, olive oil, vinegar, lemon juice, salt, and pepper in the bowl of a food processor and process until pureed. Add the parsley, cilantro, and mint a little at a time and pulse until the mixture is incorporated, scraping down the sides of the bowl with a spatula as needed. Check for seasoning and add more salt if needed. Place in a serving bowl, cover with plastic wrap, and set aside until serving.

Carve the steak, starting by cutting the larger loin off the bone, then carve the tenderloin off and cut both steaks into finger-width slices. Season with salt and pepper and serve with the chimichurri.

Spatchcock Squab with Hot Pepper and Plum Agrodolce

Drying out squab, or any bird, pig, cow, or lamb product, will make it taste better. The drier the meat when cooking and grilling, the better. Having patience and foresight is really important, especially when you are going to grill a couple squabs for the family. And you should, 'cause these are my all-time favorite bird. There's something about the spicy, sticky, acidic, juicy plum sauce that just really complements this nice little bird.

SERVES:
4

PREP TIME:
2 HOURS AND 15 MINUTES, PLUS
2 DAYS INACTIVE TIME AND TIME
FOR FIRING UP THE GRILL

FOR THE SQUAB:

4   whole squab (about 1 pound)

3   teaspoons kosher salt

2   teaspoons freshly ground black pepper

FOR THE AGRODOLCE:

1   pound (450 g) plums, skin on, pitted, and chopped

2   halved and seeded poblano chiles

4   halved and seeded bird's eye chiles

⅓   cup (70 ml) apple cider vinegar

⅓   cup (70 g) brown sugar

2   tablespoons soy sauce

2   garlic cloves, minced

1   tablespoon grated ginger

½   teaspoon dried red chile flakes

    Sea salt, for finishing

recipe continues

Partially debone the squab: Place the squab breast side down on a secure cutting board, with the legs toward you. Run the tip of your knife down the right side of the backbone, inserting the blade so it runs across the backbone. Starting at the head of the bird, take smooth slices with the tip part of your knife to release the meat from the bone, following the rib cage all the way around to where the breasts meet and leaving the breast skin attached. Next, cut through the shoulder joint to release the wing (keep the wing attached to the boneless breast). Now, at the butt end of the bird, run the tip of your knife through the hip joint to release the leg from the rib cage, leaving the leg attached to the breast as well. Repeat the process on the other half of the bird, making sure when you release the second breast you don't cut through the skin. Now you have a boneless spatchcocked squab. Place on a wire rack set over a plate skin side up and refrigerate, uncovered, for 2 days. This will dry out the skin and help you achieve the ultimate crispy skin when you cook it.

Prepare the grill: Build a 12 by 12-inch (30 by 30 cm) coal bed 1 inch (2.5 cm) deep, starting the fire about 90 minutes before cooking. It's really important to have a large coal bed to feed your ember bed as you are cooking. You don't want to be cooking over burning logs; you want to burn the wood down until you have glowing embers in order impart a clean charcoal flavor to the squab.

After the 2 days of resting, season the squab with the kosher salt on the skin and meat side. Season the meat side with pepper and allow the birds to come to room temperature before grilling.

Make the agrodolce: In a medium saucepan, combine the plums, chiles, vinegar, brown sugar, soy sauce, garlic, ginger, and chile flakes and bring to a boil over medium-high heat. Turn down heat and simmer for 25 minutes, or until the sauce has thickened slightly. Remove from heat, transfer to a blender, and blend until smooth. Pour half of the sauce into a small saucepan and cook to reduce by half to get it nice and caramelly for glazing the squab. The other half will be reserved for plating.

Grill the squab: Set your grill grate 1 foot (30 cm) above the embers; you want to cook the squab slowly, skin side down, in the center of the grill, allowing the bird to take its time to reach medium-rare. Allow the skin to get naturally crispy without letting it burn. As the fat starts to render and the squab starts to warm through, lower the grill. Flip the squab and cook the meat side for 2 minutes to warm through, then flip the squab again and give the skin another hit to crisp up and char a little, 12 to 15 minutes.

Finish the dish: Pull the squab from grill; it should be medium-rare; if it isn't put it back on the grill for a couple minutes. Glaze both sides of the squab with the agrodolce until the squab is sticky. Allow to rest on a wire rack for 8 minutes.

Pour the reserved agrodolce into the center of plate until it pools to about the size of the squab. Place the whole squab into the center of the plate and sprinkle with sea salt. Plate the rest of the squab in the same way.

Chicken Thighs with Peas and Aligot Potatoes

SERVES:
4

PREP TIME:
1½ HOURS, PLUS 12 HOURS INACTIVE TIME AND TIME FOR FIRING UP THE GRILL

Grilled chicken is an incredible gift, and with the greatest potatoes ever, peas, and gravy, it's just a world-class meal. I think it breaks the norm enough to make supper exciting. I love grilled chicken thighs without any sauce basted all over. Rarely you'll see just grilled chicken—and guess what you can taste? Chicken and crispy skin. For this, once again, you can dry out the thighs in the fridge overnight or up to 3 days. Start the potatoes before you fire up the grill, and keep them warm.

FOR THE CHICKEN:

4   chicken thighs
     Kosher salt

FOR THE GRAVY:

2   tablespoons unsalted butter
2   tablespoons all-purpose flour
1   cup (240 ml) Chicken Stock (page 51), or store-bought, at room temperature
     Kosher salt and freshly cracked black pepper

FOR THE PEAS:

¼   cup (55 g) unsalted butter
2   cups (360 g) frozen peas
     Kosher salt
     Lemon juice

Aligot Potatoes, or Cheesy Stringy Potatoes (page 108)

recipe continues

Prep the chicken: The day before making the dish, clean the chicken thighs by removing the thigh bones and any cartilage found in the meat. Pat the skin dry and place on a plate skin side up. Refrigerate, uncovered, overnight to dry the skin out (this helps the skin get super crispy on the grill).

Get the grill ready: Add charcoal, preferably Binchōtan, to a konro grill—if you have just a Weber and normal charcoal, that is fine, too. Apply lighter fluid (to help light the charcoal faster). Once part of the charcoal is lit, fan it to ignite all the charcoal. It takes time to really fire up the grill. When all the charcoal is lit and you can't keep your hand there for more than 2 seconds without feeling a hard burn, the grill is ready to cook on. Place the metal grill grate on and allow it to come up to temperature, so the chicken doesn't stick.

Make the gravy: Melt the butter in a medium saucepan over medium heat. Stir in the flour and cook, stirring constantly with a whisk and scraping up the browned bits, until the mixture is light golden brown, about 4 minutes. Gradually stir in the chicken stock and bring to a boil, stirring constantly with a whisk; whisk until the gravy thickens. Season with salt and pepper and adjust the consistency of the gravy with more stock as needed to desired consistency. Cover and set aside to keep warm.

Grill the chicken: Once your grill is hot, season all sides of the chicken thighs with salt. Place on the grill skin side down and grill 70 percent of the way through, creating a beautiful golden chicken skin and allowing the fat to render down. You can move the chickens around to help prevent flareups and fan the embers to keep the coals roaring hot. Once you've achieved the perfect skin, flip the thighs and allow the coals to cool down, enabling the chicken to stay nice and juicy; cook for about 7 minutes. Remove from the grill to a plate and rest for 10 minutes.

Make the peas: As the chicken is resting, melt the butter in a medium saucepan over medium heat. Add the peas and warm them through, glazing them in the butter. Season with salt and lemon juice.

To serve: Spoon a huge dollop of the potatoes into the center of a plate and use the back of the spoon to create a well in the center of the potatoes. Fill the well with a chicken thigh and place the buttery peas on top of the chicken. Ladle chicken gravy around the potatoes, forming a pool. Repeat with the remaining potatoes, chicken, and peas.

Chorizo Verde and Tomatillo Salsa

MAKES:
2 LARGE
SAUSAGE COILS
(6 SERVINGS)

PREP TIME:
2½ HOURS, PLUS TIME
FOR FIRING UP THE GRILL

Making sausage at home sucks, and if your grandparents are still alive and still making sausage once a year, maybe try to jump on that train and make chorizo verdes. Or just go buy them like anything else in cookbooks. If you just make the sauce, that's good enough for me. I just want you to cook something, if you can. Grilling sausage is kinda difficult 'cause you don't want it to burst. Be extra careful, but don't undercook your sausage, either. Take your time and build a hot side and a low side: Grill them on the hot side just until there's some color on them, then move them to the low side to finish cooking, just chilling and bubbling away. I love this dish so much. It screams summer and rooftops and smokes and drinking vinho verde, but I don't do any of that anymore. Chorizo verde reminds me of my years cooking at La Palette and hanging out on rooftops till the sun came up. I love how food reminds me of all the years and lives I've lived. Food is memory for me.

FOR THE SAUSAGE:
- 3   poblano chiles
- 3   jalapeño chiles
- 3   green bell peppers
- 1½   pounds (680 g) pork shoulder
- ⅔   cup (135 g) pork back fat (you can also ask your butcher to grind the fat with the shoulder to make the recipe easier)
- 1   bunch marjoram, leaves chopped
- 1   bunch cilantro, leaves and stems chopped
- ½   bunch oregano, leaves chopped
- 5   garlic cloves, chopped
- 2   teaspoons kosher salt
- 2   teaspoons ground cayenne
- 2   tablespoons paprika
- 1½   cups (360 ml) lager beer
-     Hog casings

FOR THE TOMATILLO SALSA:
- ½   pound (226 g) green tomatoes
- ½   pound (226 g) tomatillos
- ½   white onion, finely chopped
- 3   tablespoons apple cider vinegar
- ½   cup (25 g) chopped cilantro
-     Olive oil
-     Kosher salt

FOR FINISHING:
- ½   cup (25 g) chopped basil
-     Olive oil
-     Sea salt

recipe continues

Prepare the grill: Build your coal bed, starting the fire about 90 minutes before cooking. It's really important to have a large coal bed to feed your ember bed as you are cooking. You don't want to be cooking over burning logs; you want to burn the wood down until you have glowing embers in order to impart a clean charcoal flavor to the sausage.

Roast the chiles and bell peppers: Place the poblano and jalapeño chiles and bell peppers directly over a gas flame, turning regularly until blistered and blackened all over, about 5 minutes. Put all the blackened peppers and chiles into a bowl, cover with plastic wrap, and let steam for about 10 minutes, to loosen up the skin and make it easier to peel. Cool until you are able to handle them, then rub off the blackened skin and slice open to pull out the stem and seed pods. Roughly chop and set aside.

Start the sausage: Set up your meat grinder with a medium-size die hole. Dice the pork shoulder and pork back fat so it fits nicely into the grinder. Grind the pork into a large stainless-steel bowl set over another bowl of ice. It's important to keep the meat as cold as possible. Add the chopped chiles and bell peppers, the marjoram, cilantro, oregano, garlic, salt, cayenne, paprika, and beer and mix well. Chill in the fridge for 20 minutes.

Make the tomatillo salsa: While the pork mixture is chilling, chop the green tomatoes and tomatillos into beautiful uniform, small cubes and place in a medium bowl. Add the onion, vinegar, cilantro, and a splash of olive oil and season with salt. Mix well and taste for seasoning; set aside until plating.

Grind the meat and stuff the sausage: After the pork mixture has chilled, grind it through the grinder again, back into your bowl, and chill in the fridge until you are ready to case your sausage.

Give the hog casings a good rinse and let them sit in a bowl filled with water for 20 minutes before using.

Set up your stuffing station atop a lightly wetted work surface. You'll need the wet surface later, so keep a bowl of water near in case it dries up.

Pull the pork mixture from the fridge, mix it again with your hands, and form it into a large ball. Add the sausage to a sausage stuffer and push down on the mixture, removing all the air pockets. Press down the sausage stuffer until the mixture starts to come out the end tube.

Grab the casing from the water, place the casing over the end of the tube, and push the casing down all the way until the end of the casing is the only thing left off the tube. Pull a thumb length of casing back off the tube and tie a knot. Then push down on the lever of the sausage stuffer and begin to fill the casings with the pork mixture. As the casings fill, slowly swirl the stuffed sausage into a spiral on the wet surface. Once the coil is the size of two hands, pull off the casing a couple inches and use scissors to cut the casing neatly, and tie another knot to lock in the sausage. Repeat with the remaining sausage mixture.

Use a pin to prick a few tiny holes into the sausage to help prevent it from exploding during cooking.

Grill the sausage and serve: Start with your grill gate close to the embers and grill the sausage for 2 minutes on each side. Adjust the grill higher over the embers, grill for 6 to 8 minutes per side. Pull from the heat and allow to rest for 5 minutes to lock in all the juices.

Place the sausage onto a serving plate and spoon the salsa all over. Garnish the sausage with basil and a drizzle of olive oil and sprinkle with sea salt.

Squid and Romesco

SERVES:
2

PREP TIME:
15 MINUTES, PLUS TIME FOR
MAKING THE ROMESCO AND
FIRING UP THE GRILL

Grilling squid rules if you can get good squid—not bleached or sticky, tasteless frozen trash. Please develop a RELATIONSHIP WITH A FISHMONGER SO YOU COULD EVEN ORDER IN SPECIAL PRODUCTS FOR YOURSELF. Make sure to get that pesky cartilage spine out of the squid's body—shove your fingers in and just pull it out, like a long hard rock out of your nose.

1   **large (1½-pound/680 g) whole squid (get your fishmonger to clean it, but leave it whole)**

      Kosher salt

      Romesco Sauce (page 139; make it smoother by processing the roasted peppers and chiles with the other ingredients)

      Lemon juice

1   **teaspoon ground fennel**

Prepare the grill: Build your coal bed, starting the fire about 90 minutes before cooking. It's really important to have a large coal bed to feed your ember bed as you are cooking. You don't want to be cooking over burning logs; you want to burn the wood down until you have glowing embers in order to impart a clean charcoal flavor to the squid.

Place the grill grate 1 inch (2.5 cm) over a thick bed of coals. The coals need to be super hot to achieve a beautiful char on the squid in a short period of time. Once the grill is hot, season the squid with kosher salt and place it on the grill. Cook for about 3 minutes on each side, until just tender.

Remove the squid from the grill. Spoon a large spoonful of romesco sauce onto a plate and use the back of your spoon to create a small well shape the size of the squid. Place the squid over the sauce. Season with a splash of lemon juice and sprinkle with the ground fennel.

Whole Sea Bass and Fennel Mash

SERVES:
4

PREP TIME:
2 HOURS, PLUS 2 HOURS
INACTIVE TIME AND TIME
FOR FIRING UP THE GRILL

Grilled whole sea bass says springtime is here, with a fennel confit that is so sweet and beautiful and acts as a great condiment for the smoky fish. Grilled fish and fennel cooking down in bubbling butter is a very good smell on a chill night. Or cook the fish outside so the house smells just of butter and anise. That sounds wonderful.

2	quarts (2 L) cold water
	Kosher salt
1 to 1½	pounds (450 to 680 g) whole sea bass, gutted and scaled
1	pound (450 g) unsalted butter, cubed
2	bulbs fennel, cored and diced
1	tablespoon lemon juice, plus more as needed
	Canola oil, for brushing
	Zest of 1 lemon
	Sea salt
1	teaspoon ground Espelette pepper
	Pickled small red chiles (served on the side)

Prepare the grill: Build your coal bed, starting the fire about 90 minutes before cooking. It's really important to have a large coal bed to feed your ember bed as you are cooking. You don't want to be cooking over burning logs; you want to burn the wood down until you have glowing embers in order to impart a clean charcoal flavor to the sea bass.

Pour the water into a large bowl, add 2 tablespoons kosher salt, and whisk until it's all dissolved. Drop the whole fish into the salt brine and leave for 1 hour in the fridge. Brining helps the fish stay juicy and crisps up the skin as it grills.

Pull the fish from brine, pat dry with paper towels, and prop it upright, belly side down. Allow the fish to air dry for 1 hour at room temperature.

In a medium saucepan, melt the butter over medium heat and allow it to brown a little. Add the fennel, turn down heat to low, and cook very low and slow for 1 to 1½ hours, allowing the fennel to sweeten up and impart deep caramelized flavors. Use an immersion blender to whip the fennel into a smooth sauce. Season with a dash of kosher salt and lemon juice; keep warm.

Once you have a nice bed of embers, build a 12 × 12-inch (30 × 30 cm) square bed of coals 3 inches (7.5 cm) thick. Place a fine mesh grill grate 3 inches (7.5 cm) from the embers. Brush the fish with a thin layer of oil and grill your fish, allowing it to cook 75 percent and flipping the fish once, 8 minutes per side. Test for doneness by inserting a cake tester into the thickest part of the fish for 5 seconds then touching the cake tester to your bottom lip. If it is warm to the touch, the fish is cooked. Remove from the grill.

Season the fish with lemon juice, lemon zest, sea salt, and Espellete pepper. Serve fennel mash on the side with pickled red chiles.

Grilled Sardine and Cabbage Sando

SERVES:
2

PREP TIME:
30 MINUTES, PLUS TIME
FOR FIRING UP THE GRILL

When I was in Japan I had this grilled sardine sandwich in a small coffee shop in a back alley in Shinjuku-ku. It was so perfect. Another time I had a grilled sardine sandwich in Melbourne at another Japanese café. They were both outstanding. Grilled, well-seasoned sardine fillets; a salad of thinly sliced onion, napa cabbage, and coriander; sourdough bread treated like a grilled cheese and butter-fried in a pan; and Kewpie mayo and fresh wasabi in place of mustard. If kids are eating tuna melts, then let's try and feed everyone grilled sardine sandwiches. That's a great plan, and now you can follow this recipe and make everyone happier.

¼	head white cabbage, cored and sliced as thin as possible
½	white onion, sliced as thin as possible
1	jalapeño chile, seeded and sliced into super-thin rings
1	cup (50 g) cilantro leaves
8	fresh sardines, cleaned and butterflied, tails left on (ask your fishmonger to do this)
	Canola oil
	Kosher salt and freshly cracked black pepper
4	slices Japanese milk bread or Texas toast, crusts removed
¼	cup (60 ml) mayonnaise (preferably Kewpie)
2	tablespoons wasabi paste

Add charcoal, preferably Binchōtan, to a konro grill—if you have just a Weber and normal charcoal, that is fine, too. Apply lighter fluid (to help light the charcoal faster). Once part of the charcoal is lit, fan it to ignite all the charcoal. It takes time to really fire up the grill. When all the charcoal is lit and you can't keep your hand there for more than 2 seconds without feeling a hard burn, the grill is ready to cook on. Place the metal grill grate on and allow it to come up to temperature, so the skin of the fish doesn't stick.

In a medium bowl, combine the cabbage, onion, jalapeño, and cilantro and set aside for plating.

Skewer the sardines through the tail up into the head, brush the skin lightly with canola oil, and season with salt and pepper. Place on the hot grill and cook skin side down 75 percent of the way through, then flip and cook through to medium, just a couple minutes. Remove the sardines from the grill and place on a wire rack.

Immediately build your sandwiches: Lay 4 slices of bread on a clean work surface. Spread the mayo on 2 slices and the wasabi paste on the other 2. Place 2 sardines on top of the mayo side flesh side down. Place equal amounts of the dry cabbage slaw onto the sardines. Place the remaining sardines flesh side up on top of the cabbage and top with the wasabi-coated slices of bread to complete the sandwiches. Slice each sandwich into three equal pieces and then turn the slices on their sides, revealing the sardine layers within.

Clams with Nduja Butter and Bread Crumbs

SERVES:
2 TO 4

PREP TIME:
20 MINUTES, PLUS 12 HOURS
INACTIVE TIME AND TIME
FOR FIRING UP THE GRILL

Spicy pork and clams are truly meant to be together, and these are better than any clams casino in the world, trust me. If you make these for any occasion, you'll be loved and adored. Nduja, a spreadable and delicious salume, is the perfect pork product for this because of the high fat content, so it acts as the butter. All you have to do is cook the clams, then spoon the pork on top. The bread crumbs are the easiest and most rewarding recipe in this chapter, for sure. You know I'm not a liar. Make these once and you'll be hooked.

24	littleneck clams
4	quarts (4 L) cold water
½	cup (75 g) cornmeal
1	garlic clove
5¼	ounces (150 g) day-old Focaccia (page 34)
3	tablespoons unsalted butter, at room temperature
⅓	cup (75 g) nduja
	Sea salt, if needed
1	orange, cut into 4 to 8 wedges

The day before making the clams, put the clams in a bucket, cover with the cold water, and swish in the cornmeal. Refrigerate overnight so the clams spit out any sand that is in their bellies.

Get the grill ready: Add charcoal, preferably Binchōtan, to a konro grill—if you have just a Weber and normal charcoal, that is fine, too. Apply lighter fluid (to help light the charcoal faster). Once part of the charcoal is lit, fan it to ignite all the charcoal. It takes time to really fire up the grill. When all the charcoal is lit and you can't keep your hand there for more than 2 seconds without feeling a hard burn, the grill is ready to cook on. Place the metal grill grate on and allow it to come up to temperature, so the clams don't stick.

Preheat the oven to 350°F (175°C). Line a baking sheet with parchment paper.

Rub the garlic over the focaccia. Cut the focaccia into small cubes and place in a medium bowl; mix in the butter, spread onto the prepared baking sheet, and toast until golden and crunchy, about 8 minutes. Cool, then break them up by rubbing them in the palms of your hands to create a bread crumb texture. Set aside. Turn up the oven temperature to 375°F (195°C).

In a small skillet over medium-low heat, cook the nduja, breaking it up with the back of a wooden spoon, until the fat is rendered and the sausage is fairly smooth. Set aside, warm, with the nduja fat separated from the paste.

Strain your clams from the cornmeal water and rinse thoroughly. Once your charcoal is burning-hot, place the clams on the grilling rack, cover with a large bowl, and grill until they open (you do not have to turn them), 6 to 8 minutes; discard any that do not open. Remove top shells, keeping as much of the juice as possible in the bottom shells, and transfer the clams to a serving tray.

Spoon a dollop of the warm nduja onto the clams, cover the clams with bread crumbles, and throw in the oven; bake for 5 to 7 minutes, until the bread crumbs are golden brown. Remove from the oven, season with sea salt if needed, and serve with the orange wedges.

320   Home Style Cookery

Shrimp Banh Mi Dog

SERVES:
4

PREP TIME:
35 MINUTES, PLUS 2 HOURS
INACTIVE TIME AND TIME
FOR FIRING UP THE GRILL

You're wondering how I thought of this dish, aren't you? It came to me in a fever dream, and I knew it would be perfect. Make a prawn hot dog like a prawn mortadella, then grill it and top it like a banh mi! KABOOM, right? How have we not made this yet or seen it? This is such a perfect lunch for kids, and adults, and anyone who's lying around like a golden retriever. Let the dogs eat, bruh, let the dogs eat a dog!

1	small daikon, julienned
1	carrot, julienned
1	cup (240 g) rice wine vinegar
½	cup (110 g) granulated sugar
1	tablespoon kosher salt
1	pound (450 g) black tiger shrimp, shelled and deveined
3	tablespoons pork lard
2	egg whites
1	tablespoon onion powder
1	teaspoon sea salt, plus more for finishing
1	cup (100 g) chopped cilantro leaves and stems, plus more whole leaves for serving
2	tablespoons seeded and diced bird's eye chiles
	Canola oil
4	hot dog buns (preferably Martin's)
1	cucumber, sliced and julienned
	Drizzle of sriracha

Put the daikon and carrot in a nonreactive container. In a glass measure, combine the vinegar, sugar, kosher salt, and ¾ cup (180 ml) water; stir to dissolve the sugar and salt. Pour the liquid over the vegetables—they should be submerged. Cover and refrigerate for at least 2 hours; this makes 1 quart (1 L) of pickle, and it will keep in the refrigerator for at least 1 week.

Get the grill ready: Add charcoal, preferably Binchōtan, to a konro grill—if you have just a Weber and normal charcoal, that is fine, too. Apply lighter fluid (to help light the charcoal faster). Once part of the charcoal is lit, fan it to ignite all the charcoal. It takes time to really fire up the grill. When all the charcoal is lit and you can't keep your hand there for more than 2 seconds without feeling a hard burn, the grill is ready to cook on. Place the metal grill grate on and allow it to come up to temperature, so the shrimp doesn't stick.

Place the shrimp and pork lard in the bowl of a food processor and pulse until well combined. Scoop out of the processor and place into a medium bowl with another bowl filled with ice underneath. Slowly fold in the egg whites. Add the onion powder, sea salt, cilantro, and chiles.

Form 4 hot dog–shaped shrimp cylinders in plastic wrap; twist each end to make them tight, similar to a torchon. Then place in boiling water for 7 to 10 minutes and cook through.

Once the grill is ready to go, lightly oil the grill rack. Unwrap the shrimp dogs, place them on the grill, and grill until lightly charred and crisped up around the edges. Flip the shrimp dogs and repeat on the second side until fully warmed through. Season with sea salt.

Place a whole shrimp dog into a hot dog bun and add sliced cucumber, pickled daikon and carrot slaw, sriracha drizzle, and cilantro leaves. Repeat with the remaining shrimp dogs.

Lamb Chops with Scotch Bonnet Pepper Sauce

SERVES:
4

PREP TIME:
30 MINUTES, PLUS
TIME FOR HEATING
UP THE GRILL

Grilled lamb chops are perfect well-done. That's how they should be made. And well doesn't mean hammer-fucked, either. That's the thing with most cooks: They think well-done needs to be disrespected and thrown on the floor, or smashed with tongs, or some cowboy-ass shit. You can cook lamb chops or any piece of meat well and still cook it gently and lovingly and not just because it's not rare. You don't have to act like we stole your firstborn and now you have to take revenge on us through hammer-fucking the well-done protein.

8   bone-in lamb chops
     Kosher salt and freshly ground black pepper
1   (16-ounce/455 ml) jar Mateo's habanero salsa or your favorite scotch bonnet pepper sauce
     Sea salt

Turn your gas grill to its highest setting and heat to 600°F (315°C) with the lid closed.

Season the lamb chops with kosher salt and pepper on both sides.

Once the grill is smoking hot, open the lid and lay down the chops. Grill for 4 minutes without moving them. Flip the chops, turn down heat to 75 percent power, and brush the chops with the salsa until they are nice and glazed. Close the lid and cook for 3 minutes. Open the lid again, flip the chops, and brush and glaze the chops on the second side. Close the lid and cook for another 4 minutes, or until cooked to medium.

Remove the chops from the grill and place on a serving tray. Sprinkle with sea salt and allow to rest for a couple minutes before serving them at any outdoor BBQ gathering.

Swordfish and Peppers with Couscous and Salsa Verde

SERVES:
4 TO 6

PREP TIME:
1 HOUR

Swordfish is the big steak of the fish world. It cooks like a T-bone. The first time I ever had swordfish it was at the Five Fishermen in Halifax, and it was after a funeral or something. I forget. I was pretty young, and my grandparents were there, so it was something like that 'cause we were all in suits. I remember my dad got the swordfish, and being a kid, I thought it was a mythical creature with a long sword for a beak. When it came out I remember being like, Where's the sword? Kind of a letdown. But for some reason, I always thought of swordfish as a special-occasion or expensive-night-out fish. Making food at home is always a special occasion to me, so once in a while, I buy a large bone-in swordfish steak and cook it in a raging-hot oven, or fry it in a pan, or stew it, or grill it.

FOR THE COUSCOUS:

3	tablespoons canola oil
1	cup (240 g) chopped fennel
1	cup (240 g) diced white onion
1	cup (240 g) diced leeks (white parts only)
3	tablespoons sliced garlic
1½	cups (240 g) couscous
1¾	cups (420 ml) Chicken Stock (page 51), or store-bought
14	cippolini onions, peeled
½	pound (225 g) rainbow mini sweet peppers

FOR THE SALSA VERDE:

1	cup (50 g) parsley leaves
1	cup (50 g) tarragon leaves
¼	cup (35 g) finely chopped shallot
1	tablespoon minced garlic
2	halved and seeded jalapeño chiles
⅓	cup (70 ml) canola oil
½	cup (55 g) almonds, toasted and chopped
½	cup (55 g) cashews, toasted and chopped
2	tablespoons lime zest
2	tablespoons lime juice
	Kosher salt

FOR THE SWORDFISH AND SERVING:

1	pound (450 g) swordfish loin
	Kosher salt and freshly ground black pepper
1	tablespoon olive oil
	Sea salt
	Lemon wedges
½	cup (25 g) parsley leaves
½	cup (25 g) mint leaves
½	cup (25 g) basil leaves
½	cup (25 g) tarragon leaves

recipe continues

Get the grill ready: Add charcoal, preferably Binchōtan, to a konro grill—if you have just a Weber and normal charcoal, that is fine, too. Apply lighter fluid (to help light the charcoal faster). Once part of the charcoal is lit, fan it to ignite all the charcoal. It takes time to really fire up the grill. When all the charcoal is lit and you can't keep your hand there for more than 2 seconds without feeling a hard burn, the grill is ready to cook on. Place the metal grill grate on and allow it to come up to temperature, so the fish doesn't stick.

Make the couscous: Heat 2 tablespoons of the canola oil in the bottom of a Dutch oven over medium heat. Add the fennel, onion, leeks, and garlic and cook for about 10 minutes, until softened but with little to no color. Add the couscous and toast, stirring, for 3 minutes. Add the chicken stock, increase heat, and bring to a boil. Turn off heat, put the lid on the Dutch oven, and allow the couscous to steep for 10 minutes.

In a large skillet, heat 1 tablespoon canola oil over medium heat. Add the cippolini onions and cook for 5 minutes, or until they start to brown. Add the mini sweet peppers, turn heat to high, and char the peppers and cippolini onions for about 8 minutes, until they have a beautiful color. Transfer the peppers and onions to the Dutch oven and spoon them all over the couscous. Cover and set aside.

While the grill is getting hot, make the salsa verde: In a blender, combine the parsley, tarragon, shallot, garlic, jalapeños, and canola oil. Blend on medium speed until you have a loose salsa verde. Pour the salsa verde into a bowl and fold in the almonds, cashews, lime zest, and lime juice. Season with salt and set aside until serving.

Season your swordfish with kosher salt and pepper, brush a little olive oil over the fish, and place on the hot grill. Now grill the swordfish like a steak, 4 minutes per side, flipping 3 times in total, and cooking for 16 minutes in total. Once a nice crust has formed on the fish, take it off the heat and place on a cooling rack for 5 to 10 minutes.

Slice the swordfish 1 inch (2.5 cm) thick, season with sea salt, and place on a platter with lemon wedges.

Plate the couscous with a generous sprinkle of the parsley, mint, basil, and tarragon. Keep the salsa verde in a separate bowl and place everything in the center of the dining table for a family-style meal.

Lobster Thermidor with Béarnaise and Salt and Vinegar Chips

SERVES:
2

PREP TIME:
1 HOUR AND 40 MINUTES, PLUS
12 HOURS INACTIVE TIME AND
TIME TO HEAT UP THE GRILL

I will show you how to make béarnaise, and if there happen to be lobsters, then we are making lobster thermidor. Grilling a raw lobster is tricky; definitely pre-blanch your lobster. I always say four minutes for this, period, no matter the size, which will cook it halfway. Then place the lobsters in an ice bath. Transfer to the fridge and grill later in the day. If you want to blanch a day before grilling, that's fine as well. I think that good potato chips make sense for this in place of French fries. The crisp and salt of them; the moist, smoky lobster; and the fluffy, airy béarnaise is a perfect combination that will fill your house with love.

FOR THE SALT AND VINEGAR CHIPS:

1	pound (450 g) Yukon Gold potatoes
2½	cups (590 ml) white vinegar
4	quarts (4 L) canola oil, for frying
	Sea salt

FOR THE BÉARNAISE:

1	cup (240 ml) white wine vinegar
1	shallot, sliced
1	tablespoon black peppercorns
3	whole sprigs tarragon
1	pound (450 g) unsalted butter
4	egg yolks
	Kosher salt
	Lemon juice

FOR THE LOBSTER:

1	Atlantic lobster (alive and feisty, from a local fishmonger), pre-blanched (see headnote)
	Kosher salt
2	tablespoons unsalted butter
	Canola oil

recipe continues

Make the potato chips: Slice the potatoes super thin and put them in a large container. Add the vinegar and 2 cups (480 ml) water, cover, and allow to soak in the fridge overnight.

Pour the canola oil into a large Dutch oven to come halfway up the sides of the pot. Turn heat to medium-high and bring the oil up to 325°F (165°C).

As the oil is coming up to temperature, drain the sliced potatoes in a colander and place them on a baking sheet lined with lots of paper towels to absorb all the moisture. Place another paper towel on top to really dry the potatoes out.

Once the oil is up to temperature, place a handful of potatoes into the hot oil; the oil will bubble to the rim of the pot. Do not overfill with potatoes, or the oil will boil over and be super dangerous. Using a long-handled metal spider, continuously stir the chips so they cook evenly. Once the chips are all golden brown and crispy, remove with the spider and place on a baking sheet lined with paper towels. Immediately sprinkle with sea salt.

Make the béarnaise: In a small saucepan, combine the vinegar, shallot, black peppercorns, and tarragon and turn the heat to high. Reduce by half, then remove from heat and strain through a fine-mesh strainer into a small bowl. Cool in the fridge for 10 minutes.

In a medium saucepan, melt the butter over low heat and slowly simmer until the milk solids have separated from the fat. Once separated, use a spoon to skim off as much foam as you can, then gently pour through a fine chinois or strainer to catch the remaining milk solids and you'll be left with a golden clear fat (clarified butter).

In a medium bowl, combine the egg yolks and chilled vinegar reduction and whisk until mixed well. Place the mixing bowl on top of a pot with simmering water (make sure the bottom of the bowl doesn't touch the water). Keep whisking to incorporate air and get the eggs fluffy to create your sabayon. Watch the heat from the bottom of the bowl; if it's too high, it will curdle the eggs. Remove from heat.

Secure the bowl with a damp kitchen towel underneath it and slowly pour the clarified butter into the fluffy eggs, constantly whisking and incorporating the butter into the béarnaise and keeping the butter stream even and slow (if you add the butter too soon, the béarnaise may split). Season with salt and lemon juice; cover with plastic wrap to keep warm.

Get the grill ready: Turn your gas grill to its highest setting and heat to 600°F (315°C) with the lid closed.

Cook the lobster: Place the lobster on a secure cutting board bell side down. Take the tip of a chef's knife and stab the lobster right through the brain. Continue cutting to split the lobster in half. Drizzle canola oil and kosher salt on the exposed meat of the lobster.

Place the lobster cut side down on the hot grill and cook for 6 to 7 minutes, allowing it to char and create flavor. Flip the lobster so the shell side is on the grill. Put a couple tablespoons of butter over the charred lobster meat and continue grilling until warm throughout the lobster. Do not overcook it. Place the lobster halves on two serving plates, crack the claws to expose the beautiful meat, and spoon large amounts of béarnaise all over the lobster meat. Serve with a large handful of salt and vinegar chips.

CHAPTER 12

Desserts

I Love Them So Much But Hate Making Them Even More

IN MY FIRST BOOK, I ONLY HAD THREE DESSERTS: MY GRANDMOTHER'S BLACKBERRY COFFEE CAKE, MY OTHER GRANDMOTHER'S MOLASSES BREAD PUDDING, AND THE PARTS & LABOUR DONUT. I put so few in because I was afraid. Dessert and baking recipes are hard. They are no joke. Breads and desserts are science. I say all the time I am not a scientist, I am a cook, and just an okay cook at that. So, fuck ya, it's scary and way more work to write out dessert recipes, test them, and make sure they work. For this book I had a little help from my partner, my lover, my friend, my wife, the mother of my children, and the greatest human I know on this planet, because Trish is an Amazon giant home cook and makes some of my favorite desserts ever.

I always try to give you guys accessible recipes with some twists that make them not too basic, ya know. It's the same with these desserts. Everyone should be able to whip up a batch of cookies, a chocolate cake, a little sundae, and maybe even a perfectly imperfect tarte Tatin. I'm sure everyone already has their go-to squares, pies, cookies, and brownies. I'm sure most people bake a lot at home, but here are my favorite desserts, brought to you by two of the people I love the most, my mother and my wife. I love Joanie's Chocolate Zucchini Cake (page 337) so much. I remember eating it as a kid. I loved stealing pieces late at night, and let me tell you, I was a sucker for stealing the dry edges of the cake.

Here are some dessert recipes that will serve as a great starting point. Learn how to make a pâte brisée that's perfect, and then experiment. Next time fill it with blueberries, raspberries, or make a rhubarb tart. Making a flan is a stepping-stone to the perfect crème brûlée. That's how you should think of all your cooking. I always say this is science. If shit hits the fan, then it's probably your fault, but that's okay, because there are so many factors when baking. Don't beat yourself up. Remember, there's always a pint of chocolate chip mint just a delivery or quick drive away or some local indie cookie delivery a DM away.

Please keep trying and keep cooking. It's all that matters. Food is life and food is love. It's the mess-ups and the letdowns that make the perfectly set lemon tart feel that much better. Good luck, and make sure your mixing bowls are always clean and dry before using. Talk to you soon! Love, the BIG DOG.

Joanie's Chocolate Zucchini Cake

MAKES:
1 (10-INCH/
25 CM) CAKE

PREP TIME:
1 HOUR, PLUS
COOLING TIME

Growing up, my mom made a lot of desserts, but this one always stuck out for me because it was, like, designed to torture children. First off, you can't even taste the zucchini, really, so why the hell is it even in there? A chocolate cake filled with vegetables is a kid's nightmare—like, what's going on, is the world ending? It was the one cake I'd always say no to, and then five minutes later I'd crawl onto the counter and steal a piece and act like no one heard me earlier. I guess I really hated vegetables. It's funny, my son, Mac, loves chocolate like most kids and hates eating vegetables right now. He's almost four, and last night, he ate some of the salad we made for dinner, and he ate it pretty quick 'cause I told him if he eats all his dinner including his salad he'll get some chocolate ice cream. I know bribing your kids with sweets is horrible, but what's the worst that can happen? Will he turn out to be a serial killer 'cause he got ice cream for eating his salad? I guess we'll keep watching the news and see.

Baking spray
1⅔ cups (240 g) all-purpose flour
¾ cup (225 g) high-quality cocoa powder
2 tablespoons (28 g) espresso powder
½ cup (120 g) unsalted butter, at room temperature
½ cup (120 g) melted and cooled coconut oil
1¾ cups (350 g) granulated sugar
1 teaspoon vanilla extract
1 teaspoon baking soda
½ teaspoon baking powder
½ teaspoon kosher salt
2 eggs
⅓ cup (75 ml) plain Greek yogurt
1½ heaping cups (215 g) shredded zucchini
⅓ cup (80 g) bittersweet chocolate chips
⅓ cup (75 g) chopped 70% dark chocolate
⅓ cup (75 ml) heavy cream
1 tablespoon light corn syrup
1 teaspoon sea salt, for sprinkling

Preheat the oven to 325°F (165°F). Grease a 10-inch (25 cm) round cake pan with baking spray.

Whisk together the flour, cocoa powder, and espresso powder in a large bowl; set aside.

In the bowl of a stand mixer, combine the butter, coconut oil, sugar, vanilla, baking soda, baking powder, and salt and beat until smooth. Beat in the eggs one at a time until smooth again. With the mixer on low, alternate adding yogurt and the flour mixture just until combined. Fold in the zucchini and chocolate chips with a spatula and spoon the batter into the prepared pan.

Bake for 40 minutes, or until a toothpick inserted in the center of the cake comes out clean. Just be aware that there are melted chocolate chips and you might hit one. Pull the cake from oven, let cool for a minute, then take the cake out of its pan and place on a wire rack to cool to room temperature.

Place the chopped dark chocolate in a large metal bowl. Heat the cream and corn syrup in a small saucepan over medium heat until it comes to a light simmer. Remove from heat and allow to cool for 2 minutes. Pour the hot cream over the chopped chocolate and let stand, untouched, for 5 minutes, then stir until smooth.

Pour all the ganache over the cooled cake and let drip off the sides for a rustic look. Sprinkle with sea salt.

Trish's Hello Dollies

MAKES:
12 SQUARES

PREP TIME:
45 MINUTES

These are my favorite of Trish's desserts ever, for real. I know I say everything is the best, and I know that everything is my favorite, but these squares are by far my most favorite, and I love them fresh out of the oven, at room temp the next day, or after being in the fridge and chilled to almost like fudge. I really love them, and I hate nuts in desserts, and in most things, really. Trish doesn't put walnuts in them for me like I'm a child and that makes me love her even more. I love the squares of graham-cracker crust with condensed milk, caramel and chocolate chips, and toasted coconut. It's literally perfect with a huge glass of ice-cold milk. OMFG, I'm in heaven.

1   cup (225 g) unsalted butter, melted
1   (14.4-ounce/408 g) box graham cracker crumbs
1   (12-ounce/326 g) bag butterscotch chips
1   (12-ounce/326 g) bag semisweet chocolate chips
1   (8-ounce/227 g) bag unsweetened shredded coconut
1   (14-ounce/397 g) can condensed milk
½   cup (55 g) chopped walnuts

Preheat the oven to 350°F (175°C). Line an 8-inch (20 cm) square baking pan with parchment paper.

In a large bowl, combine the butter and graham cracker crumbs and mix until the graham crumbs are soft and pliable.

Pack the wet graham crumble mixture into the lined pan. Layer three-quarters of the butterscotch chips, chocolate chips, and coconut over the graham mixture. Pour the can of condensed milk over the mixture and top with the remaining butterscotch chips, chocolate chips, and finish on top with the rest of the coconut and the walnuts.

Place in the oven and bake for 25 minutes, or until the condensed milk starts to bubble. Remove from the oven and place on a wire rack. Slice into squares and serve warm or at room temperature. To serve cold, cool completely, place in the fridge and allow to set, then slice into squares.

Apple Tarte Tatin

SERVES:
6 TO 8

PREP TIME:
2 HOURS AND
10 MINUTES

If your apples aren't glowing orbs of caramel-glazed perfection, then I'm sorry, but start over. Tarte Tatin should be almost an opaque mandarin orange in color, and if it's gray, mealy soft, and flat then your apples were shit and your caramel was not hot. You have to make tarte Tartin hot and the apples have to be perfect. They don't have to be perfectly sliced and fitted into the pan—even mine is not perfect in formation. The consistency is what's key and what really matters. This is perfect with a slice of cold sharp Cheddar or a really good vanilla bean ice cream . . . or both, really.

FOR THE PÂTE BRISÉE:

1⅓ cups (190 g) all-purpose flour, plus more for rolling

¼ teaspoon salt

¾ cup (180 g) cold unsalted butter, cut into small pieces

⅓ cup (75 ml) sour cream

1 egg, beaten with 1 tablespoon water to make egg wash

FOR THE CARAMEL:

½ cup (110 g) granulated sugar

FOR THE APPLES:

4 pounds (about 9 small) Granny Smith apples or any kind of baking apple

3 tablespoons lemon juice

½ cup (120 ml) Devonshire clotted cream, for serving

recipe continues

Make the pâte brisée: In a large bowl, combine the flour and salt. Blend the cold butter into the flour mixture with a hand mixer to get a grainy texture with the butter forming into pea-size bits. Add the sour cream and mix, lifting and turning the mixture with a spatula to prevent some spots from becoming wetter than others. Add water one spoonful at a time until the mixture holds when pressed between your fingers. Cover the dough with plastic wrap and refrigerate for at least 30 minutes.

On a clean floured work surface, using a rolling pin, roll out the dough to ⅛ inch (6 mm) thick. Place on a baking sheet and store in the fridge until you're ready to bake.

Make the caramel: Put 2 tablespoons water into a heavy-bottomed pot. Cover with the sugar, place over medium-low heat, and heat until the sugar dissolves. Don't stir, as this can cause the sugar to crystallize. Turn up heat to medium-high and heat until the sugar starts to turn golden brown and turns to caramel, 8 to 10 minutes. Pour the caramel into a 10-inch (25 cm) cast-iron skillet to coat the bottom and allow to cool. The caramel will set and harden.

Preheat the oven to 350°F (175°C).

Make the apples: Peel, seed, and cut the core out of the apples with a melon baller, then cut the apples into quarters, leaving 1 half-apple slice for the center apple. Place the apples in a bowl of water with the lemon juice as you cut them to prevent browning.

Remove the apples from the lemon water and transfer onto the hardened caramel in the skillet. Line the inside rim of the skillet with apple quarters, packing them in tightly, then make a second compact ring moving toward the center. Place the half piece of apple peeled skin side down in the center of the skillet.

Take the pâte brisée out of the fridge. Place the dough on top of the apples and use a small sharp knife to cut off excess dough all the way around the outside of the skillet so the dough is flush with the rim.

Brush the top of the dough with an even layer of egg wash edge to edge. Place the tarte Tatin in the oven and bake for 35 to 40 minutes, until the crust is golden brown and some caramel is bubbling up around the edges. Remove from the oven and allow to cool on a wire rack for 10 minutes.

Place a serving plate on top of the tarte Tatin and gently hold it against the crust. Make a quick flipping motion, place on the table, and remove the skillet to reveal the glistening apple orbs.

Serve warm, with a dollop of Devonshire clotted cream.

Lemon Tart

MAKES:
1 LARGE (11-INCH/
28 CM) TART

PREP TIME:
2 HOURS AND
25 MINUTES

Back in the days of La Palette, we would always have a lemon tart, a flourless chocolate cake, and a trio of crème brûlée with different berry compotes. This is dessert you should know how to make and make often at home. It's relatively easy as long as you blind bake your dough and there are no holes for the royal (the filling) to go through. A lot of other things can happen: The dough can split when you pour the royal into the baked shell, or you can end up with air bubbles. If there are any air bubbles, use a blowtorch to remove them or you'll end up with an ugly tart. And no one likes an ugly tart. The key to most desserts is just a little salt, and I think a little lime goes a long way with a lemon tart.

1	recipe pâte brisée (see page 341)
1	egg yolk, beaten, to make egg wash
½	cup (140 g) unsalted butter
	Zest and juice of 6 lemons
	Zest and juice of 3 limes
2	cups (500 g) granulated sugar
8	eggs, lightly beaten
	Plain whipped cream, for serving

Using a rolling pin, on a clean floured work surface roll out the pâté brisée to ⅛ inch (3 mm) thick; place on a baking sheet, cover with plastic wrap, and store in the fridge until you're ready to bake.

Preheat the oven to 350°F (175°C).

Grease and lightly flour an 11-inch (28 cm) flan ring pan, line the pan with the dough, and carefully push the pastry into the corners.

Put baking beans or pie weights on the bottom of the crust and blind bake the tart base for 10 to 15 minutes, until the edges start to turn golden. Remove the beans, brush with the egg yolk to seal the pastry, and bake for another 3 minutes, or until set and dry. Pull the crust and allow to cool on a wire rack.

Turn the oven temperature down to 290°F (145°C).

Melt the butter in a small saucepan. In a separate pan, gently heat the citrus zest, citrus juice, and sugar over low heat. Whisk in the eggs and stir in the melted butter. Mix well and allow to steep for 20 minutes. Strain through a fine-mesh strainer.

Carefully pour the citrus mixture into the pie crust and bake for about 30 minutes, watching after 20 minutes. Once the tart goes from a ripple effect when you gently shake it to a jiggle consistency, pull your tart and cool on a wire rack.

Gently remove the tart from the pan and slice with a long sharp knife into perfect pie slices. Serve with plain whipped cream.

Banana Cake

MAKES:
1 (12-INCH/
30.5 CM) CAKE

PREP TIME:
1 HOUR

Another Trish dessert that rules. I love banana bread, and who doesn't love banana cake with chocolate in it? This cake is maybe the moistest cake ever. I know "moist" is a gross word, but this bread is soft and moist and sticky and kinda dense but not too dense, and when the chocolate hits it's crazy. I love taking a slice and putting peanut butter on it. I love sweets so much. I'm a glutton for sugar, I'm sorry. These desserts are all big winners and are from our house to yours.

¼	cup (60 g) unsalted butter, softened
⅓	cup (70 g) granulated sugar
2	eggs
1	teaspoon vanilla extract
2	cups (300 g) all-purpose flour
1	teaspoon baking powder
1	teaspoon baking soda
¾	teaspoon kosher salt
2	tablespoons sour cream
1	cup (240 g) mashed overripe banana
½	cup (56 g) walnuts
1	cup (150 g) chocolate chips
3	ripe bananas, cut into ⅓-inch (8 mm) coins for the top of the cake

Preheat the oven to 350°F (175°C). Grease and flour a 12-inch (30.5 cm) round baking pan.

Put the butter in a stand mixer fitted with the paddle attachment and beat until fluffy at high speed. Gradually add the sugar and beat until light and fluffy. Beat in the eggs one at a time, then add the vanilla.

Sift the flour, baking powder, baking soda, and salt into a medium bowl. Add to the sugar mixture, alternating with the sour cream. Add the banana, walnuts, and chocolate chips and mix just until blended. Scoop out the batter with a spatula into the prepared baking pan. Top the cake with the banana coins, working in a circular pattern starting in the middle of the cake.

Bake for 40 minutes, or until the center springs back or a toothpick inserted in the center comes out clean.

Let the cake cool in the pan for 5 minutes, then transfer to a wire rack.

Dean's Cow Bay Frogs

MAKES:
12 TO 16
COOKIES

PREP TIME:
35 MINUTES

Making desserts without instructions is very risky. It's like building a shed without blueprints: You can probably do without, but if you maybe just read the instructions it would certainly be level. Same goes for making cookies, or what I called "frogs" growing up that are kinda like coconut macaroons. I call them "Cow Bay frogs" 'cause we made and ate them at my buddy Dean's house, with his girlfriend, Isa. We just took oats and flour and chocolate and a banana and some sea salt and hoped for the best. These are what we came up with, so once again, this recipe is just a shot in the dark, made one beautiful morning while looking out at the Atlantic Ocean. I find these pretty special 'cause my mom made a version that she also called frogs, which were just coconut and oat cookies, really. But we called them frogs, so hey! That's it. I love my mom, and I love Dean, and I love Cow Bay, and I love frogs.

1	ripe banana
4	tablespoons (55 g) brown sugar
2	eggs
3	tablespoons molasses
2	tablespoons canola oil
1	teaspoon sea salt
1	teaspoon baking soda
2¼	cups (228 g) sweetened flaked coconut
1	cup (150 g) all-purpose flour
1	cup (110 g) oats
¾	cup (130 g) dark chocolate chips

Preheat the oven to 325°F (175°C). Line 2 baking sheets with parchment paper.

In a stand mixer with the paddle attachment, beat the banana, sugar, eggs, molasses, and canola oil on medium speed until smooth. Add the salt and baking soda, then stir in the coconut, flour, and oats and mix until the mixture just moistens. Fold in the chocolate chips.

Drop heaping tablespoon-size balls of dough 2 inches (5 cm) apart on the prepared baking sheets. Bake for 10 to 15 minutes, or until golden and the centers still have some chew. Pull from the oven and let cool before diving into these buddies.

Trish's Chocolate Chip Cookies

MAKES:
ABOUT 36
COOKIES

PREP TIME:
30 MINUTES

OMFG, I love these pillowy cookies. I know flat, crunchy, chewy cookies are white-hot, but I wanted to show off these fluffy chunkers. They are perfect for dippin' while sippin' on some ice-cold whole milk. I love it when, after a long night of cooking, feeding kids, doing dishes, bathtime, storytime, and, finally, bedtime, Trish and I slip downstairs, sit on the sofa with a blanket, pull a little side table close to us, and dip our yummy chocolate chip cookies in milk while we watch *The Office*. Just living our best lives.

2¼	cups (340 g) all-purpose flour
1½	teaspoons baking soda
1	cup (240 g) unsalted butter, softened
½	cup (110 g) granulated sugar
1	cup (225 g) light brown sugar
1	teaspoon kosher salt
2	teaspoons vanilla extract
2	eggs
2	cups (225 g) semisweet chocolate chips

Preheat the oven to 350°F (175°C). Line 2 baking sheets with parchment paper.

In a small bowl, whisk together the flour and baking soda; set aside.

In the bowl of a stand mixer fitted with the paddle attachment, combine the butter with both sugars; beat on medium speed until light and fluffy, 5 minutes. Reduce the speed to low, add the salt, vanilla, and eggs, and beat until well mixed, about 1 minute. Add the flour mixture and mix until just combined. Stir in the chocolate chips.

Drop heaping tablespoon-size balls of dough 3 inches (7.5 cm) apart on the prepared baking sheets. Cover and chill the remaining dough so the butter doesn't start melting and the dough doesn't get too soft, which can cause the cookies to spread too much.

Bake until the cookies are golden around the edges but still soft in the center, 8 minutes. Remove from the oven and let cool on a baking sheet for 2 minutes. Transfer the cookies to a wire rack and let cool completely. Let the baking sheets cool, then continue making cookies with the remaining batter and cool them as you did the first batch.

Molasses Cookies Stuffed with Dulce de Leche

MAKES:
9 SANDWICHES

PREP TIME:
55 MINUTES

Molasses cookies rule, and so does dulce de leche. This dessert is great for lunches and for late nights. Hell, you could eat these in the morning with a cup of hot milky tea. Now that I'm thinking of it, imagine adding some freezer jam on top. OMG, I die! Okay, do that and I bet you'll love yourself so much more.

1	egg
¼	cup (120 g) unsalted butter, melted
¼	cup (55 g) granulated sugar
¼	cup (60 ml) dark molasses
2	tablespoons dark brown sugar
1	cup (150 g) all-purpose flour
1	teaspoon baking soda
1	teaspoon ground cinnamon
½	teaspoon ground ginger
½	teaspoon ground cardamom
½	teaspoon kosher salt
1	cup (225 g) turbinado sugar
1	tablespoon unsalted butter
½	cup (120 ml) dulce de leche

Preheat the oven to 375°F (190°C). Line a baking sheet with parchment paper.

In a stand mixer with the whisk attachment, whisk together the egg, butter, granulated sugar, molasses, and brown sugar until smooth.

In a small bowl, mix together the flour, baking soda, cinnamon, ginger, cardamom, and salt. Add the flour mixture to the egg mixture and mix on medium speed until just combined.

Chill the dough for 30 minutes to 1 hour to make it easier to portion.

Place the turbinado sugar in a shallow bowl. Scoop tablespoon-size pieces of dough and roll into balls. Roll in the turbinado sugar and place on the prepared baking sheet 2 inches (5 cm) apart.

Bake the cookies, about 8 minutes, until the cookies puff and crack and the edges are just set. Pull the cookies and transfer to a wire rack to cool. Do not overbake the cookies, or they won't be chewy.

Melt the butter in small saucepan over low heat. Add the dulce de leche and stir until the butter is mixed in. Remove from heat and spread on the bottom of a molasses cookie, then top it with another cookie. Repeat with the remaining cookies.

Crème Caramel

As you can see, I'm trying to get some classics in with sentimental desserts. Here's a classic that you should know how to cook. I think we should all know the classics before getting all freaky-deaky with them. So make this timeless dessert over and over again and remember that these are the classics for a reason. I also always love a feud: Was it created in Spain or France? Guess what, I don't really care, 'cause it's amazing and everyone wins and no one should know who was the first to pour caramel into a pan followed by cream, eggs, and sugar, and to bake then flip it out onto a plate 'cause that could have happened anywhere. Imagine if crème caramel was actually made by some chef in Africa or Ireland.

1	cup (200 g) granulated sugar
3	tablespoons cold water
2	cups (480 ml) whole milk
½	teaspoon vanilla extract
2	tablespoons Grand Marnier
3	egg yolks
1	sheet gelatin, dissolved in 2 teaspoons water

Put ½ cup (100 g) of the sugar in a small skillet. Add the water and heat over medium heat, stirring gently with a metal spoon until the sugar has dissolved. Increase heat to medium-high and allow the syrup to bubble and thicken. Do not stir at this point or the sugar could crystallize. When the syrup starts to turn golden, about 10 to 12 minutes, swirl your pan to ensure even coloring. When you've achieved a rich golden color, remove from heat.

Pour the hot caramel evenly into 6 (6-inch/15 cm wide, 4-inch/10 cm deep) ramekins and allow to cool and harden.

Preheat the oven to 325°F (165°C).

In a medium saucepan, combine the milk, vanilla, and Grand Mariner. Bring to a simmer over medium heat. Remove from heat and allow to cool for 10 minutes, while you prepare the eggs.

In a medium bowl set over a pan of simmering water, whisk the egg yolks with the remaining ½ cup (100 g) sugar to the ribbon stage (once the eggs and sugar are incorporated, it will have a fluffy consistency). Take off the heat and slowly pour the milk mixture into the eggs a little at a time to prevent curdling the eggs. Once the eggs have been tempered, pour in the rest of the milk, add gelatin, then pour the custard mixture into the caramel-lined ramekins.

Place the ramekins into a roasting pan and pour boiling water into the roasting pan halfway up the ramekins. Bake for 15 to 20 minutes, until the custard is just set. Pull from the oven and allow to cool completely, then cover and refrigerate. For best results, chill in the fridge overnight.

To turn out each caramel, run the point of a sharp knife around the edge of each ramekin, place a serving plate on top, and invert. Give the ramekin and plate a quick jiggle and carefully remove the ramekin off the crème caramel.

Chocolate Chip Mint Ice Cream Sundae

MAKES:
2 TO 4
SUNDAES

PREP TIME:
1 HOUR

Saved the best for last. Guess what, I said Trish's Hello Dollies (page 338) are my favorite dessert that Trish makes; well, this one is my favorite that I make. I love chocolate chip mint, and I love hot chocolate fudge, and I love brownies, and I hate nuts, so there are no nuts. This is a no-bullshit sundae, all killer no filler. So soak it up, this book is done, and now you have lots of ideas and reasons to cook. I'm gonna go jump in a pool on the side of a mountain in the West Indies, and tonight I'm gonna eat a chocolate chip ice cream sundae for all of you!!!!!!! Thank you, I love you!!!!!!!

FOR THE BROWNIES:

1	cup (240 g) unsalted butter
1	cup (225 g) granulated sugar
2	eggs
1	teaspoon vanilla extract
⅓	cup (40 g) unsweetened cocoa powder
½	cup (75 g) all-purpose flour
¼	teaspoon salt
¼	teaspoon baking powder

FOR THE HOT FUDGE:

1½	cups (335 g) granulated sugar
1	cup (150 g) unsweetened cocoa powder
1	cup (240 ml) heavy cream
½	cup (120 g) unsalted butter
2	teaspoons vanilla extract
¼	teaspoon kosher salt

FOR SERVING:

1	quart (1 L) store-bought mint chocolate chip ice cream
1	cup (250 ml) heavy cream, whipped
4	high-quality macerated cherries
	Sea salt

Make the brownies: Preheat the oven to 350°F (175°C). Grease and flour an 8-inch (20 cm) square baking pan.

In a medium heatproof bowl, combine the butter, sugar, eggs, and vanilla. Place over a pot of simmering water (make sure the water doesn't touch the bottom of the bowl) and whisk gently until incorporated. Whisk in the cocoa powder, flour, salt, and baking powder and whisk until the mixture comes together. Spread the batter into the prepared pan.

Bake for 25 minutes, or until a toothpick inserted in the center comes out clean. Pull from the oven and cool on a wire rack to room temperature. Cut into even squares for the base of the sundaes.

Make the hot fudge: In a medium saucepan, combine the sugar, cocoa powder, and cream and whisk until incorporated. Turn heat to medium and cook, stirring occasionally, until it comes to a boil. Add the butter and continue to simmer until the fudge starts to thicken, about 5 minutes. Remove from heat and whisk in the vanilla and salt. Allow to cool for 5 minutes before building your sundaes.

To build your sundae, have all the ingredients ready and in front of you. Start by adding one square layer of brownie, then cover with hot fudge, then ice cream, then whipped cream and hot fudge again. Garnish with cherries and a sprinkle of sea salt. Eat right away.

The Final Word

United we stand

Divided we fall

You got to keep the faith

Ray "Raybeez" Barbieri

November 27, 1961–September 11, 1997

Todd Youth

May 15, 1971–October 27, 2018

RIP, never forget

DFTS, DFTS

Thank-Yous

My family: Patricia, Macarthur, Rizzo

Joanie, Steve, Sarah, Cail, Cam, Jamie, Jackson, Nathan, Steve Jr., Natalie, Junior JR, Dooms, Adam Jeffrey

Bill and Carol, Rebecca, Jeff, Evan, Rhys, Judy, Mark, Sandy, Alyssa, Nate, Deanna, Rob

The Conjuring: Lisa Kanamoto, Coulson Armstrong, Keenan McVey

Book crew: Garrett, Deb, Danielle, Sandman, Annalea, Larry, Quentin, Kristin, Christina, Kate, Traeger for the smoker, Ryan Baddeley

LA family: Vinny and Sarah, Sonny and Roman, Jon and Cheri, Natalie and Owen—for lending cooks and always supporting everything I do. And extra special thank-you to Sariy, Colton, and Paulette for their help during the shoot.

Trust Tree: Lisa Kanamoto, Jacqueline King, Ellie Altshuler, Nick Dierl, Sam Arraj, Raj Anand

Not-my-family family: David and Ranit and Liat and Lev Thorek, Gary and Nicole and Rocco and Max and Giacomo Quinto, Basilio Pesce and Matteo, Nick Auf Der Mauer and Alannah Kerr and their baby Axl, Ray Natale, Jon and Tasha and Kai Ocean Roth, Amrida, Siena, Avee, Shlomo Buchler

Thank-you to Shane Harper and Deirdre Frasier from the Farm at Pearl Morissette for providing the beautiful vegetables, flowers, and herbs that we shot at my home

Special thanks: Chris Bianco, Chad Robertson, and the whole Manufactory crew for letting us in your space

Index

Editor: Garrett McGrath
Designer: Danielle Youngsmith
Production Manager: Larry Pekarek

Library of Congress Control Number: 2020931035

ISBN: 978-1-4197-4748-9
eISBN: 978-1-64700-173-5
Indigo Edition ISBN: 978-1-4197-5234-6
Signed Edition ISBN: 978-1-4197-5335-0
B&N Black Friday Signed Edition: 978-1-4197-5334-3
UO Edition: 978-1-4197-5336-7

Printed and bound in the United States
10 9 8 7 6 5 4 3 2

Abrams books are available at special discounts when purchased in quantity
for premiums and promotions as well as fundraising or educational use.
Special editions can also be created to specification. For details, contact
specialsales@abramsbooks.com or the address below.

ABRAMS The Art of Books
195 Broadway, New York, NY 10007
abramsbooks.com